"Many of us have big dreams that are just that, dreams. Heather Penny is convinced they can become reality. What I like most about this book is that it's a pathway, not just a promise. Here are the practical steps to get started on creating the life you've always wanted."

Michael Hyatt, Wall Street Journal *best-selling coauthor of* The Vision Driven Leader

"If you have any interest in becoming a better, happier human, this book is for you."

Sharol Josephson, National Director, FamilyLife Canada

"Heather's guidance helped me pursue a successful career change along with four (yes, four) promotions, and the confidence to keep dreaming and moving toward new adventures."

Misty Chiboucas, Senior Wish Manager, Make-A-Wish, Northeastern & Central California and Northern Nevada

"Heather Penny has put her heart into this book. In a world that's full of ruts that get us stuck, Heather teaches us how to live intentionally. Read this book with your heart open and a willingness to think in new ways. Thank you, Heather, for contributing to the growth of so many of us as we live our day-to-day lives."

James Warrick, Coach and Leadership Consultant

"Heather Penny has been an influential voice in my own leadership journey. With this book, her invaluable expertise is accessible to aspiring leaders everywhere. I know her voice will inspire you as it has me."

Kate Wallace Nunneley, Pastor and Co-founder of The Junia Project

"Would you like a charming, therapeutically-informed guide to living more richly from your true self? Heather's clarity, warmth, and emotional intelligence will inspire you to release what no longer serves you and to invest in your God-given gifts with intentionality. If you are a growth-minded person, I highly recommend this read."

Kelley Gray, MA LPC, Intensive Soul Care Psychotherapist, Restoring the Soul, Lakewood, Colorado

"During a fork in the road years ago, Heather encouraged me to embrace my fears and have the courage to lean in to the unknown. I found clarity and empowerment through the process that has led me to focus on living my best life every day."

Jennifer Stolo, President and CEO, Make-A-Wish,
Northeastern & Central California and Northern Nevada

"Heather's coaching has helped me to connect my head and my heart, has taught me how to find clarity in who I am, the confidence to believe I am enough, and the courage to keep showing up. In her book, she lays out the core concepts of the 3Cs she has taught me and how to apply them in a practical way."

Joe Kaufman, International Teacher

"Heather Penny knows the state most of us live in—messy, confused, hurried, and oh-so-tired—because she's lived it. With a powerful message of hope grounded in clear action steps, Heather shows us how to 'spiral up' and out of those soul-crushing behaviors and beliefs. This book is for you if you are looking for something research-based that will make a practical difference."

Abbi Palsma, Regional Operations Director, CLA (CliftonLarsonAllen LLP)

"Somehow Heather has managed to see inside my mind and to ask questions that I hadn't yet realized were there. She takes you on an exploration of where you are and who you want to be. It's a journey well worth taking. It might just profoundly change your life for the better. I didn't realize my own sense of dissatisfaction with the status quo until Heather's 3Cs encouraged me to sit under the stars and find my tire swing. Now begins the work of implementing new mental and practical habits to put this into practice—to reach the reward of a more fulfilled and joyful me."

Susan Barton, Organizational Development Consultant

"While many books touch on the concept of living a life with purpose, the foundations of 3C Living actually provide a road map for the journey. In these pages, Dr. Penny weaves together an inspiring blend of practical strategies, fresh perspectives, and heart-felt stories that will leave you ready to fully embrace the life you're made for."

Tiffany Loeffler, DPT, Executive Director,
The Alliance: Defending the Cause of Kids & Families

"Heather Penny's book *The Life You're Made For* has made a tremendous impact on the way I 'show up for life,' both personally and professionally. With a limited number of hours in our day, we rarely take time to focus on ourselves. Within the pages of this book, Heather guides us on a remarkable journey that enables us to free up space to live with purpose, find new perspectives, and blanket ourselves in true life joy."

Kelly Long, Co-founder and Partner, Manifold

"The life you dream of isn't out of reach—it's just waiting for you to pursue it with clarity, confidence, and courage. In *The Life You're Made For*, Heather Penny reveals how to achieve your biggest dreams and best future!"

Allen Arnold, Creativity Coach and author of The Story of With

"Heather has helped me realize more of my potential and has made me a better leader. She has helped me gain clarity on my goals, make steady progress toward them, and change some thought patterns that were holding me back. Heather has the uncanny ability to help bring out a clearer purpose that would have been difficult, if not impossible, to accomplish by myself. Working with Heather as my coach has been a remarkable journey, and I look forward to continuing it."

David W. Smith, Chief Inspector, Neptune Aviation Services
Northeastern & Central California and Northern Nevada

"I highly recommend Heather Penny's gem of a book to any person who is a leader, co-worker, parent, spouse, friend, or child as it is chock full of tools to help move beyond surviving to thriving so you can experience a more meaningful and fulfilled life. In her friendly, unassuming manner, Heather shares her own insecurities with humor and offers practical steps for how to get 'unstuck.' Heather's professional experience as a successful coach is evident and her insights from coaching clients and work as an educator lend credibility and create rich examples we can all learn from. I am excited to apply 3C living to my own life, create my own thrival plan (my favorite part of the book!), and see how my family, work, and community life blossom as a result."

Paula Allison, Associate Vice Chancellor,
Resource Development, Los Rios Community College District

"Heather is both a soothing cup of tea and a shot of espresso. In *The Life You're Made For*, she invites us on a journey that's not easy but worth it. With the warmth of a trusted friend and the expertise of an executive coach, each chapter provides examples and tools to guide us to lasting change. For anyone who has ever asked, 'Is this all there is?' Heather offers a way to stop just surviving and to choose living our one, unique, joy-filled, purposeful life."

Heather Johnson, Bridgeway Christian Church,
Missional Communities Coordinator

"In a world inundated with books offering advice, self-help, and tracks to happiness, *The Life You're Made For* stands out. Heather uniquely taps in to the questions of the heart whilst honoring the journey of the mind. She speaks freely about her own journey to wholeness and offers a clear path to live the life we all hope for but dare not dream possible. She gently peels off the layers of what blinds us, guiding and encouraging us to the source of life. *The Life You're Made For* is a wake-up call, a message of hope, and a road map to whole-hearted living."

Samantha Kaufman, International Teacher/Librarian and STEAM Educator

"This book does not have the answers you might be expecting, but it just might have the ones you need. It's possible to miss the life you're made to live, this book may be your best chance to be sure that doesn't happen."

Nancy Ortberg, CEO of Transforming the Bay with Christ

"Heather has made a significant impact on how we approach leadership development. As a result of Heather's coaching, I have recognized in order to lead your team, you must have truth and transparency. Heather has been instrumental in helping us create a truly growth-minded organization."

Jennifer Draughon, President, Neptune Aviation

"Heather Penny's on fire with passion for life. From years of experience as a professional coach, she understands the human condition. She asks questions that shift your inner dialogue from criticism to connection, awaken your heart, and bring a smile to your face. Pause for time around the campfire with Heather, and then take flight and soar!"

Kimberly Miller, therapist and author of Boundaries for Your Soul

"If you're on a quest to live a more meaningful and productive life, this is the book for you. In a compelling, conversational style, Dr. Penny walks readers through practical strategies and real-life examples that will help you live with intentionality in the present and face the future with hope and anticipation for what is possible. The questions and exercises at the end of each chapter are worth the price of the book! There is something here for anyone who would like to live with more clarity, confidence, and courage."

Dr. Gail Wallace, Co-founder of The Junia Project

"Are you like me? Have you felt stuck in life? Have you ever felt you may be missing or wasting your life? Are you looking for practical and tangible steps that you can take to move out of a rut and into a life worth living . . . a life of calling, meaning, purpose, and impact? If you answer *yes* to any of these questions, this book is a must-read for you as it was for me. It is a compelling invitation to go on a personal growth journey through 3C Living to become the best version of yourself and live the life you were meant for. I wholeheartedly recommend it."

Cory Botts, Policy Consultant to the California State Senate

"In her new book, *The Life You're Made For*, Heather Penny stirs us from our sleeping selves. She awakens us again to the dreams that have been snuffed out by the realities and demand of our everyday living. She calls us to action, reminding us that our truest, most courageous self is exactly what this world is longing for. But this isn't simply one more book for dreamers that won't deliver results. As she reminds us to dream, Heather also gives us actionable steps to move toward them by reclaiming clarity, building confidence, and harnessing our courage. We at UNCMN Creative Works are thrilled to help Heather introduce this book to the world. It has been transforming us as we work to creatively bring the book to life for her followers. We believe you will find life within its pages."

Dawn Neldon, Ryan Ross, Cody Vermillion, UNCMN Creative Team

THE
LIFE
YOU'RE
MADE FOR

Finding Clarity, Confidence, and Courage to Be Fully Alive

HEATHER PENNY, PhD

To my family.

You cheered me on every step of the way. Darren, it was your consistent optimism and belief in me that encouraged me to write. Thank you for your confidence and sharing it so generously. Luke, thank you for teaching me what it means to "be all in" and live with deep authenticity—so grateful to be your mom. Selah, your kind and peaceful ways are grounding to the human spirit and have been a gift to me as my daughter.

To each client I have worked with.

Thank you for inviting me into your journey and trusting me to partner with you. You know who you are. And for all the times when I was the only one witnessing how bravely you were living—take a bow. Well done. You showed up for your life and inspired me with your strength as you taught me about increasing clarity, confidence, and courage. I have considered it an honor.

CONTENTS

FOREWORD

Bob Goff

My wife and I live down by the bay in San Diego. We are usually gone on the 4th of July and miss the fireworks, but this year we were home. As the sun sank low in the sky, we moved out onto the lawn, which spans a small part of the several mile bayfront, in anticipation of what was to come. We weren't the only ones waiting for the show. More than one hundred thousand people had headed to the bay to watch the fireworks.

Darkness set in and stillness came with it. Even the conversations of the onlookers turned whisper quiet in expectation of what was to come. This is what anticipation looks like. Here are two questions I have for you: When was the last time you lived with this kind of anticipation? And what step have you taken toward your most lasting, updated, and worthwhile dreams?

Most of us emerge into our adult lives filled with anticipation about what would come next. We knew something spectacular was about to happen. But then life happened. Some of us got distracted. Or we became disappointed or disillusioned. Sure, a couple things worked out, but perhaps there was a big public failure or an even larger private one. We didn't stop showing up, but we started numbing out and settling for less than we should. We traded in the life we were made to live for the one we're settling for. We stopped looking for the fireworks.

Heather is a friend and teacher of mine, and she has a little pyromaniac in her. Let me tell you what I mean. She is a person who lights fuses for a living. She has lit mine, she's done it for hundreds of people as a leadership coach, and in these pages, she is going to ignite a few fires in you too. She calls what she does "3C Living" but for me, it has felt like she has invited us to a fireworks show. Not just to watch, but to participate in.

She wants us to live with more anticipation, more focus and purpose, and to find our way to the spectacle. She wants us to bring all the sparkle we've got and to stop comparing our rockets to everyone else's. Heather wants us to find a new gear if the old one isn't working any longer.

Here is the important, flammable message Heather has for each of us. We are not the combination of our successes, and we certainly are not the sum of our failures. This book is a reminder to ask ourselves what ambition we have that we haven't pursued with enough intensity, passion, and resolve. She wants us to identify what has been holding us back, then do something about it.

All fireworks shows have a grand finale and the show we were watching off the bay didn't disappoint. Just when it seemed that all of the fireworks had been hurled into the air, a rumbling of fireworks began to explode near the ground, then another layer was added, then an additional tier of larger, brighter fireworks were added while the lower levels continue to explode in extravagance. Finally, the night sky was ripped in half with football-stadium-size rockets. This massive crescendo continued well past any reasonable amount of time had passed. It was as if they'd left the machine on full blast and forgotten about it. But I believe they had something else in mind. They wanted everyone to experience something they had perhaps never seen before.

This is a picture of the engaged, extravagant life Heather is inviting us into and what the 3C Living looks like. Is it going to be easy to get there? Of course not. But buckle up, Heather is about to light a fuse in your life.

INTRODUCTION

Finding the Way to Your Dreams

You've been on this journey called life for a while now. So let me ask: Are you closer today to the life you've dreamed of than you were last month?

Okay, maybe the past month was a rough one. And a month is only four weeks. So let me rephrase the question.

Thinking back to where you were a year ago, are you closer today to attaining those dreams than you were then?

Maybe a better question is: Do you even remember what your dreams are? The world has a way of running us hard and wearing us out. Sooner or later, the goal is just to get through the day. There is no thriving. It's just survive today so we can wake up and do it all over again.

But there's more at play. We don't tend to care for ourselves very well. There's no blame here. Most of us were never offered a better way to approach life. We gave it our best shot, but now we're running on empty with little life and downsized dreams.

This way of living isn't sustainable.

If the above paragraphs describe you, I can promise you this. The path you're on won't one day magically lead to where you want to go. Years of traveling in the wrong direction only takes you to a place you never planned to be. And the journey itself will be filled with stress, regret, and a loss of hope. Here's the sobering reality. If you continue in the status quo, doing what you're doing now, life won't even just stay the same. It will likely get worse.

But here's the good news. That isn't the life you were made for. You actually have a choice about which road to take and where it will lead you. You are the driver of your journey, not the victim of circumstances.

The goal of this book is to help you chart a new course toward what makes you come fully alive. It will provide practical ways for you to gain traction in living that better life so you look forward to waking up and living out each day.

I call this process 3C Living.

What are the three "C"s that can change your world? I thought you'd never ask.

Clarity. This is about knowing *who* you are and *where* you want to go.

Confidence. This is about what you are believing. If you believe in your potential and the unique strengths you have to offer, it opens up a whole world of new possibility.

Courage. This is about taking action and bravely stepping out in new ways. This journey isn't for the timid or halfhearted.

The goal isn't to be partially alive, to settle for a ho-hum-blah existence, or to simply just survive. That isn't the life you were made for.

The goal is to be fully present to the life in front of you and live it out well.

Taken together, 3C Living helps you achieve that. It's not about doing more. You're probably already doing too much—or perhaps you're simply not getting the traction you need to get unstuck. It's about resting more, and then discovering how to do more of what you love while letting go of all that's holding you back! Before we're done, you'll discover how to make the choices you need to supercharge your growing Clarity, Confidence, and Courage.

These proven concepts have transformed my life and the lives of the many students, groups, clients, and companies I have worked with over the years. In fact, you'll hear some of their stories throughout this book.

Remember, you're where you are now because you weren't ready for all the hairpin curves life has put in your path. But you're also closer to breakthrough than you might think. You've just needed a guide (that's me!) to help you get out of that rut and step onto a better path.

Speaking of me, allow me to introduce myself. I'm a teacher, coach, research geek, and regular person who has lived both the "stressed-out life" and the "stuck life," eventually figuring out a better way by using my inborn curiosity and love for personal growth. I geek-out gaining insights on how people grow and develop the same way some love chocolate cake, craft beer, or a deep massage. I know. I'm unique this way. But it's a good uniqueness because I don't just get curious about observations, research, and trends by themselves. My passion is bringing in the human element and applying those findings with ways that lead to us living a better life.

In the early days, I focused my research on the emotional health of high-functioning women as they transitioned from college to the working world. Most studies showed significant signs of depression, anxiety, and fear. Discussions consistently focused on women in this transitional phase as spiraling down. Researchers began identifying this social phenomenon in similar findings across the board.[1] Each research article I read ended with "more research is needed" to address this issue.

I wanted to understand this more so I could help. And logic told me that if people can spiral down, we can also learn to spiral up.

This inspired me to study what made people spiral up rather than down as I focused on two areas: emotional well-being and career fulfillment. Studies frequently focus on the negative point of view, and I was growing tired of reading all the rationale behind what was causing the adverse reactions. I was determined to research how we all—women and men—can live stronger, happier, and more fulfilling lives. I discovered common themes and even created my own terms for what I found. What started out as an initial focus on women actually became applicable to all humanity as I coached people of all ages and genders over the years.

And on a more personal note, my faith is important to me. It centers me and aids me in growing my clarity, confidence, and courage. But it is sacred to me, which I assume it is for you. This is why I don't discuss it throughout this book. I'll leave that for you to integrate as you see fit. But I will reference

---

1. There are many studies that outline this issue. To read more about this, see references listed in endnotes.

it briefly at the end simply to share authentically behind the scenes of what has exponentially worked for me. I do this simply for you to get to know me on a more personal level and to be transparent about what has helped me grow.

So that's me. *I fuse proven research with practical insights for positive change.*

I do this by focusing on what's right—rather than wrong—with people. I take great joy in helping others spiral up, while making the journey enjoyable as they step into their life with renewed purpose. My coaching technique is intentional and purposeful, fueled by love and grace instead of shame or guilt. I focus on you achieving a positive future based on what uniquely fuels *you*. And I want you to know you're never alone on this journey. Over the course of this book, I'll be your guide. But even after that, it's not all up to you. I believe we have people who meet us in our journey exactly when we need them.

So where do we begin? We'll first head to a crossroads where we will pause and catch our breath (doesn't that sound nice?). Then I'll introduce you to some life-changing concepts like Mind Chatter, Tire Swings, Staying Powers, Crossroads, the Belief Snowball, Invisible Pulls, and the Peace of Being.

Our goal isn't to get anywhere fast. It is to get to the right place as a changed human being. Doing so will open our life up to more peace, greater joy, and deeper fulfillment. 3C Living is the map that got me there. It can be your map, too.

I've infused this book with some unique components. For instance, you'll find an allegory—or short story—introducing the book and referenced throughout. Why include it alongside the tangible research, coaching stories, and practical tools? Because I know how powerful stories can be, especially when we are trying to understand new ideas. This simple story allows people to see themselves from a fresh perspective. The story represents the findings of my research in a way that's easy to understand, and it helps me introduce the language I need to talk about complex issues. Using story as a vehicle helps us make the connections necessary to understand the multifaceted issues we are grappling with. I also provide key questions, exercises, and even some helpful "cautions" at the end of every chapter to empower you in staying on track.

This is your invitation to live with new purpose, fresh perspective, and consistent energy. Are you ready to join me on that journey to the life you're made for? If so, turn the page. We'll begin with a story about the things that weigh us down . . . and those that bring us joy.

Opening

THERE ONCE WAS A LITTLE GIRL.

She loved to play outside. She would run after the birds as they flew, hunt for eggs, create clubs with her friends on the great rock, and design all kinds of beautiful art.

And at night, she would lie on her back and watch the stars.

But her favorite place to be was on the tire swing that was tied to a branch of the great oak tree. She would climb the hill to the tree where her tire swing hung. Pumping her legs made the swing go higher and higher, until she could almost touch the clouds. And as it carried her through the air, she would throw her head back, basking in the feel of the breeze on her face and the wind in her hair.

It was in these moments she felt most free.

The little girl was gentle and kind . . . yet passionate and wild.

One day, she received a special gift from someone who wanted to show their love for her. The Giver handed her a beautifully wrapped box. As she opened it and put on the gold bracelet, the Giver explained the great honor bestowed upon her. The gift was a way for her to feel loved and know her immense beauty.

But with this gift came an expectation. She would need to wear the bracelet at all times, to honor both the Giver and herself.

She took this responsibility quite seriously. During the day, she would watch it glisten in the sun. At night, she'd fall asleep as it rested on her arm. The bracelet made her feel loved, noticed, and valuable.

As the little girl grew, there were many Givers in her life, and with each passing season, she received more and more bracelets from Givers who loved her and from those who wanted her love.

Her arms grew heavy from the bracelets, and soon, she had to stop running barefoot through the grass and playing on her beloved tire swing. The more bracelets she received, the more her joy began to fade. She realized that each Giver expected her to wear their gift at all times.

Already, her arms felt heavy, and with each added bracelet, she became more restricted. But not wanting to hurt the Givers' feelings, she continued to smile and slide the bracelets up past her elbows.

One day, a beautiful bird caught her eye. A forgotten longing stirred deep within her. She wanted to follow the bird and find out where it lived, just as she had done so often when she was young.

As she ran outside to explore, the weight of all her bracelets stopped her short. Out of breath and with deep sadness, she stared after the bird until it was a small spec in the distance.

Standing in the sunlight, she remembered the care-free days of childhood and the tire swing that swayed from the great oak tree.

She sighed. It wasn't just her arms that were heavy. So was her heart.

After other attempts, she stopped trying to pursue what brought her joy. It was impossible to do what she loved with that many bracelets; however, she dared not take them off. She not only feared disappointing her Givers, but she liked how the bracelets had begun to make her feel valuable, cherished, and loved. Who was she without the bracelets? She no longer knew.

And she no longer had time to dream about her future. She was doing so much—yet felt she was becoming less.

The young woman became dutiful to the expectations of others and continued to wear the bracelets as she tried to take comfort in the worthiness she felt. She stopped looking out the window. She stopped going outside. She stopped dreaming of beautiful ideas. She stopped playing. She stopped feeling free. She looked to her Givers for love and approval . . . and on the inside, she began to disappear.

No one wanted the little girl who ran free and wild, no one misses her, she thought. *I must be a woman with many bracelets because this is who people love. This is now who I am.* So the young woman became embarrassed of who she had been as a little girl and collected more and more bracelets to hide who she truly was. She even began to give bracelets to herself.

But the sadness within her grew until she could contain it no longer. She longed to stop disappearing; she longed to be free again. But most importantly, she longed to be cherished for who she'd been before receiving all the bracelets.

The Givers—and their gifts—had become the measure of her worth. Somewhere along the way, her own desires and dreams had slowly disappeared. She knew better who others wanted her to be than who she truly was.

Unclear about what to do next, she remained doubtful of her purpose. Late one night, while sitting under the stars, she found herself weary and disheartened, yet unwilling to remove all the bracelets that told her who she was.

The stars shimmered, providing a stunning light show. This view was a gift with no expectations. She laid back and took it all in. The young woman knew she couldn't go on living this way . . . but she didn't know what to do.

"Take off your bracelets . . . I did not give them to you."

"Who said that?" the surprised woman exclaimed.

"I am the Giver of Life," responded the voice. *"I give all and I create all. I created you without bracelets, and I never gave you any. Instead, I gave you your spirit. It is a spirit that is wild, tender, gentle, and free . . . Take off your bracelets, for they dishonor the greatest gift you have ever been given . . . your beautiful, free spirit . . . and they dishonor Me,"* spoke the gentle voice in the wind.

It was then that the woman realized she had a choice to make. *Shall I keep the bracelets on or take them off? If I keep them on, I have a purpose with very little risk. But if I take them off, the risk is greater. What if I don't know who I am? And what about all those I disappoint?* Then an exciting new thought began growing within her. *What if I get to know my beautiful spirit again and find a purpose outside the bracelets?*

With this new clarity, she left the thought to simmer so she could build the confidence she needed. Before the weary woman fell asleep under the stars, she asked the Giver of All Good Things to give her the courage to love her greatest gift of all . . . her spirit.

PART I
Clarity

The First C: Choosing to Know

After other attempts, she stopped trying to pursue what brought her joy. It was impossible to do what she loved with that many bracelets; however, she dared not take them off. She not only feared disappointing her Givers, but she liked how the bracelets had begun to make her feel valuable, cherished, and loved. Who was she without the bracelets? She no longer knew.

Every great journey has a memorable beginning. This one begins in search of Clarity.

Without Clarity, how can we see the steps before us? When we're in a fog about where to start, the journey quickly stalls. Then, to make matters worse, we just go faster trying to get somewhere, anywhere. Yet we never arrive at a place that matters.

It's time to take a different journey. A journey to find the life you're made for.

Rather than a race, this trek begins with rest. The prize doesn't go to the fastest. It goes to those who take the time to face the truth and really *know* what is going on in their life.

For the overachievers, I hear your protests. *Rest? Who needs rest? Let's get on with it. Make things happen.* You've pressed the accelerator to the floorboard so many times, it's permanently stuck there. Others are stuck in neutral, finding it almost impossible to start moving or make big decisions. But hesitancy from nervous indecision or pushing through just to stay in motion isn't our goal. That never leads to a spirit at rest. Internally, you are looking for peaceful resolve that comes from seeing things clearly. Regardless of which end of the spectrum you're on, this isn't the life you were made for. I'm here to help you find a better way. But you can't begin a journey of this magnitude from a place of weariness. Or striving. Or paralysis.

That's why rest is the first requirement for what's ahead. It's not a delay to the journey—it's the very foundation of your journey. You must know where you're going and why. With everything coming at you, you need a compass that helps you find True North for what matters. One that can slow you down or speed you up as needed. That compass is Clarity. It helps to remember what your dreams are *and* who you are. Because, let's be honest, you've forgotten.

You're heading to the crossroads where you'll pause long enough to catch your breath and recover your story. Your past decisions have made up the pages and chapters and themes of the story. Yet somewhere along the way, you allowed others to take creative license with your story so that it no longer resembles who you are. Fatigue, weariness, betrayal, and ego have eroded your ability to stay on track. Along the way, the focus became surviving rather than thriving.

Clarity reminds you that the pen is in your hand—and always has been. You have the freedom to write the story you want to live. To remember, you must reduce mind chatter, restore through the power of rest, distinguish between the gifts that lift you up and those that weigh you down, and spend time under the stars.

The enemy to Clarity is confusion. It's impossible to get anywhere that matters without Clarity. So let's begin there.

THE NEED TO REST

Discovering the Secret of RESTorative Rest

You are running on empty.

It's okay. I won't tell anyone. This is a safe place to let your guard down.

You might be fooling those around you. Over the years, you've mastered the art of appearing successful, in control, and calm. On the outside, at least. But you're a mess inside.

Or perhaps you're visibly weary and bleary, tired of juggling more than you can handle. Forget thriving, you're just trying to make it through the day without one more plate crashing.

You may be wondering how I know. No, I haven't been reading your email. We've likely never met. As a professional coach, however, I know the human condition. And nearly 100 percent of us are overwhelmed, exhausted, weary, and ready for relief. Simply living in this fast-paced world takes an immense toll on the heart.

There's no shame in running on empty. You just don't want to camp there.

But before lasting change can occur, we need to name the problem.

Whether you're desperate for relief or still in denial that things are about to go off the rails, I want to offer you a way to a fuller life. This isn't a shortcut, one-minute makeover. Those sound great but never last.

You actually don't need relief—something to numb your pain. You need rest—something to restore your soul.

Let's Start with a Road Trip

Did your family take road trips when you were a child? Did you look forward to setting out to see your country cousins, your eccentric aunt and uncle in the city, or perhaps your grandparents several states away? Maybe the goal was to see epic sites—the Grand Canyon, the Redwoods, or the Outer Banks. Wherever it was, let those memories come to mind.

Or maybe your family never took road trips. If that's the case, the good news is we are taking a road trip through this book. It's a journey of the heart rather than to an external destination. I'm glad we get to do this together.

When I think back to my own road trips, I remember the good times. I see a little bit too much of myself in my dad's determination to get in as many miles as is possible between rest stops. He'd drive until my siblings and I were about to go stir-crazy. Only then would he pull off the highway . . . for a moment.

Rest stops were pure freedom, a reprieve from the confinement and monotonous pace of our journey. We'd pile out of our station wagon, leaving behind all the car games, funny smells, and lines we drew between us. (Okay, maybe I was the one who drew the lines, especially when I got stuck sitting on the middle hump with siblings bumping me from either side!)

But ahh, the rest stop. I can still see the green signs on the side of the freeway announcing the next stop. As children, we cheered, begging our father to pull over. It was where we could run, play, stretch our legs, get a snack, and feel the wide-open spaces. To feel the steady ground under our feet instead of watching the world whiz by—hour after hour.

And if we were caravanning with friends, when we piled back into our cars, we'd shout, "We'll meet you at the next rest stop!" It brought me comfort knowing that though the miles ahead would separate us, we would find each other at the next rest stop where we would gather to share a meal, go over maps, or simply enjoy the camaraderie of being on an adventure together.

Even the most driven people realize pulling over at rest stops or stopping at a gas station to fill up is a necessary component for breaking up a trip. A momentary pause that refuels both the vehicle and the people in it. When the journey continues, everyone seems more alert and relaxed. Ready for what's next.

In life, we forget to take those pauses. Instead we speed up because we feel behind . . . or just don't like someone else ahead of us in the fast lane. Eventually our accelerator can even get stuck.

This is your invitation to slow down for some much-needed clarity.

After all, each of us have cravings for richer lives with more meaningful days filled with passion and purpose. We just forget rest is a part of the journey.

CLARITY

It's not hard to find a rest stop, so what's preventing you from pulling over?

Back to the Bracelets

Do you wonder what the young woman will choose? She had reached a major decision point. Let's slow down a bit to fully appreciate the struggles she faces.

Most people I share this story with hope she'll choose a life with fewer bracelets and more tire swings. They want this outcome for her. But more, they want this freedom for themselves.

It's just unclear how she—or we—can get there.

I understand. I was weighed down by too many responsibilities for too much of my life. So are most people I know. As a coach, I listen intently to people's pain and lost dreams. I see it play out with those who cross my path on a daily basis. And I'll occasionally catch glimpses of it looking back at me in the mirror.

The hardest part is realizing that in all those cases, we have a choice.

We can take the bracelets off. We have the power to choose the life we *truly* want.

We were never meant to be stuck in this rut. Yet it somehow happened, bit by bit. Think back to the girl on the tire swing. Did you notice how the pressure snuck up on her?

One bracelet at a time.

I'm guessing you know the feeling. Do you fall into bed most nights weary and wondering how you got to this point? You want to change your circumstances, but you're not sure if you have the knowledge, power, or courage to do it. But pay attention. The fatigue that you hate serves a valuable purpose.

Like a warning sign flashing on your car dash, it's the cue that life is no longer working.

The choice is yours. You can assess the problems. You can examine what weighs you down. You can pursue rest and clarity.

If you want more life, those choices are essential. Because it's impossible to enjoy what brings life (your tire swing) when you can't even walk up the hill to what you long for without being exhausted.

As long as you have the power of choice, you don't have to live as victims stuck in a story that drains your dreams, emotions, gifting, and joy.

To take back your life, you must see clearly where you have acquiesced your power of choice.

What Pace Are You Keeping?

We all long to feel clarity in an uncertain world. Yet many of us live as if we have no control over the pace we keep—as if our accelerators are stuck. But clarity doesn't come as we whiz through life. It comes when we discover how to slow down, pull to the side of the road, and consider big questions.

Don't misunderstand. This isn't about momentarily stopping just to start again. It's not a pit stop where tires are changed in seconds to keep you in the race. It's about doing your life differently. It's about the value, pursuit, and power of rest. Right ahead of you on this road trip is a rest stop. It's the perfect place to gain clarity about the direction you're traveling.

Living with more clarity means learning how and when to pull over and take a break. It feels disruptive when you've been taught to push harder and do more, doesn't it? Get as many miles in as you can each day because that's the measure of success. It sure feels true. It's what the world tells us. But it's a lie. This way of living only creates more confusion, more anxiety, and weakens your sense of direction.

Here's the good news. Change is easier than you think. Your pace is up to you. You can pull over whenever you want. It's not about keeping up with the warp-speed you (or others) may be running, but rather slowing down and doing less. It sounds counterintuitive to slow down when you want to accomplish so much, right?

But consider the cost when you push too hard. You lose clarity regarding what you care about and where you are going. You waste valuable time spinning your wheels, and you often burn out or crash.

Slowing down regularly and pulling over to reassess where you are going and how best to get there—whole and well—cultivates a life of ever-increasing clarity.

So, let's tap the brakes for a bit, shall we?

A Recipe for Disaster

Managing your busy life while not changing the pace is a recipe for disaster.

I want to share a moment that forever shaped my understanding of rest. It happened at an event where I was the keynote speaker on the topic of work-life balance. A familiar subject—but honestly, oftentimes a dull one. There is much discussion around this concept, but from my observations, there is little practical application or inspiring life change that appears to be happening in a way that really sticks.

The standard seems to be too low. *"Just help me manage my busy life better, but don't mess with the pace I am keeping."* It's as if people want me to run interference to clear the roads while keeping the toll gates up. It makes me sad. I'm hesitant to even join these conversations. And often I don't.

Yet, I fervently believe in the power of slowing down as a way of life.

I had agreed to speak at this venue. After being introduced, I began to talk about the idea of rest. In an introductory reflection, I asked participants to imagine themselves beside picturesque still waters and green pastures. The emphasis was on the idea that we can rest through trusting that all will be well. A beautiful metaphor. One to bask in, for sure.

This introduction to work-life balance wasn't what anyone in the room expected. I wasn't giving ideas on prioritizing tasks or how to make better to-do lists. No ten steps to greater productivity. We need to remember what rest is and how it feels to actually be RESTored.

We need more voices helping us get off our hamster wheels and downshift out of fifth gear. Can we please quit racing toward wherever it is we're headed and instead pull the car over?

Yes, rest is needed, but not just any rest. RESTorative rest. This is the kind of rest that allows the spirit to feel refreshed and makes us want to get up again the next day rather than endure another moment of tired misery.

And here's where my keynote speech took an interesting turn.

A brave woman suddenly raised her hand and began to talk before I had even called on her. "What do you mean by rest?"

I loved this courageous act. It was authentic, vulnerable, and held a desperate hope for new answers. But it also startled me. I'd never been interrupted like this before in front of a group of 250+ people. As I decided how to respond, it dawned on me how we've lost awareness of what true rest looks like as a society. Many of us have abandoned all hope in being able to rest with any sense of restoring qualities. The ability to rest holistically—mind, body, heart, and spirit—has been lost. And out of frustration, guilt, shame, and fear, we spend most of our energy finding ways to push harder and achieve more.

For heaven's sake, why?

At the risk of oversimplifying a multifaceted issue running rampant in our world, we lack trust.

And without trust, we cannot rest.

Let me say that again. And for the sake of clarity you may even want to read these eleven words out loud: *Without learning to trust, you will not be able to rest.*

Yep. Trust is lacking big time.

In all likelihood, you're probably like 99 percent of the population where pausing and resting is not a normal habit done to gain clarity. Most don't even consider it an option. Many simply try harder, set higher goals, run faster, and write more to-do lists to make life work.

Except it isn't working.

Rest is what's needed. Even more, rest is required for a life of significance.

No Trust, No Rest

I'll get back to how I answered the woman's question in just a minute. But I need to pause and give you some backstory first.

I want to share where I learned about the link between *trust* and *rest*. The breakthrough occurred while I was working with at-risk children. If a child cannot trust that their room will not be haunted by an abuser, they cannot rest. If a child does not feel safe from the violence in his or her neighborhood, they cannot rest. If a child cannot trust that they can learn in a classroom without ridicule or bullying, they cannot rest.

And as adults, if we do not trust that there are green pastures, still waters, and restorative places and practices available, then we simply will not rest.

Somewhere along the way, our trust has been damaged and we have forgotten how to trust . . . and, thus, to rest.

We need to regain trust in the journey. Trust in one another. Trust that situations will work out. Trust in a beautiful plan for our lives. Trust in green pastures and calm waters. Trust in our decision-making abilities.

Trust that if we rest, all will truly be well. In other words, we need to rest in the fact that we can rest because life isn't all up to us.

But this is hard when life has thrown you one too many gut-punches, right? We've all been let down. We've experienced betrayals, loss, and pain from being misunderstood. You answer the phone expecting good news only to hear the worst. A friendship doesn't turn out like you hoped. You realize your spouse never really committed to the vows the way you did. You leave for vacation only to come back to the news you were demoted from your dream job.

Life doesn't always turn out like we planned in our childhood visions of being a "grown-up."

Actually, that's putting it mildly.

Life *rarely* turns out like we hoped it would.

And oftentimes we respond to these gut-punches by either giving up or working harder—shutting down our hearts, believing life is up to us.

We stop believing that rest impacts how we live. It feels like a waste of time. Something that puts us behind. So, we pick ourselves up by the bootstraps and press on.

And we slowly lose clarity about the story we are living.

Our focus becomes fuzzy about what we want and how we hope to create the life we had planned. The disappointment is real, but our interpretation of life isn't. And we lose much of what it means to truly rest RESToratively: mind, body, heart, and spirit.

Dealing with disappointment means taking time to find the answers you need about what your life has become. Pulling into a rest stop lets you recover and reorient. But to do this, it requires trust. Trust in the journey. Trust in yourself.

Without trust, all we know to do is press on or give up.

Teaching English and drama to at-risk junior high students in East Los Angeles taught me this. I learned quickly that if they could not trust, they could not rest. And if they could not rest, they could not have the clarity they needed to learn.

This was a conundrum—what to do? I couldn't change the world they lived in and the harsh realities of their lives.

In my teacher training, I was intrigued with the research around engaging the right side of the brain and how it allows us to heal and find comfort. It's a form of RESTorative Rest I had been personally exploring in my own journey. I thought about how to help my students trust, how to rest their minds and hearts in a harsh world that gave them every reason to feel unsafe.

I vowed that at least for one hour each day, they were going to feel safe. And it would be in my classroom. I did this by starting the first ten minutes of each period with art. Art soothes the heart and is a balm for the weary spirit. I dimmed the lights while playing classical music. I let them draw in peace. Then the lights would slowly come on and we would move into literature, poetry, or a three-paragraph essay. Within the first year, test scores went up. In the second year, the passing rate increased from 30 percent to 70 percent. Unexpectedly, I was even named Teacher of the Year and asked to serve as Literacy Coach for the district. We learned together the synergistic connection between trust, rest, and clarity.

The Brave Soul Who Raised Her Hand

Now we can return to the story. I turned to the woman who had asked the disruptively beautiful question, "What do you mean by rest?"

After a pause, I said, "We have lost our trust. And without trust, we cannot rest."

A hush came over the room. She had a blank look on her face with an expression that seemed to convey a feeling of *thanks for nothing*.

But I wasn't finished answering. Teaching students had taught me that we learn by doing. For this group, the idea of rest was still in the head. It needed to shift to the heart to make it real. The answer would be found in experiencing rest together.

I was grateful for this courageous woman. She set me up quite nicely. In this particular coaching workshop, I actually planned to lead the group in a RESTorative Rest exercise. It incorporated what I had learned in teaching—how to rest our mind and heart by engaging the right side of the brain through art and music. After thirty minutes of music playing, dimmed lights, and doodling with art supplies, the group was able to experience rest outside the familiar context of just sleeping.

Whenever a group begins this exercise, people begin to fidget. They grow restless. It feels . . . wasteful. Until the moment everything shifts. Then the feeling goes from wasteful to wonderful. No one wants it to end! Some even get downright cranky when I turn the music off and tell them our time is up. I don't blame them. I've supervised this exercise with thousands of groups—both adults and children—and each time there is surprise at how quickly thirty minutes pass. This is often what happens when we engage the right side of our brain, we "lose time" because we are living from a place of ease and desire.

This is such a powerful experience because life drains us, and we are in desperate need of refueling.

Then, as we moved into our discussion groups, new clarity emerged about RESTorative Rest and how each person needed it. New answers came from new questions being asked. The focus shifted from "how to balance life" to "how to rest restoratively."

We were now finding answers that brought peace because we were asking a better question.

Are you starting to see how shifting your focus from a place of rest can bring clarity?

This is what clarity offers. The ability to ask questions that help you rather than harm you.

Questions that direct you toward how to rest rather than how to keep up with a life that only brings daily angst. Our world does not need new systems, plans, or to-do lists that keep you racing through life without brakes. The result of that—as you well know—is anxiety, chaos, and hopelessness.

Many of us live with stuck accelerators. We forget that brakes are an option. When we shift the question from keeping up to slowing down, however, the conversation changes.

The woman who bravely raised her hand came up to me afterward and was beaming. "Now I know how to give myself what I never knew I needed. I didn't realize I could find ways to restore my spirit!" she said with tears in her eyes. It was her aha moment in learning that not only did she have brakes, but she could apply them as needed. She could find a rest stop and pull over. The next time I spoke with this woman, she was excited to tell me how much more she was enjoying life. The people in her life liked her better, too. She had found the brakes. She was living in rest, and there was restoration to her story.

There can be for yours as well.

The Art of Slowing Down

Here at the rest stop, it's critical that you step away from the car, breathe deep, and slow your pace. Take time to notice your surroundings. These simple acts will begin to unclench the knot in the pit of your stomach—the one that's been there so long it's started to feel almost normal.

This process of discovery honors the intuition within you that's been saying for years there has to be more than chasing validation while simply surviving. You were right. There is.

But none of this can happen if all you're doing is worrying about keeping up. Later we'll talk about how the power of asking the right questions is important. That's essential if you want the right answers. But for now, simply recognize that rest brings the clarity needed to have better discussions.

During this pause, let's take a look at what's weighing you down. Why? Because that's a signal the bracelets have begun piling on. If you're wondering what these have to do with rest, let me explain.

Many of you need to give yourselves a permission slip to rest. To consider that the myriad of responsibilities you're holding may be preventing you from jumping on your tire swing and enjoying life. The bracelets seem pretty, harmless, and perhaps even good or sentimental. After all, you spent so much time earning them.

And yet they are weighing you down. How can that be good?

Lean close. I want to make sure you hear this. I'm concerned you still may not know what I mean by "rest." And if you don't understand this one word, you won't be able to continue this journey, much less finish it well.

Rest isn't possible when you're pouring everything out every day and then falling over exhausted at night just to get up and do it all over again. Resting—mind, body, heart, and spirit—is about what you do that brings you to a place of peace. The exercises you enter into that cause you to breathe easier . . . not faster. You don't need to go to a workshop to experience this. Everything you need is in this book. But it usually doesn't come easily.

Your Place of Calm

Experiencing RESTorative Rest is like stepping into an atmosphere of calm. When you do, you instantly start to feel refreshed and clear-minded. It may illicit the same feelings you get when you're hiking in nature, getting lost in a good novel, playing guitar, or spending time on a craft like woodworking.

It's important to be mindful of what refuels you; what makes you feel like you just pushed the refresh button.

Simply stated, if rest isn't restoring you, it's not the rest I'm talking about. The goal is to shift out of the left side of your brain where all the logic is busy trying to work things out and into the right side where you can find a creative outlet. Find that and you've found your tire swing.

Sometimes RESTorative Rest is active—that's what I call your tire swing. Sometimes it is more contemplative, like staring at the stars. Spending regular time doing both, on tire swings and staring at stars, helps increase your clarity. It's how you will know which bracelets to take off and which to keep on. I will go into more detail on this later, but for now, make the connection that RESTorative Rest is unique to each person. Finding the rest that restores *you* is of utmost importance.

This is what can make the journey *sooo* challenging. Learning the type of rest you crave is a commitment. It means experimenting until you find what brings you greater clarity, peace, and joy.

Allow me to add a word of clarification here. Some practices may bring you comfort, but they do not bring restoration. For instance, activities that medicate you, like eating a plate of brownies, or drinking a glass of wine, or watching television, or (insert your preferred vice)—these are escapes. They numb you. In moderation, these things are perfectly enjoyable and have their place. Yet, they are very different from practices that will restore you.

Does this mean only tire-swinging or stargazing can restore you? Nope, that's like saying there's only one color or word or food that brings you joy. There are many! Most are just undiscovered at this point. Through this journey, you will find new things that restore and refresh you. I'm excited for you to discover them!

For me, this rest might be listening to a song on an early morning run, getting lost in a painting while classical music plays, spending time in nature, taking a walk with an inspiring audio book, reading poetry, listening to a podcast on my back patio, lying on my favorite couch with a good book and dozing off, or enjoying good conversation with a friend who "gets me" and likes who I am. Just thinking about these things makes me breathe easier and releases the tightness in my chest. I'm exhaling now.

The next step is to determine how you rest RESToratively.

Some activities can be done daily, but others require more time. This is navigating your work-life harmony. How often do you pull over to the rest stop? How long do you stay? And what do you need to feel restored before you get back on the road? You get these answers by intentionally examining your life.

Are you ready to try this on your own?

CLARITY

CLARITY QUESTION
How do you rest RESToratively?

Name three things that might help you feel refreshed. Don't overanalyze it or worry if they are practical. Just take your foot off the accelerator, pull your car to the side of the road, and give yourself space to try them this week.

1.

2.

3.

CAUTION: Pay attention to the thoughts or voices pulling on you, telling you you're not allowed to rest. Give yourself permission to trust in a new and better way to be restored mind, body, heart, and spirit.

PERMISSION SLIP: I, _____, who holds the authority and power to make free-will choices for ME, give myself the permission to RESToratively Rest on a daily basis.

_____   _____
(signature)   *(date)*

CLARITY

Congratulations! You've made it through the first chapter. I hope your tank already feels a little fuller. Running on empty is no way to live.

Remember, we're on a road trip together—one that spans time, space, and any past limitations. Be kind to yourself. There are bumpy patches ahead, some new terrain, and a lot of places where you'll need to trust me. I'll purposely be taking you out of your comfort zone, all for the sake of your heart and greater clarity. But we will go at a peaceful pace.

It's going to be a spectacular journey. One that will refresh you and invite you into a fuller life.

You've already discovered the importance of rest stops along the way. It's good to slow down as you travel and be intentional about where you're going and who you are becoming. Like the brave woman who raised her hand wondering about rest, you must ask yourself, "What does it look like for me to truly rest?"

It's a heart question that will require slowing down to fully answer. For it is your heart that helps identify what is driving you and nipping at your heels. It is your heart that knows what is preventing you from pulling over and trusting you can rest. Or perhaps even believing you deserve to rest. If you don't know how to listen to your heart, no worries. We'll get to that, too.

The next part of our journey involves the issue of mind chatter. It is an enemy of clarity . . . and the topic of the next chapter.

MIND CHATTER

How to Hear the Right Questions

For too many years, all I saw were my faults.

When things didn't go well, it was my fault. When things went from bad to worse, it was *even more* my fault. Even on the best days, I felt I was blowing it somehow.

I lived with the internal haunting question, "*What is wrong with me?*"

I beat myself up when misunderstandings occurred or relationships got sideways. Like when I put my foot in my mouth at a party, missed a social cue with a close friend, or shared an idea at work that went over like a lead balloon.

No one was harder on me . . . than me. I concluded that I must be the problem because I was the only common denominator in every situation. And the mind chatter was running rampant.

It never dawned on me that other circumstances were at play or that there was another way to see things. It's actually rather self-centered to think that I could be the cause for everything going wrong and that all the awkwardness or discomfort in situations were probably my fault. As if the universe revolved around me, and I bore responsibility for every encounter.

About that time, I noticed an interesting phenomenon in my work as a researcher, teacher, and coach. Others were wrestling with the same toxic thought. When life got hard and confusing, the question I heard over and again from my clients and friends was a variation of, *"What is wrong with me?"* Some spoke it out of deep despair, others with rage, and some with disheartening inquisitiveness. Many whispered it under the weight of crippling anxiety or overwhelming fear.

Countless people, including me, were asking the same question, but the question was not getting them the answer they were looking for. In fact, it was keeping them stuck.

"What's wrong with me?" doesn't invite healthy curiosity and positive solutions. It's a question that increases shame, simultaneously crippling us as it demands we run faster or do better. And the mind chatter only increases.

That's when I realized not all questions are created equal. Some questions help bring clarity. Others unleash unhelpful mind chatter. And many are so toxic that they cause deep damage to the heart. The goal of this chapter is to see how the right questions can lead to greater clarity.

Stick-Figure Revelations

Have you ever wondered why you don't fit in?

Does life seem harder for you than for others?

Do you feel you'll never achieve your dreams?

All of these questions are actually variations of: "What is wrong with me?"

It is this core question most of us struggle with. Especially when life gets hard, confusing, and heartbreaking. When the pressure is on and life is falling apart, it's easy to go there. As I confessed earlier, that was my story for many years.

It took a while, but after two decades, I finally realized this type of question was harming me and creating a deep sense of inadequacy and shame. The good news is I became obsessed about finding a way out of this pit.

That led me to ask different, better questions.

So what if I didn't always fit in?

So what if people didn't always understand me?

So what if things got awkward at times?

My heightened focus on all that was "wrong" with me caused me to see the world through a lens that was the very opposite of clarity. I didn't believe others, even friends, would like me unless I got it right . . . but I never was quite sure what the ever-changing metric of "right" was each day. Living that way was extremely conditional and stressful. I went to bed at night utterly exhausted under the weight of an ever-increasing anxiety, depression, and shame.

I was unconsciously creating the foundation for a weakened identity with an anxious mind.

Another breakthrough came a bit later when I was at an appointment with my counselor. She was tired (as was I) of me talking *around* the issues and doing all I could to avoid what I was truly feeling. And I was weary from the effort it took to "answer" her questions in ways that allowed me to stay hidden. Emotions made me feel weak—and I didn't like feeling vulnerable.

In her wisdom, she decided to try a different tactic. She stood and said, "Since you can talk circles around me, I'd like to leave you with your thoughts and have you draw those feelings." Then she walked out of the room.

Dang. She was on to me.

I noticed a drawing pad on the table in front of me. With no one to talk to or to convince, I was fine—which we both knew wasn't true. I picked up the pencil and began to draw. Being a stick-figure type of artist, I attempted to create an image. After I was done, I didn't like what stared back at me. It was a picture of me hitting myself on the head with a baseball bat.

Sigh. When had this started? Looking at that picture was sobering. I had to find a better way. A path that would lead me deeper into myself through grace, kindness, and finding a way to befriend myself. Somewhere along the way, I had set an impossible standard to achieve. And something inside of me was breaking. I became more resolved to deal with whatever this was. I even felt hope begin to rise within me.

Instinctively, I knew this was not sustainable. I was not made to live this way.

And neither were you.

Asking Better Questions

I needed a new question. One that would help me stop beating myself over the head. I needed a question that invited in grace, curiosity, kindness, and peace. It was time to lay down the bat. It was time for me to pull the car over and regroup. I was in desperate need of a rest stop.

Taking time to listen to the mind chatter and the questions we are asking is what happens at rest stops. It gives us the space not only to listen, but also the time and energy to shift unhelpful questions into helpful ones.

Asking a new question, such as: *"What is right with me?"* allows us to move forward as we shift our inner dialogue. This helps open new doors, offers creative solutions, and builds new energy. Peace and confidence begin replacing fear and anxiety as we are released from the pressure of "getting it wrong."

We cannot flourish when we constantly live in a question that keeps us stuck. If you aren't sure whether a question is harmful, here's a good test. Does asking it keep you stuck? Does it stir up feelings of shame or anxiety? If so, my advice, at least for now, is to avoid those questions.

Changing harmful questions into helpful questions is a universal need. Because when we ask the right question—without shame and judgment—we are able to get the answers we need to move forward.

Let's take a moment to practice this. How would you answer the following question?

What is right with you?

Before you respond, observe a few things.

First, do you notice how much easier it is to name what's wrong with you? Unfortunately, we all have far more practice with this question.

Second, does it feel odd to say kind things about yourself? Why do you think that is, especially if what you're saying is true?

So, what is right with you? (Seriously, pause and reflect on this for a couple minutes. Go ahead, write some things down.

I'll leave some space below. If this is hard for you, reflect on what people who love you say about you. Maybe even ask them!)

_____

_____

_____

Do you sense hope rise as you respond? Is there a bit more clarity to who you really are—and a more balanced sense of how life is going? Perhaps you're breathing a little easier. Maybe even smiling. That's the effect of a good question.

Spend some time with the words you wrote before moving to the next section. There's a lot of healing to be had here.

Life Can Be So Hard

Sometimes another person's story can help us see our own more clearly.

Here's how one man I coached shifted his question from a harmful one to a helpful one. I was on a phone call with Jack. He was struggling with balancing all the responsibilities in his life. Career, kids, marriage, school, and to top it off, his parents were both sick and it was up to him to care for them—all while living overseas. It was taking a toll on him.

In exasperation, he asked, "Why is this happening to me? How do I keep up with all this?"

Ouch. It hurt to hear the desperate strain in his voice. I know. Life can be so freakin' hard. It was the fifth conversation I'd had that day where I listened to how the stress of living was wearing people thin. With compassion, I gently changed the question to: "How do you want to make the space you need to thrive in this challenging season?"

He knew where this was heading and was deciding if he was up for it. I was greeted with silence on the other end of the line. No judgment. We were simply at the rest stop together, and I was committed to waiting with him.

I know what it feels like to ask a question that feels more like I'm hitting myself over the head with a bat. I needed to ask him a question that offered hope and kindness rather than harm from piling more on.

He sighed. "I need to invite help into this because I am falling apart trying to figure it out on my own. Even though I don't feel like asking for help, I guess I need to."

I risked another question. "How do you want to move forward?"

"I love getting out in nature and going for a run. I'm going to start each morning this way. During that time, I'll consider what help I need rather than trying to figure it all out on my own."

That began a powerful shift in Jack's life. Over the following year, we talked about daily practices he could use to ground himself in his new question and steer himself clear of the lie that life was all up to him.

Is his life perfect? No, it's still challenging. He's in the same career that pulls on him with responsibilities that continue to grow. But he's figured out how to get some of the bracelets off, spend time on the tire swing, and rest under the stars.

And it all started with a question that offered help instead of harm.

Revisiting the Rest Stop

A key to Jack's breakthrough was his willingness to pull over at a rest stop.

That isn't easy. It isn't something most people even believe they have permission to do.

When I first started resting more intentionally, everything was still a little fuzzy, mainly because I had been running too hard for too long. And slowing down was a new behavior pattern that I didn't know how to do consistently.

I learned to slow down out of desperation. I really didn't have a choice; I'd run out of fuel. But experiencing the effects of running on empty has made me more mindful about when to pull over because I don't ever want to run out of fuel again.

The world wants us to believe it's normal to work until we're ready to drop, then recharge as fast as possible to do it all over again. In other words, the world says rest comes only at the end of hard work and is a means to get us back to doing more hard work. That's a lie.

RESTorative Rest is so much more. It is the first step of our journey to find the clarity we need. I don't know if it's been an hour or a week since you read the first chapter, but assuming at least some time has passed, let me ask: How is your RESTorative Rest going? Have you been able to identify what makes you feel refreshed? I'm always intrigued by what replenishes a person. No matter how many folks share their answers with me, they are never quite the same. Like our fingerprints, each person's experience with rest is completely unique. Give yourself permission for that to be true with you.

If you aren't quite sure yet what restores your spirit, that's okay. Simply stay with it. Good things await!

Resting has now become a way of life for me—just like eating and sleeping. Without it, I don't operate well. My anxiety grows, fears increase, and I become more vulnerable to harsh treatment toward myself and others. It's so much more enjoyable for me, and those around me, when I remember to fuel up at the rest stops and keep an eye on my tank.

Here's what I learned about slowing down on a regular basis. The proactive practice of rest gives my questions the space to surface.

It helps me hear the questions my heart has been trying to ask and the issues my mind keeps chattering about. Rather than try to silence them so I can get on with my day, I listen and distinguish between the questions that help me gain traction with creative new solutions and the questions that simply spin my wheels.

The art of listening well is an acquired skill. Simply put, if the question inspires loving yourself and others better, then it is a helpful question. If a question influences self-hatred and bitterness for others, then the question is harmful. Asking the right question grounds our presence in this world.

Personally, it helped me say, *"I know I'm not perfect, and I'm no longer trying to be. Rather, I'm focusing on what is right with me, trusting that who I am is needed and valued in our world."* This new paradigm opened up a whole new life. My business grew with just the type of clients who needed my expertise, new friendships formed that aligned with this positivity, and I had more to offer my family.

The right questions ushered in new clarity. Clarity helped me explore where I wanted to go in life and identify what strengths I had to offer. Apologizing was easier, too. Without the pressure of trying to get it right, I was clear where I needed to take responsibility and where it was beyond my control.

This isn't a five-minute process. I've been on this journey for years and am a new person because of it. Be kind to yourself. It does take time. The good news is, you can begin today. You can change the questions now. Just know that it may take several passes for you to calm the internal chatter. That's okay. Don't give up.

The Woman with the Bracelets

As she grew up, the young woman with the bracelets had lost her sense of self. Because life is always changing, clarity comes with consistently asking this helpful question: What is weighing me down and what do I need to let go of to find the life I want?

Our hope is that she'll see things more clearly, address what is keeping her stuck, and be free to enjoy life again. We want her to dare to *believe* that she gets the promise of a life with unabandoned joy and passion. And we yearn for her to, please, for the love of all that is good and true, not go back to her life of too many bracelets, which forces her to live day-to-day without the beloved tire swing.

"Listen to your heart!" we call out to the woman wearied from life with the bracelets she wears.

Do you feel the tug on your heart?

We all get worn thin by the responsibilities and obligations we hold and somewhere along the way we've lost who we are. We've stopped visiting our tire swings and have gotten pretty good at suppressing the tugs at our hearts. We've stopped asking the helpful questions while accepting the harmful ones.

We live in our heads and silence our hearts. But that is never enough. To find clarity, we must listen to both the head and the heart. Yet many of us leave the heart behind or stuff it down because it is complicated, vulnerable, messy, and oftentimes just plain irrational. It complicates our plans. But living without a heart-connection starves clarity because clarity needs the nutrients of what the heart offers.

And an awakened heart is what gets us to the good questions.

In the 1960s, my mother was told she would never be able to have children. For five years, the prognosis proved true. Then one day, she felt sick and visited the doctor. Pregnancy was, of course, ruled out as the reason for her nausea. It was a mystery. The doctor wanted her to get an x-ray. On the day of the appointment, her anxiety skyrocketed. Listening to her heart, my mother told the doctor she didn't know why, but she couldn't go through with the x-ray. Everyone thought she was being irrational. Some folks at the doctor's office became upset with her over the decision.

No one knew at that time she was pregnant with twins. At that stage in the pregnancy, an x-ray would have done damage to the babies in utero. (Thanks, Mom. I'm certainly glad you paid attention to the tug on your heart.)

The heart doesn't always make sense. But ignoring it can cost us. Just like ignoring the logic of our mind can cost us, too. Both head and heart are needed to be fully engaged so that clarity can be strengthened in our lives.

The cost of ignoring our hearts is high. When we do, who we are begins to shrink as the mind chatter grows—causing anxiety, fear, depression, and frustration. We've all heard the statistics. This is the most stressed-out, medicated generation with depression and anxiety at an all-time high. And social research doesn't offer much hope. It seems to be trending in the wrong direction. Psychotropic meds are increasing in usage with prescriptions being written for younger and younger patients. Our humanity is suffering.

In the process, we end up losing heart. Yet it is the heart that helps us form new questions, moving us forward to live more fully alive. That is why I'm so passionate about breaking the cycle we're in—starting with RESTorative Rest and asking better questions.

Peace with Time

One of my favorite questions to ask is: *How do you make peace with time?*

My client Heidi taught me this concept as we were commiserating about all the things we were trying to accomplish in a day. The list was way too long. The frustration with lack of time for all she wanted to "check off" was all too familiar. Something clicked as I realized how much energy she was expending by fighting time with the harmful question, "Why is there never enough time?"

Bemoaning the lack of time was keeping her in an antagonistic relationship with herself and the moments that made up each day. But . . . what if she changed the question to make peace with time rather than fighting it?

She tried it. And what a difference it made. Consciously starting the day by befriending time allowed her to show up with a new presence. It made space for peace to ask for wisdom and guidance regarding how she was to step into her day.

So, this is where it gets real. How do you keep yourself anchored in the question that *helps* and not drift into the question that *harms*?

It requires time at the rest stop, away from the clutter and chatter and distractions of daily life. A place where you can truly *hear* the tugs on your heart and get the clarity you need. A place for the right questions to rise to the surface.

Why is it so important to know the type of questions you're asking? Because one keeps you stuck and one moves you forward.

This new awareness began a ripple effect as I started to assess the questions everyone was asking. It was like I suddenly had a new filter to process what kind of questions I—and those around me—were asking. This was what lay behind the mind chatter so many of us were facing. And my radar went off when I heard questions like: *How will I ever keep up? What if I fail? Why do I always disappoint? Why am I never enough?*

Just to reiterate, these are harmful questions that only provoke the mind chatter disintegrating your clarity because: 1) they usually aren't true, 2) they exaggerate the bad, 3) they paralyze you from moving forward, keeping you anxious, fearful, and stuck, and 4) they almost never take into account the big picture that provides larger context for where you are going and what you need to get there. Hence, your clarity is only replaced with mind chatter that is trying to keep up with harmful questions.

Helpful questions, on the other hand, strengthen your core identity. You gain new clarity on who you are meant to be in this world. More importantly, helpful questions quiet the mind chatter that can keep you anxious, distracted, and unfocused.

Understanding whether a question is harmful or helpful allows you to change the question and silence the mind chatter. But you have to pay attention to what is going on at the heart level. Trying to rationalize or think your way out of it only keeps you stuck. The habit of listening to your heart is needed.

CLARITY

Now it's time to try it out. Please don't skip over this part. It's a necessary step if you are serious about growing in your clarity.

CLARITY QUESTION
What is a question that is causing mind chatter?

Maybe it's about keeping up with daily tasks like Heidi or needing help like Jack.

What's a better question to replace it with? (i.e. *What's right with me? How do I make peace with time?* or *How do I invite in help?*)

As you reflect on a new question, what is your clarity?

I started this journey several decades ago. I was stuck in a cycle of harmful questions and zero time for heart care. I caught myself one day saying this simple sentence.

There. Has. To. Be. More.

I eventually found my "more." More comfort, more peace, more joy, more fulfillment, and more hope. And it began when I pulled over to a rest stop long enough to face the mind chatter and stop asking, "What's wrong with me?" and start asking, "What's right with me?" Good questions like these help us address the mind chatter that tends to overwhelm us, and they assist us in focusing on what we need to move forward.

CAUTION: Notice when you are drifting back into harmful questions that provoke the mind chatter and keep you distracted. When this happens, take a minute to ask a better question that helps instead of harms. This will require some practice, but stick with it. Research shows that it takes one-to-three months to change a thinking habit when you practice it daily, but it is so worth it![2]

2. C. M. Leaf, *Switch on Your Brain*. BakerBooks, Grand Rapids, 2015.

Congratulations! You've made it through the second chapter. Mind chatter is quieting as you ask better questions. The next step in our journey toward clarity is an intriguing one—discovering your tire swing!

YOUR TIRE SWING

Finding the Time and Space to Be You

The ice cream oozing down my hand instantly takes me back to my ten-year-old self. Back then, I'd quickly try to eat the ice cream faster than it could melt. But I never quite succeeded, and that was okay. It was one of my favorite parts of summer.

Maybe that's why ice-cream trucks still make me smile.

Think back to *your* childhood summer days. School is finally out and the days and nights take on a new rhythm. It's a time to run barefoot on the wet grass while hopping from one foot to the other on hot cement. Or meet your friends at the community pool, with the radio blaring and the unmistakable smell of suntan lotion and chlorine permeating the air.

How about waking up at noon wondering why no one else is hungry for breakfast. Playing at the park long into the night as fireflies dance around you. Climbing in treehouses, riding bikes, and watching matinees.

One of my favorite days of the year when I was a kid was July 4th, when we'd spread blankets on the grass and watch fireworks as I painted the sky with my sparklers.

Have you ever wondered why these memories hold such universal appeal? I think I know.

Childhood summers were so simple. It was easy to spend time doing what we loved. Every morning held a tantalizing invitation to enjoy the day stretched before us. There was freedom. Laughter. Play. Long naps. Sleeping in and staying up late.

And of course, there were tire swings. At least there were in my neighborhood. I can still see the tall oak trees with big rubber tires, hanging from a thick rope, swaying in the breeze.

So many good memories. And while we can't return to our childhood summers, we can tap into the power of the tire swing as a new way to gain clarity—and joy.

What I Mean by Tire Swing

I can already hear the protests . . .

"This is silly. Give me a serious assignment."

"There are no trees in my neighborhood."

"How can swinging back and forth on a tire bring clarity?"

"I can't even fit into a tire swing. I'll break the branch."

Okay, so take a deep breath and let me explain what I mean. I'm using the tire swing as a metaphor.

The tire swing represents your idea of spending time doing what you love to do. Not what someone else enjoys. Not what gets the applause of others. Not even what you feel you should do. Those are obligations, and while there's a place for doing what's needed, this isn't that.

Your tire swing represents what awakens your heart and brings a smile to your face. That's it.

So, think with me for a moment. What used to bring you joy that somehow got lost as you grew up? Playing an instrument? Jogging? Reading comics? Crossword puzzles? Sewing? Cooking new recipes? Drawing? Playing board games? At what point did you give that up to focus on the more practical aspects of life?

Perhaps you know exactly what it is, or maybe you have no idea. That's okay. For now, just ask yourself how you'd love to spend a free day. Assume you're rested, that chores can wait, and money is no object. The only rule is you need to be able to pursue it daily. So while a trip to Hawaii would be nice, that can't be your tire swing.

If you know what your tire swing is—or might be—say it out loud. Seriously, it's okay. There is power in our words. Just speak what it is.

And again, if you don't know, just speak that. Maybe think back to earlier days to help shine a light in the dark corners of your mind where you put those long-forgotten passions or talents. Speak that desire out loud. Then take a deep breath, and give it time.

Now that you know what I mean by tire swing, I'll share why it is the perfect metaphor.

Pulling Back to Go Forward

For those who never got to spend time on an actual tire swing, let me explain the art of swinging well.

First, you had to get it rocking. You could do that on your own, but it was super helpful to have someone pull you and the tire back and then release.

The same principle holds true for your tire swing today.

Spending time on it allows you to pull back and pause from the demands and responsibilities of adulting. And why is that important?

Because it helps provide some clarity. Let me say this again because it is very important, and it runs counterintuitive to the beliefs we often hold about the pace we keep. *Jumping on your tire swing is what stills the mind chatter that keeps you running at a ridiculous, unsustainable pace.*

Have you ever noticed how, as adults, we search endlessly for our purpose? But do children ever have to "work" at finding their passion or their purpose? Do they reflect on their lives in melancholy moods, wondering, *How did I get here?* I smile even as I write this, because children are beautifully uncomplicated. They just live. No, these are questions we ask as adults.

Jobs and responsibilities replace the carefree days of summer. Returning to the allegory, we are given bracelets that naturally come with growing up. Some we like, some we don't. But for many of us, this begins the process of losing touch with our tire swings. Heck, we might even chop the tree down because we find out the roots are tearing up the cement. Adult problems.

Children don't notice the broken cement; they are focused on the tire swing.

When we are simply trying to keep up with life, we don't have the bandwidth to find the clarity to chart a new course or come up with creative solutions. Slowing down and enjoying our tire swing allows us to decide which bracelets we keep and which ones we toss. It's the way to bring more balance into our busy lives.

Learning how to spend time on the tire swing will increase your clarity on a regular basis.

In our youth, we instinctively knew that time on the tire swing restored the spirit. We wouldn't have used those words back then, but we were drawn to the tire swing for joy. And it's impossible to have deep joy without a healthy spirit.

Have you ever been in a classroom of fourth-graders when the bell rings for recess? Let's just say, don't get between them and the door. They are on a rampage to get out and play. Instinctively, they know the value of their tire swings and refueling their spirits. I can still remember the mud pies I made on the playground as an eight-year-old and the disappointment of not being able to finish my task when the bell rang to go in.

Somewhere along the way, we lost this authentic ability to refuel. We stuff our days with growing responsibilities and then wonder why we are unhappy.

The transition doesn't happen overnight. It sneaks up on us, doesn't it?

Perhaps it is the longing for something we once had and the sadness that we might never get it back that hurts the most.

The Heart of the Matter

Early in this chapter, I asked you to think back to what brought you joy when you were younger as a way to help you identify your tire swing. I want to share one woman's experience in identifying hers.

Speaking with an executive leader recently, the first words out of her mouth when she got on the line with me were,

"Heather, I am completely stressed-out! Can you help me find my tire swing?"

She was having an intense time at work, and her two children were having an equally intense time in school. She found her days filled with a series of unending crises. Exhausted, she realized her need to establish some boundaries to limit her work and her kids from being able to access her every moment. With limits in place on the demands, she was able to seek out her restorative time on the tire swing of her choosing, which for her meant slipping into a bubble bath, complete with music, candles, and occasionally a good book.

I have another friend who steps away from the daily pressures almost every evening by jumping on his mountain bike for a restorative ride through trees and trails. Can't we all relate to this? Whether it's bubble baths or bike rides, our tire swing is the place that restores the heart.

But now let me offer a deeper cut on this topic.

The tire swings of your youth may differ from the tire swings of maturity. I'm guessing playing with dolls or toy soldiers doesn't hold the same appeal as an adult. But those early joys often hold a clue to what would do your heart good as an adult. It just requires further exploration.

Because regardless of age, your heart still matters. Ignoring it will come at great cost to you.

Some activities do stay in your childhood, but consider that some things might have been forgotten and are ready to be rediscovered.

This is why children run for the door when it's time for recess. When we are refreshed, we are centered. We can see things more clearly. Reach back and remember those emotions and motivations.

You were a child once. This deep truth is still inside of you. Yes, things certainly change as you age, and you would be naïve, even foolish, not to change with it. You have responsibilities that prevent you from spending all your time on the swing. And yet, it is your *regular* visits to the tire swing that will keep you balanced.

The times spent doing what brings you joy are times well spent. It helps you make clear choices that support where you want to go and who you want to become. You stay fueled and energized by these visits.

I remember when I rediscovered a long-forgotten tire swing. With two young toddlers, I felt the beautiful weariness of motherhood swirling around me. I had stepped away from my job of teaching and consulting, which had required traveling and late hours. It had become a bracelet I no longer wanted that was preventing me from enjoying my family. I was ready for a change.

Deciding to take a break, I resigned to enjoy "my littles." But entering back into full-time mothering was, well, let's just say intense. A jolt to my system. Some days I wondered if it would swallow me up. I realized this was more demanding than any job I had ever had. And I desperately needed my tire swing—the constant daily pressures and responsibilities were piling on.

During this challenging season, I remember thinking back—What had I enjoyed as a child? How had I refreshed myself? Ahh yes, I remembered how much I loved to read. Picturing my teenage bedroom took me back to the relief and comfort I felt lying on my bed getting lost in adventurous stories and inspiring dramas. Back then the longer the book, the better. If there were several sequels, I was giddy. I had even created a little corner in my room, complete with a fur rug and pillows, as my special reading nook.

But that was in the past. Not only did I *not* have a special reading nook (can anyone have a special place in their home that toddlers won't find?), but I couldn't remember the last time I had read anything other than "helpful information." I had a stack of books about nutrition, mothering, career, and self-help piled high on my nightstand and coffee tables, but no novels. What stories were adults even reading these days? Was I even allowed to get lost in a story?

At some point, I had stopped reading for pleasure and had started reading for purpose, results, and fixing whatever felt broken. I had put on too many bracelets and stopped visiting my tire swing. Sigh. I missed me.

It was time to return to reading for pleasure. This was my tire swing. I reached out to some friends for novel suggestions and made a new plan. Every day at the kids' nap time, I sat down with a cup of tea and a good book. Only pleasure reading was allowed. No "self-help fix-it" books. And it was pure bliss. I had returned to my much-neglected tire swing. Just knowing I had this to enjoy each afternoon made me more present as a mother and kinder as a human being. The tire swing will do this for you.

When You Neglect Your Tire Swing

I remember times when I felt the need to be productive—whether it was returning calls, folding laundry, straightening the house, researching on the Internet, or cleaning the kitchen. Later, I would feel robbed. I was irritated, frustrated, and felt trapped. Worse, I realized that I was doing it to myself. Like self-sabotage.

It was my choice. I could enjoy my tire swing—or not. I could focus on the pull from my commitments and responsibilities knowing that it was a form of validation I often sought. But the choice was always mine. It was up to me to pull over at a rest stop and trust that it was exactly what I needed to refuel. More importantly, pushing myself was not only hurting me, but who I wanted to be as a mother and, ultimately, as a human being. I began to understand the cost of avoiding my tire swing, and it was not worth it.

The tire swing became an invaluable tool to center me and clarify who I wanted to become.

Part of my breakthrough has been deciding some bracelets, once off, are never worth putting back on.

For instance, keeping up with all the dishes from multiple snacks, meals, and drinks was a lot to, well, keep up with. I would load and run the dishwasher several times a day. Somewhere in my "ideal mother picture," I thought paper plates were lazy or somehow shirking my duties for good mothering.

This epiphany came to me after regular visits on my tire swing, and I decided this was a bracelet I was going to toss. From then on, paper plates were bought in bulk and having my kids clean up after snacks and meals became so much cheerier for all of us.

Fast-forward ten years. My kids are now in their teens, driving and needing me. But not in the ways young children do. I have more space and time, but I still try and hang around. I'm making space to engage in the challenges they face as they find their way in this world—while staying out of their way when they want to spread their wings and soar.

Learning how to stop living only in the land of "responsibility" and "productivity" ironically helped me have the balance to start a successful coaching company. It felt counterintuitive to make time for my tire swing as I built my business. Yet I knew who I became when I didn't keep my balance, and I didn't like the stressed-out, striving version of myself. And honestly, I knew my husband and kids didn't like that "me" either.

Making time for the tire swing on a regular basis guided me into the life I knew I wanted, but wasn't always sure how to get. The tire swing gave me time and space to just be me, and this is how I increased my clarity about moving forward in my work as I began to write the next chapter for my life.

Just as I learned how to re-enter my life after the kids would awaken from their naps, I did the same in building my business. Putting down my novel and getting off my tire swing—knowing I would indulge in it again tomorrow—I learned what it felt like living with a full cup or a full tank of gas.

Without the tire swing, I always felt like I was running on fumes, hovering barely above empty. As I learned (still learning, honestly) how to mother with a full tank, I also discovered how to live day-by-day with balance as a businesswoman, wife, friend, volunteer, and all the roles I was holding.

Time on the tire swing was teaching me how not only to hang on to myself but become the person I wanted to be.

To be clear, some days were harder than others. They still are. But what makes it different is I know what helps. And I let my weariness, frustration, irritation, anxiety now cue me for my need on the tire swing instead of pushing me away from it.

What is it for you? Perhaps it is going for a run, getting lost in a project, enjoying a story, curling up on the couch with a favorite book, or spending time at the beach. It's that activity that makes you forget the worries and responsibilities of life while refueling you to step back into your world with more energy and renewed hope.

It came naturally as a child. But it can happen again if we seek it as an adult.

Children don't have to be told to enjoy themselves—they just do. As adults, we enjoy feeling productive and getting a job done. We love the commitment we've made to spouses, children, work, and volunteering. It gives us purpose. We wouldn't trade it for the world, right? But no matter how good a job is or how much we love someone, we can't fill our days 24/7 with it. It's just too much of a good thing. Which isn't a good thing.

Getting Practical

So, what is your tire swing and when will you step away from all the demands of your life to restore your mind, body, heart, and spirit?

Remember, if you wait too long between visits to your tire swing, irritation, confusion, and feeling trapped will nip at your heels as clarity evaporates like the steam of your morning coffee. If you don't regularly spend time on your tire swing, eventually you are left with just a cold cup of coffee. You still have your coffee—but you've lost what makes it good. Even more, the joy of being who you are begins to disappear.

The secret is consistent time on your unique tire swing.

It is your tire swing that prepares you to hear what you value most, and reminds you that life is more than pushing through or keeping up.

We are not hamsters on a wheel. There is a better way. A way that allows us to *listen*. Because it opens up new space. Space to hear what really matters. To think. To notice. And to live more connected to ourselves. Creativity opens up, new solutions emerge, compassion grows, and decisions are more clearly seen from time spent on our tire swing.

But something else can happen.

Here's the catch. Sometimes re-entering life after time on your tire swing can be sobering. Unlike childhood, you have a life full of responsibilities and choices waiting for you when you get off your tire swing. And they only grow more complex as you age. *Do I stay in this relationship? Is it time to look for a new job? Where do I vacation? What can I afford? How am I preparing for retirement? Where should my kids go to school? Is it time to move? Should I accept this new job offer? Who do I want to spend time with on the weekends? When do I go grocery shopping? Where do I commit to volunteering?* And the list goes on. (Sorry, did your blood pressure go up just reading this?) How do you step back into the world waiting for you to make decisions you never had to make in childhood? Sometimes it makes you want to run back and just *live* on your tire swing. I know this feeling. There were times when I felt as if the tire swing was only a short reprieve from the daily pressures I had to face. "Now what?" I'd mutter to myself when re-entering my full life.

Learning how to make decisions that align with your passions, values, and purpose can feel like an immense weight. You now have new clarity. However, it is not about answers and solutions but more questions and better decisions.

CLARITY QUESTION
What does time on your tire swing look like?

List three things you could do daily—from ten minutes up to an hour.

CAUTION: Resist being distracted by the busy world around you. It usually doesn't invite you onto your tire swing. Make sure to notice how the tire swing time gives you more clarity for facing the daily decisions you need to make as an adult. This will encourage you to instill it as a daily habit.

CLARITY

I love seeing you on your tire swing! This third chapter has been all about what brings you life—because that ultimately also brings clarity. In the next chapter, we'll discuss crossroads, times when you're facing big decisions.

Everyone faces crossroads, so it's not a matter of avoiding them. What's important is how you spend time at them. You want to be ready for the big decisions that shape the course of your life so you feel empowered to make choices from a place of clarity rather than confusion.

We'll get to that soon . . . but for now, simply spend time enjoying your tire swing.

CROSSROADS

Taking Time for the Big Decisions

Most days, it can seem like we're stumbling through thick fog. The landscape may be somewhat familiar, but the horizon—along with our hopes—remain fuzzy.

Yet the rays of clarity can still break through. That is the promise of this book.

With my clients, I've found it's helpful to begin sessions with a quick recap from our last conversation. Allow me to offer you the same here.

The story of the girl on the tire swing is far from over. But through it, we've learned about the bracelets we wear. Too many weigh us down and keep us from true rest. Then, we looked at the effect of mind chatter, reframing the questions we ask. And last chapter, we discovered the joy of the tire swing, short rest periods every day doing something that makes us feel more alive.

There's an intentional progression to our journey. But the choices regarding where we want to move forward require clear thinking, silencing the mind chatter, and slowing down. It turns out we don't make wise decisions going 150 miles per hour. That's where the benefit of spending time on the tire swing comes in.

Preparing for the crossroads is the next step on the journey to clarity. It involves what we've learned so far about both bracelets and tire swings.

When you hear the word *crossroads*, what do you imagine? I see a busy flow of traffic and lots of motion—not rolling hills and a lazy stream, 100 miles from the nearest town.

Are we tracking?

The crossroads is a very busy place. It's where the intersection of ideas, information, people, and vehicles come together. But they're all heading in different directions. In this place of constant motion, there is no deep rest. Forget clarity, we just have to keep moving. If we don't, we'll be pushed to the side. Or worse, run over.

The crossroads would be the last place we'd choose to set up camp.

Yet, counterintuitively, it's the perfect place to stop and make camp so we can assess whether to stay on course or head in a new direction.

You think I've lost my mind, right? Setting up camp in the middle of the crossroads sounds insane. But stay with me here.

I have fond memories of camping, both as a child and as an adult. Camping is a lot of work until you get to your site and set up all you need. After that, everything slows down to a snail's pace.

Nature soothes and comforts the weary spirit. Books are read in hammocks. Marshmallows roasted over crackling fire pits. Adventures are planned and stories are told. At this relaxed pace, we become kinder people, more attentive, and rejuvenated.

The right kind of camping brings soul-level clarity. At the crossroads of life, that's what we need most.

Yet oftentimes, crossroads provoke the opposite reaction. Our minds and emotions accelerate at the very moment we need calm to make a wise decision. The crossroads are a place of constant motion, distractions, activity, and little ability to stop and think. A bit like life on any given Monday morning, right?

During one of my camping trips, a new idea emerged. *What if I could actually camp at the crossroads?*

No, I'm not literally suggesting you head to the busiest intersection and set up a tent there. But, *metaphorically speaking*, what if camping in these high-pressure zones allowed us to approach them—and life—at a better pace? What if camping at the crossroads provided the needed pause to the pressure we're facing, bringing clarity before we made any new decisions? To put a stake in the ground and say "no" to the constant push to do more until we can stop, breathe, rest, and use this temporary pause to see more clearly.

Perhaps a story would be helpful.

Bone-Tired and Soul-Fried

Linda had lost her balance. She didn't trip and fall, but she had lost her way in life. As we spoke, she recounted numerous difficult conversations, career challenges, and health issues. It was a hard conversation—one that reminded me of how challenging life can be.

"It sounds like you are tired."

"Yes," she said. "I guess I am. I didn't even realize it until you mentioned it."

She was utterly exhausted from simply pushing through each day. Then doing it again the next day.

We can't see anything clearly when we are bone-tired and soul-fried. When the weariness is not just lack of sleep but deep exhaustion of heart and spirit, it's time to pull over and get some real rest. Only then can we gain any clarity about how to determine our next move: what to say to the person at work, how to respond to our teenage child, or where to turn for answers about health concerns.

As Linda's coach, I asked the question I knew her heart was craving. "How do you want to rest?"

There was holy silence as she sat in the question. I always like this part of the conversation because how we each choose to rest is so unique. And I've heard it all—from simple choices like taking a day off, reading more, joining a retreat, resigning from a job, or going back to school—to more creative examples like floating down the Nile, visiting an alpaca farm, or spending Christmas in Bethlehem. (Yes, these are all real examples from my clients.)

Linda let out a long sigh. "I need to take some time off. Stop doing more all the time so I can think through what's best—and what's next."

Notice how she began with the permission to admit how tired she was. That's a very good place for us all to start. It allows us to come up with the solution we need when we're honest about how we're really doing.

The next morning Linda texted me to say how freeing it was to have permission to recognize her exhaustion and explore the possibility of rest. She now had clarity on the need to place boundaries around her work hours and actually use the vacation time she'd earned. In her case, that meant taking an entire month off to travel.

Notice what your mind and heart did when you read that last sentence. How did you react to someone taking a month off just to travel? If you rolled your eyes or thought, *Yeah, nice for her, but that would never work for me*, just stay present and hopeful. You're about to have your own crossroads experience.

Our ability to creatively find ways to rest starts with small steps. It's making daily choices that restore our spirit that, over time, progress until one day, we're making big choices that support the life we've always wanted.

The idea of a month's vacation may be too daunting. Let's start smaller.

Anna is a working mother of two toddlers. Her entire waking day is consumed with the needs of two little ones. My mission was to set a low goal as a starting place, just to give her a taste of what was possible. Anna felt realistically that she could only get one minute three times a day to rest.

Anna and I had worked hard just for her to believe she was allowed to rest. This was her first baby step in giving herself the permission to find what she needed. And guess what? It worked. The one minute grew into ten minutes, then into an hour and eventually into a three-day road trip with her best friend.

See how it progresses? Don't be afraid to start small. Just start.

By the way, I spoke to Linda just last week. She came back from her month of travel a new and joyful person. It was so fun to hear her enthusiasm and new vision for next steps in life that had been birthed through camping at the crossroads. And it was a direct result of getting RESTorative Rest.

CLARITY

It Will Look Different for Everyone

One word of caution. There is no single way this process looks or works. It depends on the season of life you're in when you pull over. The experience for a mother with two young toddlers will look very different than a person with an empty nest. A single man with a trust fund and few responsibilities will have more options than a father of four providing for his family.

But you can find the way that works best for you.

Comparing how it looks for someone else—or wishing you were someone else—will keep you stuck. You will save yourself a heap of trouble if you don't look at the person next to you. You must focus on yourself. Decide what you are able to do and what works for you. That's what truly matters.

This isn't a competition. It is an individual run, or perhaps walk, toward gaining more clarity.

Remember, each new commitment in your life adds another bracelet. And each commitment makes it harder to find time to swing on your tire swing.

It is at the crossroads where we learn to choose our options more wisely. Yes, this process requires time away from the blur of life. To be clear, this is not the same as time on our tire swings (which replenishes our joy). This is time to ask the hard questions we've been avoiding, time to listen and find creative solutions, and even time to address the fears that haunt us.

What decisions are you facing in your life? Perhaps it involves a new job or moving to a new state. It may be deciding whether to marry, have children, get a pet, or simply determine who you want to be when you grow up.

I've spent a lot of time at the crossroads, both personally and professionally. And in my line of work, I meet many people here. If you're feeling hesitant at the potential of camping at the crossroads, honestly, that's normal. Crossroads can create anxiety for everyone. Well, let me take that back. Not quite everyone.

I watched my three-year-old dance through the crossroads of life without a worry or backward glance. Oh, the freedom of childhood. What causes us to be so carefree and confident in our youth and then change into nail-biting-pro-and-con-list-makers-fearful-of-making-the-wrong-decision adults?

Maybe you're one of the rare ones still dancing through the crossroads. If so, please keep going. Then write a book about how you do it. I'd like to read it!

For the rest of us, crossroads can be intense periods of analytical reflection, to-do lists, what-if scenarios, and desperate peering into the future to guarantee an outcome while being haunted by the idea of making the wrong decision. Perhaps it is realizing the cost of what we are evaluating, or maybe we have a memory of a similar situation that didn't work out so well and we don't want to fall flat on our face again.

Yes, the stakes are higher now than when we were young. And recognizing how our choices might affect those we love adds pressure. Life can take a toll on us and our decision-making processes, huh? We learn quickly the impact of one wrong turn. And we also learn the art of counting the costs.

But not slowing down is even more costly. Not examining the state of our lives and hoping more busyness will eventually lead to a life of more peace is a losing bet.

In other words, every decision—or non-decision—has a cost. I'm asking you to make the investment now that ultimately will lead to clarity and the life you want. Will you make the brave, counterintuitive decision to camp at the crossroads?

Rather than continuing to try and conjure up the strength to keep going, let's pull over and recalculate the costs and the possibilities of our journey from this point forward.

Deciding to spend time at the crossroads is a huge breakthrough. The question now is: Will you do so as a Speedy, a Melter, or a Pauser?

Speedys, Melters, and Pausers

I've observed three different types of people at the crossroads.

1. THE SPEEDY

The life motto of the Speedy is: *"The faster the better!"*

If you're in this group, you probably are skimming this paragraph. There's just no time to take it slow. Being productive gives your brain a shot of dopamine. Being weary only makes you reach for a triple-shot of espresso. And, like the Energizer Bunny, you keep going and going and going.

Maybe that's why when I see them running full speed past me, I sigh. I'm a recovering Speedy and this group reminds me way too much of my old self. I know this pace doesn't work long-term.

Eventually, the Speedy gets themselves into predicaments that require—at minimum—a course correction, and in extreme situations, a massive rescue as they end up unable to maintain the pace they set and get sidelined out of sheer exhaustion.

Sometimes an authentic exuberance for life drives the Speedy. The Speedy wants to be the best they can be and give all they can. Although it may be a good motive, that doesn't make it sustainable. Often, it is fear nipping at their heels—fear of not measuring up, getting left behind, being a disappointment, wasting their life. It's amazing how creative we can get with our fears.

How does a Speedy approach the crossroads? In record time. Not because the decisions are simple, but because who has time to waste thinking, assessing, or evaluating when they could be doing? So they cruise through the crossroads, perhaps tapping the brake a time or two, but they never really stop, much less camp here.

They don't respect the value of the crossroads as an opportunity to slow down and assess their course . . . so they receive very little from what crossroads could potentially offer.

2. THE MELTER

The motto of a Melter could be: *"I'm not sure what to do, so I won't do anything."*

I've given this person the name Melter because they "melt down" with indecision and insecurity that keeps them paralyzed with fear and anxiety.

When a Melter approaches a crossroads, they don't race through it, they hunker down and hesitate. Yet the longer they stay in this state, the worse the situation becomes. They may be at the same crossroads a year later, still unsure which way to go, and unwilling to risk making the wrong move. Even the sight of the crossroads leads to feeling overwhelming pressure and immense anxiety.

Ironically, some Melters used to be Speedys. But running down the wrong path one too many times and paying the price of poor decisions have cost them greatly. Eventually, they began to mistrust themselves, even in the small decisions. Now every crossroads is a terrifying exercise in decision-making. The longer a Melter remains in this state, the worse it becomes.

I always want to give them a hug because of their paralyzing fear of indecision since I've wrestled through this as well. To the uninitiated, these folks just seem like they can never make up their minds. But one big face-plant in the arena of life can do a number on anyone, causing them to think twice before ever running without looking again.

Fear is behind this group as well—the fear of getting it wrong, fear of disappointing, fear of missing a better opportunity, fear of the cost. The common denominator is that fear manifests itself in constant anxiety and mistrust.

A Melter gets stuck at the crossroads . . . and so rather than breakthrough, they breakdown.

Thankfully, there is a third type of person that we encounter at the crossroads.

3. THE PAUSER

The motto of the Pauser could be: *"Taking time to be fully present brings peace and clarity."*

To be honest, it actually took me a while before I realized this type even existed. I probably didn't see them sooner because I was either speeding by them or too consumed with my own anxiety over making a decision.

This type of individual actually appears to be *enjoying* the crossroads experience. Seriously, how could this be? They weren't speeding through out of fear of being left behind or melting down with anxious self-doubt. They were *choosing* to pause at the crossroads. This was a new revelation for me.

At first glance, a Pauser can appear to be a lost soul trying to find themselves. They don't seem to be on the fast track, especially to those of us swinging back and forth between anxious striving and insecurity.

A Pauser waits. Even when they linger, they exude a confidence that all will be well. They trust their decision-making process and believe they are being led and guided on their journey.

Hmm. Let's spend more time with this group to see how they navigate the crossroads.

The Secret of the Pauser

I found myself drawn to the Pauser's campfire.

How did they spend their time at the crossroads? How could this pace make sense? What were they doing while they waited? Did they know some secret I didn't?

Joining them at their peaceful pace, I learned they were waiting for clarity about what was best—and why. Around the campfire, they asked great questions filled with hope and anticipation. But they didn't just talk. They listened. Then they waited until they knew—*really knew* in their heart of hearts—the best course.

They waited long enough to set up camp and make themselves comfortable. (I mean, if we're going to be here awhile, we might as well get comfy, right?) They waited with both anticipation and faith. Anticipation that things were going to work out, and faith that it wasn't all up to them to make it happen.

The Pauser offers hope to the Melter biting their nails in angst. They give new perspective to the Speedy who believes fast is the only speed that wins the game.

And what was this new hope and perspective?

That crossroads aren't something to be raced through or feared, but places to calmly pause and discover greater clarity. The Pauser has learned how to give space to honor their past while writing the next—even better—chapters of their future.

We need the Pauser's way of approaching the crossroads to help us take a brave look at what has worked and what hasn't. They know our souls needs good questions, kind answers, and rest to properly navigate this world. The life we want doesn't come on a silver platter. It requires patience and daily practices that care for our spirit and increase our clarity.

Let me offer an example of a famous Pauser. Remember Mr. Mayagi from the 1980s movie, *The Karate Kid*? Okay, so he's not a real person. But he's the epitome of a Pauser. Mr. Mayagi mentors a young boy who wants to learn karate, by having him paint fences. The boy thinks the old man is crazy. He has no idea that the act of painting fences is actually leading him into the very life he desires. The boy has to learn to trust his mentor, the process, and stay patient with the steps required for him to reach his goals.

This is what it is like to hang out with a Pauser. They have confidence in the process and trust the winding steps in the journey. A pauser knows there is a systematic way that life works. While not always exciting in the moment, knowing that it's the small, daily steps learned around the Pauser's campfire that matters.

Becoming a Pauser

Recently, I was consulting for a group wanting to break the cycle of poverty in third-world countries by educating students and training teachers in refugee camps. Pretty inspiring stuff! It was similar to the work I had done in Belize, and I loved being a part of their conversation.

But as I listened to the founder share his vision, it quickly became apparent that his plan was scattered. He wanted the organization to work with three different countries, all on different continents, with limited contacts, no business model, and no staff or budget. When I gently suggested that perhaps we were putting the cart before the horse and needed to look at the structure first, he responded with, "I don't want to work on building the foundation! I want to get in the country now and start helping!"

Do you recognize it? His language was that of a Speedy. I couldn't help but smile. On some level, his impatience even resonated with me. It can be boring to start with the foundational stuff. It's aggravating when we're ready to chase our dreams and others tell us to slow down. That can even feel like a waste of time. I mean, "Come on, Mr. Miyagi, can't we just start throwing karate punches instead of painting fences?"

But as a practicing Pauser, I knew the cost of starting something too quickly without developing a strong foundation. Exhaustion. Chaos. Burn out. Failed Missions. This is where I usually ask people to trust me. Trust that I know the process to get them there well. Trust that they are being set up for sustainability. Trust that each step is getting them closer to the results they want. The shock is usually in the realization that they were hoping for three steps to reach their goals, and I have to tell them it's closer to 500 steps.

You cannot get the life you want running at breakneck speed. This is simply a rule for how successful living works. Ask anyone who has ever achieved outstanding results: Winston Churchill, Mother Teresa, Abraham Lincoln, and Harriet Tubman. There are no shortcuts.

It's also the reason I won't work with clients unless they agree to a minimum of several months together in weekly conversations. Why? The foundation of your identity is not strengthened overnight. It requires time around the campfire to pause and ask the right questions that will grow you into the person you want to be. To address the blocks that have kept you stuck for too long. And to create a strong enough foundation for you to maintain a big, beautiful, thriving life.

It's like a trainer saying you can lose twenty pounds in a two-hour workout session. Crazy, right? Yet many of us want to believe this and try to make life work on these terms. We all know what is true, but running fast allows us to live in denial for a little longer. Until we can't.

There are two main reasons we fear slowing down.

#1—We compare our lives with other people's lives.

Don't look at how those around you spend their time and the pace they are running. Each of us is living out a different story, and we're at different places on our journey. Pay attention to what you need and the unique role that only you can play for your life. Whether you are a full-time parent, CEO, teacher, artist, or nonprofit visionary—live *your* life.

Spend time discovering what works for you and what fits your lifestyle. From there, design your life by understanding the helpful rhythms of your day and your heart. This is the hard work I am talking about. Systematic, slow, intentional steps so that you can take off and build exponentially from a sustainable foundation.

#2—We ask the wrong people around our campfires to weigh in with their opinion. Remember, not all opinions are created equally.

Who you ask to join you at the crossroads is important. Because when you camp at the crossroads, you want to make sure you have the right people around the circle. This means friends who ask good questions and know how to be with you to rightly interpret your internal issues.

My Crossroads Community

Who we choose to have join us at the crossroads can vary. Creating categories has helped me live more intentionally. For my Crossroads Community, I look for five types of Pausers to join me around the campfire:

1. CHERISHED PARTNER

My husband plays this role. I bounce things off him and trust that he will help me stay true to my path and the mission I want to accomplish. He is someone who knows me well and not only loves me, but is committed to my success. Best of all, he will not hesitate to defend me when needed and stand by me when I falter.

2. HEART FRIEND

These are people who don't want anything from me, but simply love me for who I am. They cheer me on whether I fail or succeed. They are the source of unconditional support I need when I'm in a vulnerable place of change. They are also the ones who celebrate with me when I succeed.

3. HELPER

Usually I have a reciprocal relationship with these folks, or I pay to keep the relational lines clear. These individuals exude a peaceful calm by supporting me with activities I either can't do or don't want to do. For instance, I have the most amazing professional housecleaner who comes into my home office and cheerfully cleans around me and my busy family as she helps our home stay beautiful. Also, the individuals on my team who know instinctively how to handle, with grace and ease, all the stuff I throw their way.

4. GUIDE

Oftentimes, these are people I hire. Coaches, counselors, consultants, and people who are skilled at showing me how to get to the next level. I like getting results. And I like working smarter, not harder. For instance, I hired an awesome professional coach when I was starting my coaching company as well as an inspiring writing coach as I wrote this book. And several counselors along the way to support my inner life and all the questions I was asking. These people are experienced, trained, and know how to help me take next steps.

5. FELLOW SOJOURNER

These are people on similar journeys who I feel an instant connection with. I've connected with them through conferences, retreats, events, neighborhood gatherings, and even the gym— as well as through reading their books and listening to their podcasts. Some I've met. Others I've only read or heard. Either way, I celebrate the connections from our worlds intersecting. It is as if our paths are crossing for a specific purpose. Staying open to these connections allows us to learn from one another and often gives wisdom and hope for the journey we are taking and the choices we are facing. I experienced this recently at a leadership conference facilitated by the author of a book I had just read. Thirty leaders flew in from around the country to spend the weekend together as we learned and shared our stories—feeling connected and understood—all because the same powerful book had resonated with each of us. What a rare gift. I will likely never see most of them again, but I felt lucky to have intersected with these fellow sojourners. I was inspired by their journeys and encouraged to keep moving forward in mine.

As a Pauser camping at the crossroads, surround yourself with people who will stay with you, ensure you don't take shortcuts, listen as you find solutions, ask great questions, help you access what you desire, and ensure you build a strong foundation for your life—the one only you are made for.

This is what I want for myself. I want no less for you.

CLARITY QUESTION

How might camping at the crossroads bring you greater calm and insight?

Are you currently more of a Speedy, Melter, or Pauser? Has that served you well? Why or why not?

Who do you want to invite around your campfire? Do you already have some of these people in place? Who might you still need to find?

- Cherished Partner:

- Heart Friend(s):

- Helper(s):

- Guide(s):

- Fellow Sojourner(s):

Are you aware of the role you play around others' campfires?

CAUTION: You don't have to like literal camping to find enormous value from "camping at the crossroads." But you do have to embrace the value of intentionally pausing if you want to see your life in new ways. If this brings you anxiety or you feel you can't slow down right now to pursue this, I encourage you to try one thing before writing this off.

Find a "Mr. Miyagi" in your world. Invite him or her to lunch and ask how they learned to pause and live at a different pace. During your time with them, practice the art of asking good questions, active listening, and taking notes rather than explaining your situation and doing most of the talking. You already know your story. Hear theirs. You'll be glad you did.

One of my biggest epiphanies came several years ago with this thought:

I am the only one stopping myself from a Big, Beautiful, Thriving Life.

This poignant realization made me take responsibility for fully owning my journey and the life story I was writing. I only get one shot at this life, and I want to make it count. You do too.

Are you ready? It's time to step away from anything that smacks of simply surviving. In the next chapter, I'll reveal how you can move from a life of survival to a life of thriving. Really!

SURVIVE OR THRIVE?

Your Ability to Choose Is Greater Than You Think

D o any of these sentiments regularly invade your thoughts?

Three more days until the weekend.
Just let me survive until then.

Why bother getting to know that person? They don't care anyway.

When will my spouse stop making everything so difficult?

How come there's never enough time to do the things I want?

Life is too hard. Forget breakthrough, just give me relief.

Ugh. It's Monday, again.

*How am I going to make it through another day at this job
—much less the next year?*

Why not eat that second (or fifth) brownie?
It brings me a little joy.

What's the point of trying? Nothing ever changes.

CLARITY

Ouch. We wouldn't want any of these thoughts tattooed on our arm. Yet we've somehow allowed the sayings to be permanently embedded in our minds. That's a problem. Because survival thinking doesn't allow us any space to enjoy the moment. Survival thinking never leads to hope . . . or breakthrough.

Survival thinking is toxic because it creates a sense of loss over the past, dread for the future, and a hunker-down mind-set for today.

Let me ask you a question. Do you think like a survivalist or a thriver?

You may be thinking, *I'm not a survivalist; I'm just being a realist.* If so, let me push a bit further. Yes, by all means, be real. We all will face hard seasons that bring unexpected crises and shocking loss. And in those times, surviving might be all we can do . . . for a time.

The problem is, if we're not careful, we get stuck there. And our bodies, minds, and hearts weren't meant to live in survival mode for months and years.

Being a realist is good, as long as that means you interpret reality with clarity. Because here's the deal, you'll never simply drift into a thriving life. It requires intentionality. If you want clarity, you have to set aside time to listen to the questions of your heart, to weigh the effects of your choices, to slow down and re-evaluate the hopes and the habits of your life.

Gaining this clarity is fueled by time on your tire swing. It also includes camping as a Pauser at the crossroad. That's why I introduced those key terms first.

But even with those tools, I understand that what I'm inviting you into is challenging. I've coached hundreds of people through this very topic. This isn't about putting on rose-colored glasses and skipping through the tulips. I'm inviting you to be a realist (seeing life as it really is) *and* a thriver.

I define a thriver as one who takes time to regularly evaluate their bracelets and consistently jumps on their tire swing. Based on that definition, would you consider yourself a thriver? If not, that's okay. You're about to have the tools to become one.

A thriver lives with intentionality. Life is an ongoing, daily adventure—not a formula to learn. Just like our physical health needs regular attention with diet and exercise, so our mind, heart, and spirit require consistent care and attention. When life becomes only about the bracelets, we move into survival. Worse, we get stuck there until it becomes the new norm. Just like we can adapt to those twenty extra pounds we didn't used to carry.

As I researched this topic, I was struck with how many phrases we have around the idea of surviving.

I am surviving.

I will survive!
(shout-out to Gloria Gaynor for that song!)

We survived the experience.

I am a survivor.

Yet the language around thriving is far more limited.

I am thriving. (This works.)

Life is about thrival. (Nope.)

We thrived it. (Even more no.)

I am a thriver.
(Um . . . no again. Except when I decided to start using it.)

I'm thinking we need to start expanding on this word.

What if we spent as much energy on cultivating a life and language of thriving as we spend on merely trying to survive? We'd have to invite new words to express the new breakthroughs. Because I'm such a believer in this concept, I'll go ahead and start using these new words for us now.

Shifting from survival to thrival is what will give us the clarity we need to write the story we want for our lives. It's about a whole new way of living. Honestly, this is where most people hesitate. We are creatures of habit, comfortable with the familiar. Perhaps that's why this is so challenging. Because to begin, we must be willing to change.

And that starts with making sometimes unusual, often uncomfortable, choices.

It isn't easy. But easy is overrated. Perhaps it will help to understand why it can be challenging.

Why This Is So Hard

I'll keep this brief. Here are three reasons this journey can be complicated.

1. THRIVING LOOKS DIFFERENT FOR EVERYONE.

In a sense, it is like a chameleon. What thriving looks like changes from person to person. That's not just okay—it's good. More so, it's how it will always be. Because we are all unique.

2. LIFE IS CONSTANTLY CHANGING.

Life is not static—it's dynamic! Every day brings change. Every year brings even more change. We have to change with it, even if we never asked for change or wanted it. This is just the way life works. The sooner we accept that, the sooner we can begin to thrive.

3. WE FORGET THAT WE HAVE A CHOICE TO SURVIVE OR THRIVE.

I hope that's encouraging because when we have a choice, we have power. Choosing to thrive sets certain events in motion, while choosing to just let life happen causes us to drift away and get stuck in survival. Two opposite outcomes, but one choice, and the choice is ours.

There you have it. The summary of why this can be hard. See, I told you I'd keep it brief.

Choosing to Change

Being human means living with choices.

As I write this, my little Yorkie Terrier snoozes in the sun as my French Brittney chases down a lizard outside my window. Animals have it easy. They have so few choices to make. Their options: do I eat, nap, or play? I'm not even sure if those are choices or simply instinct. Either way, what a carefree life. They never wake on a Monday morning faced with the dilemma of what to wear, how to deal with a cranky boss, or embarrassed by the extra pounds they put on.

Humans don't get off so easily. It seems we have to make choices with every breath we take.

Some choices are small, like how to respond to the barista at our favorite coffee shop or the driver next to us. Some are bigger choices, like who to marry, how to parent, where to move, managing finances, and making the best decision for our career.

CLARITY

Deeper still, we have choices in how we engage with joy and pain. We choose how to respond to our dreams as they come true and devastating loss as it hits, sometimes in the same day.

How we choose to respond is critical. This is the nexus where humanity and life meet. This is where we choose to survive or thrive.

But most people remain stuck in their story, having long ago lost track of what brought them joy or purpose. This is what happens as the bracelets pile on and our times on the tire swing become distant memories of a life once lived.

You forget you have a choice. You are not a victim to a life handed out to you. It is *your* life. The challenge is knowing how to take charge in ways that empower us to foster the life we've always wanted.

We get to choose. That's the good news. But living in a constant state of choosing is draining. That's the bad news.

It's overwhelming to try and keep up with the pace of our world and the stories constantly unfolding. Each day holds a mix of beauty and heartbreak.

We catch our breath in wonder as we stand on the edge of the Grand Canyon surveying its, well, grandness . . . or when we experience the sacredness of a newborn baby entering the world with her first cry. Life is exquisite.

We gasp at unexpected news about a loved one. Some days, it's not just one thing but an avalanche of broken appliances, misunderstandings, illnesses, and financial burdens. Life can be excruciating.

Amidst all the unknowns, we get to choose: How will we respond? How will we engage?

The pull is to *not* make a choice. To simply go shopping, eat at the new restaurant, lose yourself on Netflix, or push through the latest workout. Anything to avoid facing the fear that lurks around the corners of what may come. Especially on the days that hold hard stories.

This is survivalist thinking. *Just get through another day and push through to the finish line.*

On our best days, we live with anticipation about what is to come. On our darkest days, we live with impending dread wondering how to put one foot in front of the other. But most days, it's just another day—moving through Mondays, Wednesdays, and weekends. Trying our best to show up in our little corner of the world.

Are you starting to see what's going on in new ways? To make it clearer, let me frame it this way.

A survival question is: "How do I get through another day?"

A thrival (yes, I'm using my made-up word) question is: "How can I live in this very moment the best I can?"

Do you see how one brings resignation while the other brings restoration? How one cuts our story short and one makes our story better? Our choices help us become the author of our life. They offer the empowerment we need to own our life story. In contrast, living in the survival question is like putting the pen down and allowing life to simply happen. It abdicates the choice we have to live better, to rise strong, and to thrive.

While we can't control the ebb and flow of life, we can be intentional about how we engage with the choices we make and the story we're living. Clarity on whether we are actively choosing to survive or thrive is an anchor for our souls and a solid foundation for our minds.

It is possible to navigate all the twists and turns life brings, to have absolute clarity about who you are and how you are meant to respond in each moment, and to make wise choices when the unexpected hits.

But first, you have to get unstuck.

Five Ways We Get Stuck

I thought it might be helpful to share five main ways we drift into survival mode and get stuck there. See which story seem most like yours.

1. NEW SEASONS OF RESPONSIBILITY

Laura was on the fast track. When I started working with her, she was a senior vice president eager for even more responsibility. Within the next few months, she secured a major promotion, and we celebrated. Yet when I caught up with her a year later, she was frazzled, had gained thirty pounds, and was exhausted from her frantic schedule. What happened?

Her advancement had sent her into a pattern of survival thinking.

The increase in her responsibilities and her desire to "get it right" drove her to do more and to be more. She had little time to visit her tire swing. She was working twelve-to-fifteen-hour days, skipping breaks, saying yes to responsibilities she could have handed off, and overeating long into the night as a reward for the day she had endured . . . only to start all over again the next day. And even that wasn't enough. She took work home on the weekends in exchange for quality time with her family.

Notice what crept into her thoughts in this season of responsibility.

Survival Thought: *I'm terrified I will mess up, so I have to work all the time because I can't afford to fail.*

But what if she'd chosen a thriving mind-set? Perhaps it would have sounded like this.

Thrival Thought: *I have everything I need to do this job well. Keeping my balance along with good daily patterns will allow me to offer my best.*

Thankfully, Laura ultimately chose to thrive rather than just survive. And that shift made all the difference. She set limits on the maximum hours she'd work based on her desires for a higher quality of life. Rather than being driven by the fear of failing, she committed to choosing self-care, believing this would produce success. How did that go for Laura?

Her results actually improved, her team was happier, and she attracted better employees—because not only was she expressing her values, she was now living them out. Even better, her family was thrilled with her enhanced presence and energy.

I have a personal experience in this category. Years ago, as a new mother, I was shocked at the amount of cleaning, caring, and feeding that came with parenting. It made me downright cranky trying to keep up with laundry, wash dishes, make sure everyone was clean, and somehow figure out how to put meals on the table three times a day as well as provide a constant flow of snacks. I could feel the pull of survival thinking and the "stuckness" of it all. But who else was going to do it?

I was stuck . . . and I felt trapped.

Here was my Survival Thought: *I'm stuck with these responsibilities for the next eighteen years. Every. Single. Day. And I can hardly feed myself!*

Then one day I decided to change my mind with this Thrival Thought: *I get to find a way to be happy in order to more fully enjoy this brief season of motherhood.*

Better answers came when I asked better questions such as: "How do I get to be happy and enjoy motherhood?"

I've already shared how I stopped trying to wash all the dishes and enjoyed the ease of paper plates. I also hired a babysitter every Friday so I could enjoy a few hours to do what I loved. Bonus, she even folded the laundry while the kids were napping. It was pure bliss—and it provided time for me to enjoy my work *and* my kids as I figured out what was blocking me from thriving. And the years where money was tight, I traded help with other mothers who were committed to thriving as well.

2. IT'S ALL I'VE KNOWN

When I started working with Blake, he was resistant to any suggestions for improvement. He responded defensively to creative ideas or new ways to see his story. Over time, his defensiveness halted all progress.

One day I stopped the conversation and asked Blake what was going on.

He sighed and then explained that he didn't like anyone telling him how to do his job. It felt controlling. He was surprised to hear I wholeheartedly agreed with his comment. I assured him I had no desire to tell him what to do. My intent was to serve as a sounding board for him to troubleshoot and explore possible solutions. He'd never had this type of partnership before and wasn't sure if he could trust it.

That's when the light came on for me. I asked if he'd ever had leadership development. He shook his head. Never.

Ahh. His perspective of leadership development was off. I explained how it was my job to come alongside him and collaborate—not control—his choices. From that point on, the conversation completely changed. But first, he had to choose to trust a new way of doing things and embrace a fresh perspective. I'm happy to share, Blake is thriving at work and is quick to reach out and ask for support on new ideas when he needs to.

Here's the shift in Blake's thinking that allowed him to come alive as a leader.

Survival Thought: *Those coming alongside me want to control me and tell me what to do, and they are a threat to avoid.*

Thrival Thought: *I get to collaborate with helpful people who are investing in my leadership development and trust they are not trying to control me, but rather are an asset to embrace.*

Do you see the difference?

Many are stuck because they lock into mind-sets of *"This is all I have ever known and this is how it will always be."* We must not base our life on false future assumptions created by past perceptions.

Change happens when we embrace a fresh perspective and shift from thoughts that limit to thoughts that move us forward.

3. EMOTIONAL CONFUSION

Drew was highly agitated when we got on the line for our coaching call. That surprised me. But what intrigued me was that he couldn't tell me why. All he knew was that when a coworker politely said he didn't want to work overtime, it provoked Drew.

I offered several possible reasons for Drew's frustration, but none seemed to hit the bull's-eye. I paused and then asked if Drew was disappointed.

"That's it!" he exclaimed. "I am disappointed for how he responded to the needs of our company." Drew placed a high value on loyalty and didn't like his coworker declining this opportunity to be part of the solution.

Do you see the clarity that happened?

Survival Thought: *I can't deal with this because I don't know what's bugging me, so I might as well ignore it and avoid him.*

Thrival Thought: *When I understand why I feel the way I do, I can respectfully express it and trust our relationship will be stronger for it.*

What could have been a confrontation or breakdown of relationship became an opportunity to build more trust and strengthen a working friendship between two good-hearted guys.

I'll share one more example.

My client Darcy was depressed and worn out with life. She was a special-education teacher who struggled to get up every day. I asked what brought her joy and she excitedly shared how she'd love to spend a couple days on a farm with alpacas. (Huh? I never get tired of hearing about people's unique tire swings.)

Eventually, she made this dream trip a reality. Darcy returned with newfound clarity. Her sadness was because her current job wasn't her passion. Her desire was to be an environmental scientist and advocate. Perhaps now it makes sense why alpacas were her tire swing.

Observe the shift in her thinking.

Survival Thought: *I have to do this teaching job because I've trained for it, they need me, I'm good at it, and I should like it.*

Thrival Thought: *I'm sad that I'm not doing what I want, so I'm going to do something about it.*

Soon after her trip, Darcy started a community garden in her neighborhood and enrolled in an environmental science graduate program. At the same time, she honored her teaching contract for the year while lining up a new job to help urban cities plant gardens and care for community centers.

Breakthrough was only possible when she chose to sort out her emotional confusion.

When you remain confused about what you're feeling, you remain stuck in survival mode. Sure, it can be scary to try and understand *why* you're feeling something—much less name it. But isn't it even more scary to remain forever frozen? Thankfully, time on the tire swing and at the crossroads allows you the space to sort it out.

Clarity comes only as we create the space to honor what we are feeling.

4. FORGIVENESS OF SELF AND OTHERS

Breanna struggled with forgiveness. Her situation was heart-breaking. A group of close friends had turned their backs on her and then falsely accused her about her intentions toward them. It reminded me of the junior-high pack mentality—except this was being done by "mature" adults.

When Breanna reached out to them, they ignored, belittled, or simply diminished her. She wanted to apologize, thinking she'd done something wrong. Yet she had no idea how she'd offended her friends so deeply. The sad truth was much more complex. She had to learn how to forgive them because it was keeping her stuck.

Survival Thought: *I have to figure out what I did wrong so I can apologize and fix it.*

Thrival Thought: *I have tried the best I can to make this right, but now it is time to release it and look for friends who share my values of trust, loyalty, and open communication. I get to offer forgiveness to myself and them as I heal and move forward.*

This took several months because it was so painful, but as Breanna practiced her Thrival Thought, she became stronger. She focused on growing her business, which had suffered due to her being distracted. She began to enjoy her family and find new friendships with those who appreciated her loving and caring nature.

When it comes to forgiveness, sometimes the issue is with others—like in Breanna's case. But more often, it is an issue within us.

When I met George, his life was filled with countless self-imposed rules designed to help him be liked and appreciated. It was important to him that he get every situation "right." Self-doubt kept him constantly apprehensive. As you might imagine, it was exhausting to hear the thinking that kept him anxious and fearful.

It soon became apparent that he was struggling to forgive himself. In his younger years, he'd treated numerous women disrespectfully. Now, years later, with a beautiful wife and daughter, he was mortified by his behavior. The shame and guilt were keeping him stuck and getting in the way of his relationships. He needed to free himself from self-loathing so he could step into a life of thriving.

Survival Thought: *I don't deserve forgiveness. To make it right, I must keep punishing myself.*

Thrival Thought: *I get to trust the forgiveness my wife freely offers as well as forgive myself and commit to being an honorable man.*

The change was powerful as George practiced this mind-set daily. He found a new peaceful rhythm that enabled him to let go of the rigid demands, and even punitive expectations, he often placed on himself. No longer was he pushing through work, refusing to enjoy his life, or running at an unsustainable pace. The ability to choose forgiveness gave him a new lease on life and freed him to enjoy relationships. He was now able to set future goals without the weight of past guilt.

5. TRAUMA & CRISIS

Experiencing unexpected trauma can mess with our sense of safety, trust, and security.

I met Gina at one of my coaching retreats—talented, kind, and ready to be married again. But one obstacle stood in the way. She was absolutely terrified to commit to a man. As we began working together, she shared how her previous husband had died unexpectedly, two weeks after her third child was born. With two young toddlers and a newborn, it was over-whelming and devastating. Yet it had happened more than a decade ago and she was still stuck in survival thinking that stopped her from pursuing her dreams.

Her thinking needed to change.

Survival Thought: *I can't get involved in another relationship because he might die, and I won't be able to go through that pain again. Plus, I feel I'm being disloyal to my former husband—and my kids could suffer with a new dad.*

Thrival Thought: *I am stronger than I know and can trust that I am being led into a beautiful new relationship with a man who will love me and my children.*

As her thinking shifted, Gina soon fell in love with a man who adored her and her children. Last I heard, they were newly married, and he was even adopting her children to make it official.

Can you see how past trauma distorts our ability to see the present or the future clearly?

It takes such courage to believe you can thrive when you're barely surviving. Yet learning the secret of choosing a thrival mind-set in the middle of chaos and confusion makes all the difference.

Moving from Survival to Thrival

Practically speaking, how do we successfully move from survival to thrival? First, we've got to practice it regularly. It's like a daily commitment to exercise, except this is a mental exercise.

I've referred a number of times to the power of being intentional. Here are three simple steps to guide you in moving from survival to thrival:

1. IDENTIFY

Identify each Survival Thought and replace it with a new Thrival Thought. Sometimes it comes easily and sometimes we need a little help troubleshooting. If you're stuck here, consider reaching out to a coach, counselor, or good friend for guidance and support.

2. PRACTICE

Practice the mind-set daily. Current research reveals that practicing your mind-set for as little as ten minutes a day for three months can change the pathways in your brain. It turns out we live out how we think.[3] Mind-set is critical for life change. Take the time to sit with your Thrival Thoughts—write them down where you can see them daily. Meditate or pray on them, say them out loud, and share them with those close to you.

3. EVALUATE

Look back and evaluate your progress after three months of intentionally practicing it. Discuss it with people who care about you and your story. Celebrate where you have grown with those who know you and support you on this journey. Make it measurable and real.

---

3. For more about this, see Dr. Caroline Leaf's book, *Switch on Your Brain*.

CLARITY

CLARITY QUESTION
Are you surviving or thriving?

IDENTIFY: Write down one of your Survival Thoughts. What are some ways you can change it into a Thrival Thought?

PRACTICE: How can you spend time actively shifting this thought each day? Be intentional.

EVALUATE: Mark your calendar for a three-month checkup so you can measure your growth.

CAUTION: Make sure you define *thriving* in terms of success that truly matters. Otherwise, you'll only be making headway toward something that might actually be fueling an addiction or unhealthy need for validation. Overworking, overeating, overdrinking, overbuying, overplaying, overavoiding . . . are just some of the passive-aggressive ways we lose our balance and slip into survival rather than thrival. If you're unsure about how you're defining *thriving*, ask a trusted friend, coach, or counselor what a healthy approach might look like, based on your unique story.

Now that you've identified your mind-set, it's time to talk about how time under the stars can further strengthen, and even shape, greater clarity in your life.

UNDER THE STARS

When the Tire Swing Just Isn't Enough

Sometimes the tire swing just isn't enough. We need more, and deep down we know it. Just like the young woman with too many bracelets, life has gotten away from us. Too much weariness from carrying them all. The responsibility of life can get to be unbelievably more than we thought we were signing up for, and the tire swing alone just isn't going to cut it.

Our hearts and minds crave stillness—time for reflection and contemplation.

Recently, I came home from a gathering with old friends. This group had held my babies over eighteen years ago, and I had held theirs. We laughed at the time I had danced nine months pregnant at Kim's wedding and how when I was doing the twist on the dance floor, I almost didn't make it back up. We reminisced about new homes, careers, and vacations together—it was a rich time. But I came home feeling "off."

I headed to my upper patio, where I love spending time under the stars, to sort it out. Was it nostalgia? Was it weariness from recent travels? Was it that my babies were grown and life just felt like it was moving too fast? What felt off?

After several minutes of sitting in stillness, the clarity began to wash over me. Yes, the nostalgia was poignant, but this was something more. I had listened to the stories we were all living and recognized the challenges each was facing. As the conversation weaved around us, I heard the weight of finances, teenager years that were so different than the toddler years, and coping with broken relationships that had somehow gotten sideways. I recognized the sorrow embedded in the joy of the gathering. I so badly wanted to do something—to make it all better. And I was weary from the suffering of this world and the strain I saw on each of their faces as they shared some of their pain. I ached for them. And I ached for myself. Their pain had touched on my own.

The last several years had been challenging and full of many unexpected emotions. Burying a parent, launching my firstborn to college, a failed business venture, caring for aging parents, and too many loved ones either getting terminally ill or passing away. Life just felt like a lot in this moment. I needed time under the stars to feel the sadness. To send out love and prayers. To love and comfort myself as I honored what I had lived through.

Time under the stars reorients us and allows us to truly notice what we're feeling so we can honor it and respond to it in a way that is authentic and true.

As the clarity came, so came the peace. Not long after, my daughter joined me outside and invited me to watch a show with her. By then I'd felt sorted out because of my time under the stars and was ready to be fully present with her. See what I mean? This time gives you the opportunity to slow down and check in with yourself as you learn to honor the beautiful complexities of your thoughts and feelings.

So, let's unpack this a bit.

Why is time under the stars important? There are three main gifts of clarity this time can bring:

1. It gives you the opportunity for an accurate and honest reflection of yourself.

2. It gives you the chance to reorient so you can get to where you want to go and be the person you want to become.

3. It gives you the opportunity for depth. Without it, it's like living in the shallow end of life. A well-lived life requires contemplation and reflection.

Ultimately, time under the stars keeps us congruent with who we say we want to be and who we truly are. It gives us time to assess how we are engaging with those around us and even ensures that the words we speak match the voice and presence we want to offer.

Have you ever known someone who keeps making the same mistake over and over and never achieves the results they hope for? And worse, they're confident that their way is the best as they attempt to convince you? People who know them shake their heads in wonderment. I know we all have blind spots, but I'm talking about those who choose to live in flat-out continual denial about who they are and the state of their life.

It's like working with a trainer who is unhealthy and overweight but keeps talking about how healthy they are and can help you get fit. We don't buy it, do we? It's confusing because what they say and what they do is incongruent.

CLARITY

Reflective Solitude

Choosing to show up well for our lives day after day and moment by moment can be challenging. We can go through our day reacting to a thousand demands pulling on us, but I want to offer a better technique. What I am proposing here is that we pause and learn to engage in reflective solitude and experience the value of deep thinking so we can respond to our lives purposefully and from centered clarity.

It's the difference between reacting to life and responding out of a thoughtful, measured clear-mindedness.

Building on the idea of the tire swing, this kind of deep thinking requires more intentionality. We need bigger blocks of time to pull away and think in order to nurture our clarity.

This is especially true when we are in the middle of big life changes. I remember spending lots of time under the stars as I moved away from teaching and consulting into starting my own coaching company. It was under the stars where I got the clarity I needed to see what I wanted. It was also where I got the strength to eventually take a much-needed risk.

Here are some questions I find myself asking under the stars:

- Am I being true to myself?
- Is what I'm offering helpful or hurtful to others?
- How do I want to respond?
- What are my values and how do I want to live them out?
- What is important to me?
- What do I need to release?
- Am I becoming who I want to be?
- Where do I want to move forward?

- What am I feeling?
- What is true?
- Where do I feel stuck and why?
- Who do I want to invite into my journey to help me move forward?

See how the tire swing isn't enough? We must pause to get clarity that strengthens our identity. And it is time under the stars that allows for reflective solitude.

What Does Time Under the Stars Look Like?

It's hard to know if you're doing something well if it's unclear what it's supposed to look like. Let's get practical by discussing what Star Time is, and isn't.

Just like the tire swing, time under the stars looks different for everyone. For my husband Darren, I've watched him slip away to enjoy a quiet hour on the upper patio, or I often find him up early in the morning with a cup of coffee reading inspirational literature or writing poetry. This time confirms who he is and nurtures who he wants to become. And when there are hard times in our relationship, it is the time under the stars we both crave to fill our spirits so we can come back to the relationship with something meaningful to offer. We know we are each better people because of it. And this makes us better together.

For me, time under the stars is about being still long enough to exhale. It may involve reading, meditating, praying, or simply enjoying my latte on the upper patio as I honor what I am meant to do today or reflect back on a day I just lived. It is about anchoring myself in who I am. To keep it simple, I may even choose a word or phrase to meditate on that prepares me to purposefully step into each moment well.

In short, this time under the stars involves activities that ground me. It is not a time where I am talking or worrying or carrying the weight of the world on my shoulders. It is a time to breathe, think, dream, relax, ponder, contemplate, and savor what matters. It is a time to be still rather than work harder as I reorient to who I am, who I am meant to be, and who I am becoming.

Some days, it might be twenty minutes (or less) of meditation, contemplation, or prayer before I launch into a flurry of activities, travel, and work. Other days, I linger with a book, music, art, or journal writing. No matter what comes after that— whether stimulating conversations or mundane tasks—my *being* is connected to my *doing* because of my time under the stars. See the connection? We need our sense of *being* and *doing* to be integrated, flowing intermingled throughout the day. When they are, it becomes the source of great clarity and personal power.

For example, when writing this book, some of my biggest epiphanies came as I was busy doing something else. I might be in the middle of coaching a client, cleaning the kitchen, or running on the treadmill, and I suddenly knew next steps regarding a chapter or story. But this was only possible because I first spent time listening under the stars. And it is *being* that ideally precedes *doing* . . . but both are essential.

As you set out to experience your time under the stars, make sure it includes these three things:

1. TIME

Structure your days and weeks to do this consistently. As I review my calendar for the upcoming week, I ask myself when

I will schedule time to reach for stillness so that I can achieve deeper clarity. You may start the day with it or end with it. Find what works for you.

2. TRUST

This is important because we have to trust that our spirit matters as well as our ability to ask good questions. We also have to trust that time under the stars will make a difference and that answers are coming.

3. TRUE LISTENING

For the sake of alliteration, I had to get that third "T" in there. But it works, right? We all know what it means to listen half-heartedly, but this time requires that we step away from all distractions so we can really listen to what we need, what we want, what we may even be grieving, and what we are being called into. Our identity is strengthened as we find out what our heart is trying to tell us.

Asking the Right Questions

A recent trip revealed to me the value of asking the right questions.

As I boarded the second leg of my flight heading to Montana, I was surprised to see someone already in my seat. I checked my seat number again. Yep. 27C. The very seat this stranger was in. The couple had been looking for me and when they saw my look of confusion, asked if I wouldn't mind switching so they could travel together. I was happy to oblige.

I went to their assigned seat and buckled in, but then another passenger came on board. He had the seat number for the seat I had just moved to. Huh? We were all confused.

The flight attendant came over to help us sort the situation out. Each of us tried to explain the issue from our point of view. She finally held up her hand for silence. Then she masterfully broke through the confusion by asking one simple question.

"Okay, let's start from the beginning. Everyone here is going to Boise, Idaho, right?"

As soon as she asked that fundamental question, my heart nearly stopped. "No! I'm heading to Missoula, Montana." No one had taken my seat. I didn't even have a seat on this plane! The passengers around me graciously helped me gather my bags, and I raced off to catch my plane. I made it just in time to sit in 27C on the flight heading in the right direction.

A brilliant move on the part of the flight attendant. She stopped the confusion and reoriented us by asking the right question—"You know where you're going, right?"

This is what time under the stars does for us. It slows us down to ask the question we need to ask instead of the question that keeps us confused. What would have happened if the flight attendant hadn't asked that question? How long would we have stayed confused? What if she had asked another passenger to simply switch seats? I would have ended up thousands of miles from where I wanted to be.

The right questions are essential. I offered some questions earlier in this chapter, so you can choose one of those or one from the list below, but go ahead and select a question that resonates with you and take it into your time as you give the space for your heart and spirit to respond.

Here are a handful of additional reorienting questions:

- *How do I feel about my current pace of life?*
- *What is the state of my heart?*

- *What do I most need from this time?*
- *Where do I want more peace?*
- *What is blocking my joy?*
- *What lies do I believe about myself?*
- *How am I becoming the person I want to be?*
- *What would I spend my time doing if money were no object?*
- *What is not sitting right with me and why?*
- *What steps do I need to take to get back on course or stay on track?*
- *What do I need to step into my day and not just survive, but thrive?*
- *What is my body trying to tell me?*

Staying in the Dark

When we avoid time under the stars, whether consciously or not, we choose to ignore the hard places in our lives. In the process, we sidestep the question we most need to ask.

We all do this at various times. You'll get no judgment from me. There have been moments I'd rather clean the bathroom floor with a toothbrush than spend time under the stars. The thought of checking in with the state of my spirit and asking scary questions for which I have no answers can create a mild panic within me. But when the uncomfortableness of my inner life becomes unbearable, I relent. The honesty floods over me, and I find my true self under the stars wondering why I waited so long. The delay only served to extend my pain and confusion.

This reminds me of my friend Joy who left her career as a full-time educator to start her own tutoring business. Leaving the day-to-day work with classrooms and state standards better supported the quality of life she wanted with three young children. I watched her pause, show up under the stars, and grapple with hard questions for which there were no easy answers. No one forced her to do this. It was her choice. She listened to her tired spirit and believed that life could be better for her. It wasn't easy to leave a secure income and a tenured position, but last I heard, she had a waiting list of parents wanting to use her services. I admire Joy for finding the courage not to settle in her career.

Pushing into our big questions can feel like pressing on a festering wound. It's much easier to slap on a bandage and forget about it. Or at least try to forget about it. The haunting never really leaves us alone, does it? It's amazing how creative we can get in trying to ignore it—staying busy, overeating, addictions, shopping, and so on. We only gain victory when we're willing to struggle with the state of our life and how we got there.

Like Joy, I encourage you to press in. Be kind to your heart but be relentless in your pursuit for clarity. Ask questions like, *Why am I so unhappy? What do I really want? Why did I give up? What steps do I need to take to get back on course?* I know this isn't nearly as fun as playing on your tire swing. It is some of the hardest work you'll ever do. But here's the good news, if you will commit to spending time under the stars and daring to ask the hard questions, you *will* get results!

Taking time under the stars helps us move from avoidance, unawareness, and pain—to new creativity, new hope, and a new vision for our lives. Everyone wants that joy, peace, and happiness, but most give up when they realize there are no shortcuts. Don't throw in the towel. Be brave and you will eventually enter into the life you've longed for.

The choice is ultimately yours, whether you seek the light this time can bring or choose to stay in the dark.

Time Under the Stars Isn't Static

The way we spend our time under the stars ultimately grows and develops just as we do. Over time, it will become more about restoring your vibrant spirit than resurrecting your crushed spirit. Sure, you'll still have hard days, but not hard *years* like you used to when you avoided paying attention to the state of your spirit.

That's because you now know what to do to prevent yourself from getting off course in the first place.

Taking this time is a preventive way to live. This is such a hopeful thought. I want to make sure we're tracking. It starts with doing the hard work of understanding your story and heart. Initially, this time helps you become aware of what went wrong and why. It is painful. There are tears. It is disruptive. But it isn't static. As we progress and experience breakthroughs, this time then becomes about how to gain traction and soar even higher. It keeps us moving in the right direction.

Until we trust the value of time under the stars, many of us are often too scared to stop and listen. We push harder to make life work rather than address what isn't working. All the while, fear nips at our heels and prevents us from ever asking what our spirit needs. We start to believe lies like: *Maybe I won't ever get clarity. I won't have true fulfillment or know what I want. Worse yet, maybe I can't get what I want.*

But press in, because both our fears and hopes can reveal what we really want.

Let me ask a few more questions.

Do you know how your spirit is doing? Is it light and free or weighted down and weary?

Strengthening your true inner self means paying attention not only to what weighs you down, but also to what sets you free. You know the bracelets have become too much and the tire swing too little when your spirit is primarily weary, frustrated, anxious, and depressed.

In Chapter 3, we talked about how time on the tire swing replenishes a tired spirit. So does time under the stars. But what is the difference between spending time under the stars and spending time on our tire swings?

Time on the tire swing is an active spirit-rest, which restores the spirit. Whereas time under the stars is a contemplative form of spirit-rest, which affirms our core identity. Both are needed on a consistent basis. Both are critical to nurture a whole sense of self.

Resist the temptation to ignore how your spirit is feeling. Don't run from it or distract yourself. Instead, make your way to that space you've set aside for lying under the stars. Then relax as you bask in the light from above.

CLARITY QUESTION
How will you care for yourself under the stars?

Name a place you can spend time "under the stars." It doesn't need to be outdoors or at night or even where you can literally see the stars. It's your reflective, affirming place.

What makes this space special to you?

What are three questions you most need to ask?

When will you spend time under the stars? How often? It may be daily or weekly, but it's what you need in your season of life. Who can you share your commitment with who will offer you support?

CAUTION: Give it a good three months before you evaluate the results. Research shows it takes three months of doing a habit consistently before you see the change. Pay attention to what is distracting you from spending time under the stars. Recognize the fears that cause you to avoid this time and the voices that are telling you to push faster and run harder. Stand against this pull and be brave. Dare to commit to this time consistently.

Well done! I can feel the energy building. It's time for you to believe there's more for you.

As good as it is to care for your spirit by lying under the stars and listening to the state of your heart, doing so is actually a prelude for something even greater. It starts with giving yourself permission. The permission to be exactly who you are meant to be. But this takes confidence, and it is the first step that leads us to our second "C."

PART II
Confidence

The Second C: Choosing to Believe

The Givers—and their gifts—had become the measure of her worth. Somewhere along the way, her own desires and dreams had slowly disappeared. She knew better who others wanted her to be than who she truly was. Unclear about what to do next, she remained doubtful of her purpose. Late one night, while sitting under the stars, she found herself weary and disheartened, yet unwilling to remove all the bracelets that told her who she was.

We've made it through the first part of our journey. Well done, you!

The temptation is to just keep going, but you know better now. Let's pause and raise a glass to this milestone. It is a huge accomplishment. I mean, come on. Most folks live their entire life in an exhausted daze. Eventually they give up or give out. And understandably so. How can anyone undertake a journey without vision?

But your eyes are now clear and your gaze is set. You've experienced the value of rest. You've discovered how to silence mind chatter. You have sought time on the tire swing and under the stars.

If you haven't noticed yet, you're a different person. All because you have gone after your clarity. That's essential . . . and it's only the beginning.

This journey began with clarity. But it was never just about that. Remember, our goal is attaining the life *you* were made for.

Did you catch the personal nature of this mission? Everyone reading these words is on a unique journey. You aren't pursuing the life your neighbor was made for. Or what your mom thinks is safest. Or that your boss believes will make you more productive. You are pursuing the life *you've* longed for. The life that makes *you* come alive because of the unique being that *you* are.

Confidence is needed for the next phase of our journey. I use the word "our" because I'm at your side as your guide. Confidence isn't optional. It's connected deeply to your beliefs—some of which have been helpful but many have been holding you back in ways you aren't aware of. The enemy of confidence is comparison. You'll never get the life you were made for if you keep chasing other people's dreams.

CONFIDENCE

We're in pursuit of the truest version of you. To find it, you don't need all the answers upfront or to wait until you feel fully ready. Yes, the terrain ahead is treacherous, but I have the survival tools that will see you through. You'll learn how to give self-permission, identify your Givers, understand the belief snowball, call upon your staying powers, and much more.

You have found ways to increase your clarity. But there is an abundance of freeing truth that awaits.

It's time to step into growing your confidence . . . as you venture to become who you are meant to be.

GIVING SELF-PERMISSION

The Gift Only You Can Give Yourself

U p to this point in our journey, our entire focus has been on clarity.

Your vision has likely improved quite dramatically from the start of this book, especially if you've spent time on your tire swing, at the crossroads, and under the stars. As you take the time to care for yourself on your journey, you have more peace about who you are and where you are headed.

Experiencing life with newfound clarity is exhilarating, is it not? And yet . . . it isn't enough.

Our goal isn't 1C Living. We're in pursuit of 3C Living. And as helpful as clarity is, it can only take us so far if we lack confidence. Clarity is the necessary foundation, but now we must check our beliefs as we focus on *becoming who we are meant to be*. This is the second "C" of 3C Living.

You may still feel wobbly in your clarity, unsure if you're ready to jump into a whole new category for seeing your life.

Or you may be anticipating what's next, eager to charge into new terrain. Whether you find yourself at one extreme or the other, or somewhere in between, I want to assure you that you are right on time.

I have led thousands on this journey, and so I have clarity *and* confidence that you are ready for this next step. Like the young woman in the allegory, you don't need confidence to begin this part. Confidence is what you foster while you are living each day at a time.

The Choice Is Yours

My life opened up dramatically once I realized that I had the ability to live my life in a way that restored and affirmed. Not only that, it was up to me how often I wanted to visit my tire swing and spend time under the stars.

Prior to this epiphany, I was frustrated because I felt stuck. I was trapped in a life that I didn't want. I was weary from wearing dozens of bracelets, but didn't believe I had a choice whether to keep them on or take them off. And, let's be honest, it's easier to avoid change when you paint yourself as a victim with no options.

Yet, before I could make a change, I had to give myself permission to even consider it.

I decided to write a permission statement and mine looked like this:

I get to remove what blocks me, pursue what offers me freedom—such as my tire swing and time under the stars—and change my actions to align with these choices.

This simple statement was a catalyst for much-needed change in my life.

But wait, I can hear you asking, didn't I already have clarity at this point? Yes, I did. Thanks to time on the tire swing and under the stars, I could see who I wanted to become. But I now needed permission to shift from *knowing* to *becoming*. Clarity is about knowing, but confidence is about becoming. I needed a new mind-set to step into the life I wanted.

Before we have clarity, our confidence is weak. How can we boldly step out when we don't know where we're going? But with clarity, we must now give ourselves permission to confidently step into our dreams.

The permission statement helped me to start becoming the person I was meant to be. Isn't that what confidence is all about? Becoming who you know deep down that you are meant to be?

Can't Get Life to Work

One of my clients recently discovered the need, and power, of this concept. Kendra had experienced years of success in the business world. She actually didn't see herself as "in the business world" but "on top of the world." She was a thriving overachiever in every aspect of her life.

But then something shifted. She became a mom. Soon she had two toddlers and suddenly she felt disorganized, behind in everything, and constantly irritated with the daily grind of life.

With her successful career a distant memory, she tried to start her own financial planning business from home. She did her best to balance work and family, but was failing miserably with both her clients and her kids.

She arrived at our first conversation burned out, exhausted, and depressed. "I feel so stuck! I'm overwhelmed with my to-do list and angry that I can't get my life to work. What is wrong with me?"

CONFIDENCE

I was intimately familiar with this feeling. She was describing my life from a decade or so earlier. Thankfully, I was also familiar with the way out.

First, we had to slow down, pull over, and hit pause.

Next, we had to coast her car to the nearest crossroads so we could calmly assess the number of bracelets she was wearing . . . and the beliefs behind them. In the midst of doing so, several key agreements began to spill out.

"I have to do everything I used to do before I had kids, all while building my career. And still be a good mother and wife with an organized home."

"Is it working?" I asked.

She sighed. "No."

"Then let's take a closer look at what you believe." I then voiced my favorite clarifying question, "Kendra, what's true here?"

"I can't keep up with my career like I used to *and* be the mother and wife I long to be."

I nodded. "We can be so hard on ourselves. But what if you had permission for what you most need?"

She locked eyes with me, trying to decide whether to risk hoping this might actually work. Thankfully, she was desperate enough to give it a try.

We then spent time crafting her unique permission statement. Here's what she landed on:

> *Because of what I learned about my beliefs not being realistic, I now realize that I get to set new expectations for how I can be successful both as a businesswoman and as a mother.*

Do you sense the power in that statement? It's a solid start because it addresses the lies that weighed her down while simultaneously helping her beliefs to work *for* her. It built her confidence up rather than tearing it down.

But I wasn't done. I had an essential follow-up question. "What do you need to be successful?"

She thought for a minute. Then responded with one word. "Time."

"Time for what?"

"Time to work without interruption. Time to keep the house clean. Time to relax with my husband. Time to enjoy the kids."

"What would that look like?"

Pause.

Before I share Kendra's response, I'm going to address something essential. Not for Kendra but for you. Notice how my question requires vulnerability. The question, *What would it look like?* assumes there's a way to attain the desired outcome, so it keeps us on the hook. It helps us envision the impossible as suddenly possible.

In this moment, it would be easy for us to cling to our previous beliefs that have kept us stuck with no solution. To stay a victim of circumstances. To say change is impossible because if it were possible, we'd already have done it.

The tendency is to throw up our hands in desperation and walk away. It's so crucial—right now, in this moment—to resist the pull to give up. That's where the permission statement is so helpful. Its solution-oriented focus acts as an anchor.

Here's Kendra's response to the question I had asked her: "What would this look like?"

"I think I could hire a babysitter twice a week so I could work at the office. And I can bring in a housecleaner twice a month so I have more time to enjoy my family and not worry about the house."

CONFIDENCE

Yes! Now, before you shut it down or maybe feel the sarcasm rise in you that you, too, could be a raging success with hired help . . . pay attention. It's not about her answer so much as it is letting herself discover what she truly needs.

Do you see the initial breakthrough? She came up with a new solution because she was rooted in her permission statement.

I probed a bit deeper. "That sounds like a great plan. But how will this work financially?" (Yes, we gotta be practical.)

"I'll need to stop working for free with friends and family," she said, "and take my business seriously to afford the help I need."

What? This was new information. I didn't know that she'd been working for free! No wonder she felt so much stress and pressure. It was a lose-lose situation.

Because she was working for free, she was not able to get what she truly needed for herself and her family.

But now Kendra had a workable plan. And as she put it in motion, it was amazing to see the dramatic change to her life in just a few short weeks. Her business grew, her family life was more enjoyable, her home became orderly and, most important, her internal peace and joy increased.

I have seen this play out over and over, particularly when children and caretaking challenges enter our lives. Once people are honest about what is not working and what they need to make it work, a new door of possibility is opened. Although they may not yet have the answer for how to do it, it is first understanding what they need that allows them to eventually find the creative solutions that work. Solutions that fit their budget and make them happy.

I have seen some decide that work was not worth it and they found fulfillment in quitting their jobs to take care of children or aging parents; for others, they had to acknowledge their job was not compensating them enough and found new jobs; and for others it was a complex hybrid of all these. What each person ends up doing is less important than giving the self-permission to be honest about what they truly want.

What can keep us stuck is jumping over the permission to be honest and going straight to the pressure of having the answer. We can avoid exploring the truth of what we need for fear of not yet having solutions. Yet living in avoidance and fear is what tears down our confidence and prevents us from moving forward.

To keep growing her confidence, it was important for Kendra to venture out in new ways with new permission. Over time, she eventually added these brief permission statements to her original one:

I get to relax with my husband and not spend the night cleaning.

I get to enjoy my kids and be fully present.

I get to savor my work and set myself up for success.

I get to make the money I need to support the quality of life I want.

I get to come up with creative solutions that support me and my family best.

I get to relax even when my home is not perfect with two small children.

I get to keep meals simple.

I get to ask for help and not try and do everything myself.

I get to find ways to partner with my loving husband who cares.

CONFIDENCE

> *I get to trust that God is helping me find*
> *the solutions I need for more peace and joy.*

You get the point. These permission statements helped her breathe easy, name what was possible, and shift to the life she desired.

Notice how all the statements start with *I get*_____?

Within four months, these simple but concrete statements helped Kendra shift her mind-set and her reality.

She was experiencing success again, but this time, it was deep, lasting success that began internally and carried over into her external world.

It all starts with listening to your heart and giving yourself permission to believe what you need is possible. That hope will start you moving forward.

The Enemy of Confidence

Just as confusion can block clarity, comparison is the enemy of confidence.

Comparing ourselves to the success or failure of others decreases our confidence. More importantly, it distracts us from the work we need to do that helps build our confidence back up.

Before the permission statements focused her, Kendra had been comparing herself with other mothers and how they "looked" successful, or what she thought success was supposed to be. Comparison was distracting her from designing the quality of life she needed as a working mother.

Allow me to share a personal example.

My husband and I decided to join a bodybuilding challenge. We had lost focus on our physical health and were excited about the tangible results this program said was possible in three months. So we jumped in with both feet and stuck to the high-protein, daily-weightlifting, calorie-burning plan.

Everything was going well . . . until our first weigh-in.

Darren had lost double the weight that I had. That wasn't fair! We'd been doing the exact same plan. In my frustration, I inadvertently allowed a seed of discouragement to take root. With each weekly weigh-in, the seed grew. I was comparing my success and results to his, which wasn't fair to either of us. Doing so was destroying my confidence—the very confidence I *needed* to get fit.

I'm not proud of it, but my barely-there enthusiasm for his success further eroded as the weeks wore on. I'm a fierce competitor—I don't like to lose even if my husband is the one winning. On my best days, I summoned the focus to push through this and cheer him on, regardless of my status, but on my less than stellar days, I got discouraged as I let the comparison get to me.

Sometimes the problem is we look too much at our own life. Other times, it's that we can't stop looking at the lives of those around us. Neither is healthy.

I didn't begin to understand until a trainer explained how men typically lose fat faster than women due to higher muscle content. Based on how women typically lose weight, I was actually right on schedule. This new interpretation shifted my focus from how he was doing to what success looked like for me.

I knew I needed a new permission statement to help my confidence here—so I created one:

Because of what I learned about muscle building, I get to enjoy the pace of my journey and celebrate the success of my husband.

CONFIDENCE

The right permission ushers in so much freedom.

Shortly after giving myself permission to simply be me, I reached my goal. In the process, I learned several things. First, the immense power of staying focused on my own journey. Second, comparison (to anyone or anything) weakens confidence. And most importantly, comparison hurts the people around us. Being free of comparison allows us to freely celebrate others without hyper-focusing on how their victory affects us. And isn't this who we all want to be?

Confidence comes from knowing that we are living in abundance rather than scarcity. There is an abundance of success for all. Comparison creates a scarcity mentality. This not only weakens our confidence but hurts relationships. Cheering on the success of others is a way of not just fighting the harmful effects of comparison, but it strengthens our confidence for the life we are meant to live.

Writing Your Permission Statement

I know we started the journey together in Chapter 1 with your permission slip, but it's time to build on that and create your permission statement.

The best place to begin is with a question. Where are you making comparisons that are hurting your confidence? It will be easy here to focus on your job (or lack of one) or perhaps your favorite sport. But broaden the possibilities. Consider how you feel when the neighbor's yard looks better or your best friend buys a new car while you're still driving that clunker from last decade. It may be that you're comparing yourself to your spouse . . . or your sibling. The ways we compare are endless. You may already know of a dozen such occurrences. If that's true, your challenge for this exercise will be to narrow it down to just one example. The best next step in this scenario is to spend a little time under the stars to gain clarity. Ask yourself which one would be most helpful right now. Then listen.

On the other hand, you may be struggling to come up with even one time of comparison. You know you've been guilty of it—but you're drawing a blank when it comes to a helpful example. My answer is the same. Spend some time under the stars. Perhaps ask those you trust to shine a light on this issue by bringing to mind some examples.

Once you have the situation clearly in mind, articulate where you feel stuck. For clarity, write it down:

_____

_____

Now, what do you need to be successful in this area? Keep this to a few words or a sentence.

_____

_____

Based on the above, create your own permission statement for this area of your life.

Because of what I learned about _____,

I now realize that I get to _____.

CONFIDENCE

Writing all of this down doesn't magically create change. But it is the foundational step for all that follows. Remember how Kendra pursued this even further by coming up with several shorter "I get to" permission statements. Those kept her moving forward. You may want to do the same.

Let's dive a little deeper with our first confidence question.

CONFIDENCE QUESTION
How much time do you spend comparing areas of your life to others?

Let's get specific. Name a recent time you compared something you have/don't have to what another person has/doesn't have.

What effect did comparing have on your heart . . . and your confidence?

How will permission statements help you overcome thoughts like this in the future? Why do you think they are so powerful?

CAUTION: Remember not to put your confidence in the bracelets you wear, what others think of them, or in how many you have compared to others. Who you are can never be accurately measured by what you do.

Stay with your permission statement. It's foundational. Coming up next is another powerful concept for confidence. It's called the belief snowball, and it works in every season of life.

CONFIDENCE

THE BELIEF SNOWBALL

The Multiplication Effect of What We Believe

What does the word "snow" bring to mind?

Some of you got cold just reading that sentence. For others, the thought of snow creates giddy anticipation. For moms of school-aged children, the thought of a snow day may create a mild panic! Depending on what part of the world you live in, you may have never experienced a winter wonderland—or you may have an abundance of snowfall.

I hope you've had the joy of experiencing a good snowball fight. Our family relishes those times. How fun to rally friends and neighbors, divide into teams, and have a good old-fashioned game of "smack your opponents with a snowball." It's a blast. Until a baseball-sized glob of snow zings through the air and knocks you upside the head.

Here's the thing. Flying snowballs can hit us whether we see them or not.

Belief snowballs do the same. But even more so because they operate in stealth mode. And these affect us all, no matter the season.

What, you've never heard of belief snowballs? Well, buckle in.

In this section, I'll reveal the power of true beliefs and false beliefs. I titled this chapter "The Belief Snowball" because what we believe tends to multiply over time. Think of a small ball of snow. It can fit in the palm of your hand. But as you roll it in more snow, it grows. The same principle occurs with our beliefs. When we accept a lie about ourselves, we act a certain way. And that leads us to believe more lies. And soon, we have a ten-foot snowball of lies that started with just one small false belief.

We're going to take a look at what you believe about yourself, the ways to identify true and false beliefs, and how to replace the false beliefs with true beliefs. Are you ready?

Bill and Ted's Amazingly Different Adventure

I'd like to introduce you to two imaginary people, Bill and Ted. They've both read the section on clarity. They've invested time on their tire swings and under the stars. And they are all in.

So they should be equally successful in pursuing their dreams, right?

Before you answer, let me share one more observation about them.

Bill is a confident person. Ted is insecure.

But hey, they both possess clarity. They know what matters.

So, will they be equally successful in attaining their dreams? Unfortunately, they won't. Sorry, Ted.

Because one has set a purposeful course for life (Yay, Bill!) while one is allowing life to happen to him (Boo, Ted!).

They've both gotten their clarity, but only one has dared to believe what is possible. And that makes all the difference in the world. Because it comes down to whether we will boldly believe and become all we are made to be.

But confidence doesn't just happen.

It is our beliefs that determine our level of confidence. In other words, what we choose to believe will either grow or shrink our confidence. Without it, we drift into a life we no longer want, ending up in places we never intended to be.

True and False Beliefs

It's important to know which beliefs grow our confidence and which beliefs decrease it. Because one helps us spiral up—and one causes us to spiral down.

Knowing which beliefs are real (true) and which are faulty (false) interpretations is the quickest way to influence your confidence.

What makes a belief true?

If the answer is yes to the four questions below, then it is true:

- Is it helpful?
- Does it move me forward?
- Does it help me connect deeper with my true self?
- Does it bring increased peace, freedom, joy, or love?

What makes a belief false?

If the answer is yes to the four questions below, then it is false:

- Is it harmful?
- Does it keep me stuck?
- Does it disconnect me with my true self?

CONFIDENCE

- Does it bring increased anxiety, oppression, grief, or fear?

Rather than keep it conceptual, let's consider a few examples.

Imagine someone who believes no one likes them. Is that helpful? Would it fuel them to move forward? Or bring more peace, freedom, love, or joy? Clearly not. But on the other hand, is it harmful or would it keep them stuck—absolutely. Ding! It's a false belief.

Let's try one more. A person believes they can attain their dream of becoming a painter if they will invest time in learning the art. Does that move them forward? Yes. Is it helpful? Of course. And it certainly connects them with their true self, which will result in more peace and freedom. They will experience more joy and love as they dive into a hobby they've longed to pursue. Ding! This is a true belief.

Oh, one more key point. A belief cannot be simultaneously true and false. That's helpful because it removes the ambiguity that often keeps us stuck.

Changing Our Beliefs

As a leadership coach, I have the honor of experiencing my clients' personal growth on a regular basis. During our time together, I'm constantly on the lookout for where they are giving themselves permission and where they aren't.

I remember an executive who had advanced unexpectedly at a young age. As the new vice president of a fast-paced, highly successful company, Carla had more than 175 people reporting to her. It was a big jump from her previous leadership responsibilities, so we tackled each issue that came up on a weekly basis.

CONFIDENCE

We had some hard conversations because she was pushing up against her leadership lid—meaning her learning curve was steep as she was understanding how to lead in new ways. It often felt like a game of real-life whack-a-mole as we tried to stay ahead of all she was grappling with.

One day, Carla remarked, "I had to tell my leadership team the same thing three times, and they still didn't listen to me. But that's okay. I just did the task myself."

Whoa. I had to interrupt. "When did it become okay for your leadership team not to listen to you?"

"It's typical, but I'm used to it. I have to get the job done whether anyone listens to me or not."

"It's typical because you *believe* it is okay to be this way," I said. "It sounds like you have to change your beliefs."

"I never thought about it that way. How do I change what I believe?"

"Try this. The next time you meet with your leadership team, hold on to this belief: '*My leadership voice matters, what I say counts, and my expectation is for my team to respect and listen to what I have to say.*' Then, as you speak, demonstrate your belief by looking around the room and making eye contact with each leader. If someone interrupts, tries to talk over you, or dismisses you, politely stop the conversation and say, '*I'm not being heard on this, and it is important that I am.*' Then start again and tell them what they need to hear."

In our next conversation, Carla came back beaming. "It worked! They stopped ignoring me and now listen the first time I say something. It's like I slowed everything down with my new belief. I don't think they realized what they were doing. It was a bad habit we'd started as a team, but I'm already seeing a change. They are not only listening to me better, but to one

CONFIDENCE

another as well. And we're all doing a better job of actually hearing each other as a team."

Her belief was holding her back as a leader and limiting her team's ability to work effectively. But real change wasn't just going to happen on its own. It was Carla's job as a leader to set the true beliefs and confront the false beliefs affecting her team. This new true belief built her confidence as a leader and created a healthy rapport for the men and women who worked for her. As Carla addressed the belief for herself as a leader, she grew the healthy communication for the entire team.

On a side note, this principle is helpful for parents, teachers, coaches—really anyone who works with young children or teenagers. If you don't believe you deserve to be heard the first time, kids can sniff this out and won't take you seriously. Parents and teachers, if you find yourself repeating directions or words that aren't being heard, slow it down, check your internal belief, and look for opportunities to communicate your expectations out loud. The change may not happen immediately, but you are resetting expectations. Imagine a small snowball that grows bigger with every encounter. And it begins the moment you align with what is true about your role and identity.

Persistent False Beliefs

What about the false beliefs that seem harder to get free from, even when you know they aren't true?

Rachel understands what that's like. She was a talented leader who was terrified to speak publicly, even to a small group of five leaders. Throughout her life, she'd bought into the lie (false belief) that her thoughts weren't worth much. Now she was in a position where speaking was part of her job, and this false belief was holding her back.

A common solution might simply be to sign her up for a public speaking class. And that would help. But it's not enough. Why? Because it doesn't get to the source of her false belief.

Together, we pressed into that first. And what came out were big agreements she'd made as a girl. When she was growing up, her mother and father often dismissed her thoughts and ideas. They focused more on her siblings, so she began to believe that what she had to offer wasn't wanted . . . or even worth listening to.

Let's look at this through the lens of our true and false beliefs criteria. Was that harmful? Yep. Is it keeping her stuck? Absolutely. Does it disconnect her from her true self and bring anxiety, oppression, grief, or fear? Yes times four. So we named her false belief. *My words aren't worth listening to, I can't speak clearly in public, and I freeze up with dread when people look at me.* Then we replaced it with her true belief. *I have something meaningful to say, people want to hear my words, and I can speak with joy and confidence.*

It took many conversations and time under the stars for this to take root . . . but over time, it did. And less than a year later, Rachel was confidently presenting leadership tools to large groups of people. Her communication abilities grew exponentially. But her true beliefs grew even more dramatically. It was those internal shifts that fueled the external changes.

Rachel now develops her own leadership tools and trains business audiences several times a year with high confidence. And yes, we worked on some skills and techniques to grow her public speaking ability, but we first had to get to the root of her mind-set.

CONFIDENCE

Can you see how it all begins with what we believe?

If you're in a situation like Rachel's, mastering all the skills in the world won't help. In fact, you'll just be spinning your wheels. You must first get to the root of what you believe and identify the false belief. Then focus on transforming the false beliefs into true beliefs. That's the foundation for all that follows.

Let's consider another example.

Tyler was a young man whose company flagged him as having management potential. When we met, he'd never had any leadership development and struggled with whether he needed it.

"Do you believe you're a natural leader?"

"Nope. I've just always said what I think."

"How do you feel about getting some coaching around your leadership?" I asked.

"I don't want to but my supervisor asked me to give it a try. He wants to advance me but feels there's something holding me back. That's why I'm here."

"That's a fine place to start," I said. "As long as you're open, we'll partner in this training."

As we worked together over several months, I first had to confront his underlying belief that he was "messing up and needed to be fixed."

His belief was: *I have to get it right the first time, and if I need any help or coaching, that means I'm failing.*

Let's view this through our true and false beliefs lens.

Was his belief harmful? Yep. Do you hear the lack of permission to learn, grow, and stay curious? This is a common false belief I hear among high achievers, and it keeps them in a pressure cooker. Would you say his belief was keeping him stuck? Most certainly. He couldn't move forward in his position or advance his team because of this harming belief. And was it bringing more anxiety, oppression, grief, or fear? Definitely. Not only was this belief filling him with negativity toward himself, but it was spilling over to his team as well. In fact, the morale of the group was at an all-time low with high levels of frustration and cynicism. It was snowballing.

This was most definitely a false belief. Tyler was in desperate need of a new true belief.

Keeping an open mind, he worked hard identifying a new true belief and changed it to: *Everyone needs leadership development to grow, and this is not about being fixed because I am not broken.*

Hmmm. Let's now evaluate this new belief.

Is it helpful? Definitely. It allows for a fresh perspective that takes the pressure off and invites in new learning. Does it assist him in moving forward? Absolutely. He was stuck as a leader and he knew it. Coaching him in skills and techniques weren't going to help a bit until we formed a new true belief to build upon. Does it bring more peace, freedom, joy, or love? Certainly. It manifested itself not only in his professional realm but in his personal life as well. His wife and children started to see positive changes in how he saw himself . . . and them.

Over the course of the next several months, we continued to work together and came up with several sets of additional false beliefs (**FB**) and true beliefs (**TB**). Notice below how there can be more than one true belief to counter a false belief.

FB: *I can't speak in front of people.*

TB: *I value this as an important skill to advance in leadership, and I can learn new skills to grow in my speaking. I can trust that the topics I speak on are in my area of expertise and be confident about this.*

CONFIDENCE

FB: *I don't know what leadership tools are.*

TB: *I can be open to learning new tools and trying out what works for me.*

TB: *I can develop my own leadership tools that fit my authentic leadership style.*

FB: *I'm not a leader. I just have a strong personality.*

TB: *I'm a natural leader, and I get to refine and develop my leadership skills to advance and influence my team better.*

With these new beliefs, Tyler's entire attitude toward leadership development changed from fear to anticipation as he realized this was an invitation to grow rather than to be fixed. And this shift in belief is what strengthened his confidence as a leader.

In a more personal example, I have worked with many marriages and life partnerships where the relationship is sadly spiraling down based on false beliefs. Kira is a good example of addressing her false belief regarding her husband, Tony. When we first started working together, she was struggling with depression. Once she started sharing, the false belief was all too clear. *"I can't tell my husband how I want to be loved because I am neither loveable nor does he care."*

One of the bravest things I witnessed her do was to challenge this false belief that she had lived in for years—keeping her stuck in sadness and only confusing her husband—and invite in a true belief to help her start the process of spiraling up. *"I am loveable, my husband truly cares, and he wants to know what I need to feel loved."*

After inviting in this new belief, the marriage began to change. Within three months, she was feeling new levels of hope and joy for the first time because she was learning to speak up and

CONFIDENCE

tell him what she wanted, and he was responding. (Yes, I know the key is that he responded—and the complexities in marriage can sometimes be overwhelming—but keep in mind that checking false beliefs in our relationship is a powerful place to start on both sides.) In our most recent conversation, Kira came to the conversation happy and light as she shared how Tony had recently surprised her. He'd made reservations at a Greek restaurant simply because she had shared her desire a few days earlier to try Greek food. It was so simple, yet meaningful to both of them. He had wanted her to feel loved but simply hadn't known how because she had stayed hidden in her false belief.

Here's the important takeaway. Our confidence can only grow according to what we believe. So, it's essential to know what we believe and then assess whether it is harming or helping us. And you'll also notice how our beliefs can harm or help the relationships around us.

CONFIDENCE

The Belief Bank

Here are some common false beliefs followed by their corresponding true beliefs. I frequently hear these in both personal and professional coaching relationships. See how many you can identify with:

FB: *I'm not ready to have the hard conversation.*

TB: *I get to schedule this important talk and trust I have what it takes to do it well.*

FB: *I have nothing to offer because I'm not an expert, so I won't speak up.*

TB: *I'm good at my area of expertise and get to ask questions that help me partner well.*

FB: *I have to lead the same way for every member of my team.*

TB: *Everyone's in a different place. I get to respect where each person is and meet them there.*

FB: *I need to get things done on my own and not ask for help.*

TB: *It's okay to ask for help and people appreciate it when I do. It's not a sign of weakness, it's a sign of strength, and it's how we can partner well.*

FB: *A new relationship will be hard.*

TB: *I get to experience new relationships. They can be fun, easy, and mutually enjoyable.*

FB: *I don't know what I'm doing as a parent.*

TB: *I get to trust that I am being led and guided and seek out wise counsel.*

FB: *I'm stuck, and there's no way out.*

TB: *I always have options.*

FB: *If I need someone, I'm failing as a leader.*

TB: *Great leadership invites in trusted advisors.*

FB: *If I compliment others, it's a sign of weakness.*

TB: *My relationships need to hear my gratitude and doing so raises trust.*

CONFIDENCE

FB: *I'm stuck, and I can't do anything about it.*

TB: *I'm never stuck, and I can make choices to take care of myself—but first I need to rest to get my clarity.*

FB: *If I'm not being productive, I'm a lazy and horrible parent.*

TB: *I need time on the tire swing and under the stars to be the best version of myself.*

FB: *I'm a terrible friend because of all the things that are being said about me.*

TB: *I'm not perfect, but I'm a good friend and not who they're making me out to be.*

FB: *I have to fix this on my own.*

TB: *I get to say my truth and trust that I am being led and guided.*

FB: *Saying the truth has to be brutal.*

TB: *I get to speak truth in a caring and compassionate way.*

FB: *I hate exercising.*

TB: *Moving my body is a pleasure, and I get to find ways to enjoy it.*

FB: *I'll never be able to make money doing what I love.*

TB: *I get to trust that I can do what I love and the money will follow.*

CONFIDENCE

FB: *I don't know what to do next.*

TB: *I will continue to move forward in ways that enrich my life and the lives of others as I stay creative, hopeful, and solution-oriented.*

FB: *Things just go downhill as I age.*

TB: *I get to age gracefully and find ways to enjoy growing older.*

FB: *I never have enough time to do what I want.*

TB: *I am in control of my time, and I can figure out how to manage it in life-giving ways.*

FB: *Your pain means I'm doing something wrong.*

TB: *I am not responsible for your pain.*

FB: *Being uncomfortable means I am messing up.*

TB: *I am experiencing growth pains, and I can stop fearing it because this is how we grow.*

FB: *I have to make this work, and it is stressful because I can't see all the moving pieces.*

TB: *I don't have to be clear on all the hurdles today to have a great day, and I get to take it one step at a time.*

FB: *I'm afraid I won't know what decision to make.*

TB: *I have everything I need to figure this out.*

CONFIDENCE

FB: *I can't tell my spouse what I secretly want so I feel cherished because it doesn't matter, and I probably don't deserve it.*

TB: *It is important to say what I am feeling—even though it makes me feel vulnerable—because I am loveable and worthy of being loved.*

FB: *Who I am in a relationship is not wanted or valuated, so why bother speaking up?*

TB: *Offering who I am is valuable and voicing it strengthens the relationship.*

I hope it's helpful to see the truths right after the lies. These lies can quickly snowball in our lives, so it's important to see true interpretations right next to them. Exposure to the light helps melt the false beliefs.

Over the years in my practice, I've created what I call a Belief Bank. These are the most common false beliefs that people struggle with. Read through them and circle the ones you most relate to. We'll revisit them in an exercise at the end of the chapter.

BELIEF BANK

I am alone and stuck in this.

I can't look at the truth because I have no solutions.

I have to take care of everyone else and don't have time to take care of myself.

I am alone in my life.

Growing old is terrible.

I don't have time to do what I really want to do.

I can't trust myself to see things clearly.

I don't deserve to be loved the way I desire.

If I stop to rest, it will cost me. Something important will get dropped.

Living out of peace is too good to be true. It's the anxiety that keeps me going.

People want me for what I do, not for who I am.

I don't have what it takes to accomplish my dreams.

I don't get to be happy.

Living in joy means I won't get things done.

I have to keep up with a pace of life regardless of how I feel.

People are counting on me, and if I pay attention to what I need, it will disappoint them.

I don't get what I really need, so I have to put up with what people choose to give me.

Friendships will always let me down sooner or later, so I have to maintain a safe distance and keep my guard up.

I just have to keep my head down and plug away.

Accomplishing my to-do list is the only way I get to have satisfaction.

Spending time on the tire swing is a waste of time and will cause me to lose my momentum for what I need to accomplish.

If I am not productive, I am not living well.

Resting does not bring clarity, it just gets me further behind.

If it feels too good to be true, it probably is.

CONFIDENCE

Growing old means losing my memory.

I'll never meet my healthy goal weight no matter how hard I try.

Take these statements seriously. What we believe will snowball over time—for better or worse. Before our confidence can grow, we must begin the journey of replacing our false beliefs with true beliefs.

CONFIDENCE QUESTION

What false beliefs have you been believing?

Look at the Belief Bank and choose three that you circled (or write your own) in the space below.

For now, recognize what is holding you back. Describe the false belief—what isn't true—in a sentence or two. Simply naming the lie and shining light on it is a great beginning.

FALSE BELIEF #1:

FALSE BELIEF #2:

FALSE BELIEF #3:

Now that you've identified your false beliefs, try shifting them into true beliefs. Some might be harder than others, so don't worry if you get stuck. We'll talk more about this and how to get to your true beliefs in later chapters. For now, just give it a try. You can always revise your answers later.

TRUE BELIEF #1 (tied to False Belief #1 above):

TRUE BELIEF #2 (tied to False Belief #2 above):

TRUE BELIEF #3 (tied to False Belief #3 above):

CAUTION: Because you've lived with false beliefs for so long, it may be hard to articulate true beliefs about yourself. Don't be afraid to ask for help. I've noticed that clients easily identify their false beliefs but have a harder time coming up with true beliefs about themselves. It's always easier to see what is helpful in others than it is in ourselves. Ask someone you trust—a friend, spouse, mentor, coach, counselor, or guide—to help shift your false belief into your true belief.

CONFIDENCE

CONFIDENCE

Up until now, we've hinted at the importance of our hearts, but we haven't taken an in-depth look at what our hearts need most. That's the focus of our next chapter. In it, we'll learn how to stay true to ourselves as we befriend our hearts.

STAYING POWERS

Boost Your Confidence as You Lead with Heart

grew up watching television shows with heroes like Wonder Woman, Six Million Dollar Man, and Bionic Woman. I know this dates me. But just thinking about them takes me back to my younger self. I would watch, absorbed and in awe of their ability to deflect bullets, outrun trains, defeat bad guys, and lift sinking ships. I loved them not just because of their superpower strength, but because I daydreamed of what it would be like if I could have their powers to right every wrong. (And look aMAZing while I did it!)

You may not have daydreamed about it since childhood, but what superpower did you secretly want? Especially when you were hoping to outwit a bully or be the hero that saved the day? Was it to fly, stretch like a rubber band, or control minds? Maybe it was to run at the speed of light or lift a car with one hand? Perhaps it was to travel through time, fly through the air, or turn invisible?

And let's get real, haven't you longed for the ability to be stronger than every bully and right every wrong? Even turn into a raging green monster when someone kept pushing your buttons? Yeah, that's revealing my deep satisfaction in justice being served.

What if I told you the ability to have powers we can call on in times of need isn't make-believe. They just aren't the kinds of powers we see in comic books and movies. Rather than superpowers, these are staying powers. And to be honest, superpowers don't hold a candle to staying powers once we learn to wield them in our daily lives.

In this chapter, I'm going to introduce you to six powerful ways to maintain confidence. They are separate yet work together. And they have an amazing side benefit—they all serve to simultaneously strengthen your heart.

Why is that important?

Glad you asked. Because if your heart goes numb, not much else matters. It's hard to change the world when you don't even want to change clothes from yesterday. You can't motivate a team when you are unmotivated and disengaged. The heart is essential if you want to lead people in a memorable, meaningful manner.

These staying powers will befriend your heart, keep it engaged, and help you stay in the game. And they couldn't be more essential. Because what you believe is who you become. Staying powers help you sniff out false beliefs and anchor into true beliefs. And they all serve to build confidence.

So cue the super-hero theme music. It's time to discover your six staying powers.

1. Stay Curious

This is our starting point. The ability to stay curious sets the foundation for who we want to be.

We grow when we ask questions. We stay humble when we seek to understand the world around us as well as those who disagree with us. We find new ways forward when we admit we don't have all the answers but remain hungry to discover more.

This posture also serves to combat the judgment, often-times harsh, that we pile on ourselves and others. And that's key, because once we get stuck in judgment, we no longer have the capacity to move forward.

Let's put this to the test.

Remind yourself of the false beliefs you identified in the last chapter. Have you shifted them into true beliefs yet? If not, that's okay. Keep with it. The important thing is to stay curious about *what* you believe. And staying curious means staying away from judgment, guilt, and shame.

I learned the art of staying curious while working with children. It was a great reminder that the younger we are, the more natural curiosity we have. But then what happens?

As we age, we unintentionally allow those around us to diminish our curiosity. If someone is ashamed of us, we begin to feel shame. If a teacher or parent is afraid, we become fearful. This is especially harmful at an early age when we don't know how to interpret the reactions of those in authority.

On the other hand, if young children are shown kindness and love, they tend to feel love toward themselves. Given that, it should come as no surprise that loving ourselves is associated with staying curious. So, see this section as an invitation to get to know yourself and love yourself better. You'll be glad you did.

CONFIDENCE

Ethan taught me this in my first year of teaching third grade. He came to me as a shut-down nine-year-old. Honestly, my first thought as a teacher was, *How does life beat up a cute little boy in just nine years?* I was determined to get to the bottom of whatever had happened and change the trajectory he was on.

As I worked with Ethan, I realized that he was "slow" in everything he did. As we've all discovered, this can get a person a bad rap in school. We learn quickly that the student who works or moves fastest is the brightest, right? Whether it's solving math problems, reading out loud, or running in sports—faster is better. Most of us never question this flawed logic. But is faster always better?

Even at his young age, a false belief had formed in Ethan's little mind: *"I'm dumb because I am slow."* I began to teach him new beliefs that countered it like, *"Those who take their time will go far in life,"* and *"Being methodical is more important than finishing first,"* and *"Just because you need more time does not mean you lack intelligence. Quite the opposite. It means you're analyzing it from every angle to ensure you do it right the first time."*

Slowly, these new beliefs began to replace his old ones. And as Ethan believed it, he blossomed. I realized I was working with a highly sensitive child who saw the world through a unique set of glasses. He began to write poetry that blew me away. His art was filled with depth and insight. He was brilliant.

He just didn't look like what schools said high intelligence should be. He was the inspiration for me to give all my students an intelligence test that reveals the nine key intelligences of: Verbal, Mathematical, Musical, Visual, Bodily, Interpersonal, Intrapersonal, Naturalist, and Existential.[4]

---

4. See Gardner's Theory of Multiple Intelligences. https://www.multipleintelligencesoasis.org.

I showed my students that only a couple of these intelligences are quantifiably measured in school, and that it is the system that limits how we define intelligence to those few. But look how many more intelligences we have. And most are never assessed on our standardized testing—including interpersonal, naturalistic, and musical intelligences. Those excelling in the unmeasured skills aren't less intelligent. Tragically, they tend to be overlooked.

I shared Ethan's poems, art, and drawings with the class to show his incredible talent. I'll never forget the day his mother came to my class and handed me a recording of a song he made for me. Tears welled up in her eyes as she thanked me for "seeing" her son. The lyrics of his song were about how I'd faithfully stood by him and believed in him every step of the way. I can still hum the melody several decades later.

Staying curious with Ethan changed me not just as an educator but as a human being. I learned that as I stayed curious about Ethan, I invited him to become curious about himself. See how this impacts our confidence? Staying curious in our interactions with one another helps grow our confidence as it gives permission for each of us to be curious about ourselves and our unique abilities. It is truly a superpower. Begin with your life and those you interact with. Where do you need to replace judgment with wonder and introspection? Start asking the right questions, not from a place of shame but from genuine curiosity.

Why do I keep gaining weight?

What is happening in my marriage that hurts?

Where do I want more hope, and what is blocking it?

Why do people consistently not want me to join their groups?

CONFIDENCE

Staying curious about what we want and what blocks us from getting there helps us with the second staying power . . . kindness.

2. Stay Empathetic

By staying curious, we become kinder people. We become more empathetic as we understand where others have come from and what they have lived through. Empathy also helps combat the shame that can overwhelm us as we either face our own issues or see them in the reflection of others.

I have a little more to share of Ethan's story.

In my first parent-teacher conference, Ethan's parents shared how his last several teachers had put him down because of how he needed extra time for everything. The feeling of weariness still washes over me decades later as I remember that conversation.

When did it become okay to push our students to keep up with some invisible standard that disrespected their pace of living? Our world needs more children methodically taking their time—not keeping up with the pack—to problem-solve, come up with better solutions, and see the world with fresh vision.

Empathy is needed to remember what people are experiencing and enduring.

For instance, with anxiety growing in our classrooms—for both students and teachers—slowing it down to engage our empathy can help us find better ways. We need to be encouraging more permission in our school systems for the pace each individual needs to maintain so they can learn, grow, and make connections. Not diminishing and dismissing them because they break the mold and can't keep up with the pack. Yes, it was my job as an educator to get Ethan ready for the next grade level. But before I could do that effectively, I needed to understand where he was coming from and meet him there. That was a far more important job, and curiosity and empathy were required to do it well.

This is the same approach I follow with my clients. Where are they in their journeys? How can I meet them where they are *now* rather than where I think they should be? This allows us to discover together what they need to move forward.

Cindy is a good example of this. When we first started working together, she was frustrated, restless, and overall irritated with her life. Initially she couldn't pinpoint the problem since her career was strong and her family was a joy to her. Honestly, it wasn't clear to me either since there were no obvious signs. So I simply stayed with her in the emotional strain and empathized with her. It was the emotions of defeat and feeling out of control that she was dismissing, avoiding, and denying. In this kindness, she allowed herself to be honest and the truth came out.

She felt trapped—stuck—and lived with a growing irritation that embarrassed her. Rather than find out why, she just kept working harder to be nicer. But we know how that goes, don't we? Empathy. "It's frustrating and discouraging to be irritated with your family and coworkers and not know why, isn't it?" I said. She sighed. "Yes, it is and I can't seem to get a handle on it."

I didn't know why Cindy felt this way, but I know that I have felt that way before. And I know how out of control it feels to not understand the "why" behind our emotions. Empathy is a powerful doorway to discover the truth within ourselves—especially when what's going on inside of us is confusing and uncomfortable.

We soon realized the underlying issue. Her false belief was, *I have to be there for everyone else, and it is selfish for me to take time for just me.* She gave all her attention and energy to work and home, and slowly she stopped doing anything for herself. She missed her daily time in the gym, date night with her husband, weekend hikes with friends, and simply choosing a restaurant that didn't always cater to the kids. Her tire swing. She'd stopped visiting it. And it had been awhile. Once she gave herself permission to put herself on the calendar again, her energy and joy significantly increased. She shifted into the true belief that kept her grounded: *Making time for myself is important and makes me a better human.*

We all need empathy. But before you can offer it to others, it is essential that you offer it to yourself while sorting out what you believe. Let your curiosity reveal how you need to treat your heart with more empathy. In that space, you will find your true belief.

3. Stay Humble

A word of caution. As we "conquer" our beliefs, experience curiosity, and offer empathy—our confidence will increase. That's a good thing. But once life starts clicking on all cylinders, we may be tempted to give advice. You know, help people have a better life by doing what we've done. I mean, come on. They're stalled now like we used to be. They need to get with the program. And we have just the answer.

Resist the temptation to be the one with all the answers because it's based in pride and it keeps us from staying truly connected to the person and what they need to move forward.

When pride takes root, we miss the opportunity to really listen and ask what *they* need. People don't need our "helpful advice" nearly as much as they long for a humble spirit to come alongside them and truly befriend their heart.

Humility reminds us what might be right for one person is not right for someone else. There isn't a formula we throw at people and then wait for miracle results.

The change needed in these situations is more often about us, not them. Learning to hold our tongues, really listen, be fully present, and ask good questions engages the clarity and confidence we all crave. From there, we hold hope that over time, they will come up with the right answer and solutions *for themselves.*

This reminds me of a lesson I recently learned with one of my clients. I was coaching Tim's leadership team at their headquarters. We'd just worked through their core values, and I was wrapping up. It had been a powerful meeting, and we were bursting with anticipation for the future. It was time for Tim to communicate the new leadership values to the team.

For me, it couldn't have been more obvious what the next steps were. Tim would announce the information to the team, sell the dream, and inspire them to be part of the values we'd come up with. I was closing down the meeting when, thankfully, I felt the need to pause.

Something in me wasn't sure Tim and I were in sync with next steps. So rather than assume I knew the answer, I asked him a question. "Tim, how do you think it would be best to message this to your team?" I'm so glad I asked. His answer surprised me.

"I'm not sure they'd feel heard or respected if I just told them what we decided, as good as that plan may be. Instead, I want to ask each team member about their values, collect the answers, and then have a larger group discussion."

CONFIDENCE

Wow! I'm glad I slowed it down long enough to ask. Tim wanted to come up with the team values together so he would have a higher buy-in—and because he knew he didn't have all the answers. Brilliant. He demonstrated such humility. And it was also humility that helped remind me not to assume everything would go the way I would do it. Unless I slowed down and asked Tim, I didn't know where his heart was headed.

To lead from your heart, you have to make space to ask good questions and listen well.

Humility makes space to learn and grow. It slows us down and reminds us that every encounter and person is unique. What worked great in last week's situation might be a disaster this time. That's why the most powerful posture is one that is curious, empathetic, and humble. We're fully present, ready to discover what's best, and eager to listen and learn rather than assume we're the source of all wisdom. And this is where true confidence can authentically grow.

CONFIDENCE

4. Stay Truthful

When our children were young, there were times they didn't tell the truth.

We weren't panicked. We knew this was a typical developmental stage all children go through. But if the deception ran unchecked, we also knew it would not just lead to a weakened character but to a lonely existence. At the same time, we'd seen how punitive behavior resulted in shame and broken relationships between parents and children over time. We didn't want that either.

Our desire was to teach the value of honesty through love. We just weren't quite sure how to do that. And then our children presented us with the perfect moment, one every parent can relate to.

It was the cookie-crumbs-on-their-face-with-a-broken-cookie-jar-on-the-counter moment. You walk in. The children are wide-eyed. And they nervously yet emphatically declare they did *not* have a cookie, with the evidence still lingering on their faces. The best we can hope for is to keep a straight face in the moment before going behind closed doors to chuckle.

They were still too young to have developed stealthy cover-ups. It was the perfect time to teach them why truth telling was so important.

As we stood in the kitchen watching two toddlers trying to lie their way out of their very obvious crime, Darren came up with a brilliant response. He bent down and lovingly looked them in the eye as he said, "If you tell the truth, you get a partner. But if you lie, you get a consequence."

It was a sight to behold. They each broke under the weight of his loving directness. Their little lips started quivering as they threw themselves into Daddy's arms, declaring what they had done.

It's a beautiful reminder about the power of love versus the power of shame. Nobody wants to live alone. Staying truthful keeps us connected to our hearts and to the hearts of others.

This set the foundation for years to come as the value of this commitment only increased over time. During their teenage years, each came to us at various times to confess when they'd been dishonest, knowing they would get a partner if they told the truth.

You see, the saddest thing about lying is that it isolates you. Because you're not just lying to others, you're lying to yourself. As our children matured, they were able to see the

CONFIDENCE

worst consequence is being alone. Even though the confessions brought natural consequences, it was essential they knew we didn't expect perfection. They had permission to mess up and get the help they needed to sort things out instead of hiding in isolating shame while they carried the pain and suffering of their guilt.

Lying does this. It keeps us away from the loving help and support we need most. Honesty is what keeps us connected not only to others but to ourselves. Let me say this again: when we are honest with ourselves, we can deal with what's in front of us and get the solutions we need to move forward. And this process allows us to befriend our hearts. Many people stay stuck because they are lying to themselves and refuse to listen to the truth of what their hearts are saying. Truth sets us free to explore the right options and get the solutions for where we want to go. Caring for our hearts requires us to stay truthful and be honest about our emotions. But first we have to know what we're feeling.

Perhaps a story would be helpful. A leader named Miguel recently showed up to a coaching session highly agitated at a coworker. I went through the obvious emotions I thought might be bothering him, but nothing resonated.

"Hang on," I said. "I have an Emotional Categories sheet, and I'll start reading some of them off to see if any fit." As I ran down the list, we finally found a word.

"How about manipulated?"

"Yes, that's it!" he exclaimed. "And mistrusting!"

"Okay, good. Now that we know what we're dealing with, tell me why you lost trust and how you were manipulated."

As he began to explain his coworker's actions and attitude toward their supervisor, we found the reason for his anger. The coworker had told the rest of the team that their supervisor didn't care about them having to work overtime. And this caused a growing cynicism on the team toward the supervisor. The team then began putting pressure on Miguel to talk to the supervisor. But when Miguel brought it to the attention of the supervisor, it got confusing. Apparently, the supervisor was in the middle of giving the team a bonus for working so hard and was also in the process of hiring a new employee to help minimize overtime. Miguel was shocked and realized it all pointed back to this disgruntled coworker who was attempting to get the schedule he wanted with weekends off. Now he knew the truth of what he was feeling *and* what he wanted to say to his coworker.

In my next meeting with Miguel, we had a high-energy conversation. He shared how empowering it was to have a discussion using truthful emotion rather than stuffing down his feelings or exploding at the guy. He confronted his coworker, letting him know that he felt manipulated and was now mistrusting of him. What came next surprised Miguel as the coworker owned up to it, apologized, and shared his fear about conflict. Even more important, Miguel became a better leader by calling out his coworker to be honest about what he was feeling and the damage he had done. I recently had the privilege of watching Miguel present at a corporate workshop. His topic? The Power of Knowing Your Emotions in Leadership.

I have no doubt Miguel's presentation will impact his entire team culture . . . and it all began with his courage to stay truthful.

5. Stay Hopeful

Why is it important to stay hopeful?

Let's take a fresh look at the four main questions for true beliefs:

- Is it helpful?

- Does it move you forward?

- Does it connect you to your true self?

- Does it bring more peace, freedom, joy, or love?

Note how all four of these questions are rooted in hope.

As you pursue true beliefs, it's crucial that you stay hopeful. I've seen this trip up many people. Here's the reason. True beliefs can't anchor without hope. And it's up to you to hold the hope, even when others can't.

Another client I met with discovered this the hard way. Aaron gave up on his team because of his own lack of hope, which, not surprisingly, stemmed from this false belief: *People can't change or grow. It's a waste of time to try.*

If you go around believing that, guess what happens? No one changes. Or grows. No big surprise, right?

The executive leadership asked me to work with Aaron on this issue, and I readily accepted the challenge. Although Aaron was open to being coached, he was not open to changing his beliefs.

And no matter how many times we pressed in on his false beliefs, he clung to them like a drowning man gripping the last life raft. Except this life raft had a hole and was going down. Everyone seemed to know that but Aaron.

His lack of hope, along with growing cynicism and despair, demoralized his entire department. Eventually he was replaced because of his team's low morale and lack of productivity. Nadine took over for him. She was someone who knew how to stay hopeful and clung to true beliefs. It was difficult changing the group culture, but Nadine was steadfast in hope for her

CONFIDENCE

potential and for her team's future. Within several months of us working together, her department had an entirely new atmosphere. Last time I was on-site, there was a contagious energy, people were engaged in their jobs, and the improvement in bottom-line results was undeniable. Her department became a model across the company for how to change culture.

But notice this—the very change Aaron was certain couldn't happen *did* happen. The stumbling block wasn't his team or the economy or the budget. It was his lack of hope and his commitment to his false beliefs.

This can transfer over to personal relationships as well. A wife who has given up hope with her husband, or a father with his son . . . hope is the anchor for our beliefs. And what we believe influences our confidence in ourselves and others.

People long for hope. Our world is starving for it. And whether we're CEOs, stay-at-home parents, teachers, or entrepreneurs, we have a myriad of ways we can offer hope. But it begins with us staying hopeful, because true beliefs are always filled with hope—embracing what ignites our hearts and moves us into the life we want with the relationships we value.

6. Stay Integrated

"I can't be strong and sensitive at the same time!" Max practically shouted into the phone. He was CEO of a multi-million-dollar company and one of my favorite clients. But he wasn't happy. He slammed his hand on the desk. I heard the vibration through the phone line.

This had been an on-going conversation that he was ready to be done with. The conversation was getting tense because I was pushing in on a false belief he'd been protecting for too long. Now we were getting to what held him back as a leader as well as a father, husband, and all-around person.

"There's no way, Heather. I can't be simultaneously strong and sensitive. It's impossible!"

"Why not?" I asked with all sincerity. Remembering curiosity, humility, and empathy are part of the staying powers, I wanted to gain new understanding by asking the question.

"Because," Max responded, "you have to be one or the other. And I choose to be strong. If I'm too sensitive, my team may perceive me as weak, and I won't be respected."

"Strength is good and necessary, but it seems to be costing you more than you realize. I'm wondering if it is time to consider a new belief."

There came a long pause on the other line.

When this happens, I'm never sure if they're going to push back, disengage, or go silent on me. But I knew I'd pushed on a nerve. Out of respect, I stayed quiet and let him work it out and say whatever he needed to say so I could then meet him there.

"Okay," he said hesitantly. "Let's say you're right. How can I be both?"

"Yeah, it's tricky to hold this tension, but so important. And as your responsibility grows, this will become even more challenging. Paying attention to how your heart is leading is critical, but first you have to accept that you can be both. This new true belief will allow you to stay integrated instead of swinging back and forth between extremes."

He sighed. "You mean there's no formula or easy answer?"

I laughed because I could hear the comic relief in his voice, and it was a common complaint we both often shared. "If only. Life would be so much easier that way, wouldn't it? But staying

CONFIDENCE

integrated and holding tensions requires the practice of leading from—and listening to—your heart."

Funny enough, that same week, I talked with Kay who was struggling with the inverse of what Max was grappling with. She was trying to balance her sensitivity with more strength since her team was not responding to her emails and dismissing her deadlines for projects. She, too, had to trust that she could be both sensitive and strong. As she balanced out her sensitivity with more strength, she became integrated. The team began to respond to her higher levels of accountability, causing the results to double within three months. Staying integrated with both her strength and sensitivity not only made the team more successful but their respect grew for her as a leader.

If only there were a quick fix. But pressing into being your best self requires the hard, intentional work of staying integrated. We'll talk more about this in the chapter "Holding Tensions," but for now, consider how increased confidence needs our ability to live integrated.

But just because it's hard doesn't mean it's impossible. Give this a try. Next time a situation comes up where you feel you have to morph into one response or another, hold on to this true belief. Ask yourself, "How do I offer both strength and sensitivity to this situation, relationship, or conversation?" As the parent of two teenagers, I have found this to be one of the more valuable questions to grow trust between us. Asking this question will help you show up better than ever before. Doing so gives your heart permission to weigh in and help guide the situation. This is what staying integrated means: being mindful of leading from both your head and heart; knowing how to hold both a strength and sensitivity; and learning how to live out of balancing both in every situation.

CONFIDENCE

Max was ready for a better way. He knew his strength was inadvertently running over his team, his wife, and his daughters. As he practiced his new true belief of being both strong and sensitive, it required on-going attentiveness to his heart. He learned to let it guide him in what was needed for a situation. Nothing was on auto-pilot anymore. There was no longer a formula to follow. It wasn't easy. But people immediately saw the difference in him. His team noticed, and more importantly, his family reaped the benefits of his growth. And Kay, too, found the value of monitoring and balancing both her strength and sensitivity to those she led.

The ripple effect of an individual staying integrated is inspiring. In a world where people demand that you fit into categories, we need more voices who dare to live integrated. Will you be one of them?

One last suggestion. Pay attention to how you talk to yourself. Does it tend to be more with love or shame—kindness or harshness? Would you allow someone else to talk to you the way you talk to yourself?

CONFIDENCE QUESTION
How do staying powers befriend your heart?

Which staying power comes most naturally to you? Why?

Which staying power is the hardest for you to implement? Why?

Looking back, can you think of a time when you used all six staying powers simultaneously? If not, can you think of a current relationship or situation where it might be helpful to try?

What is a true belief you can create based on this new awareness?

CAUTION: The six staying powers help us find our true beliefs. If the belief is helpful, keep it. If it is harmful, let it go. If it is true, keep it. If it is false, replace it. Do this and you will see your heart, and confidence, soar.

CONFIDENCE

CONFIDENCE

I hope you enjoyed testing out your new staying powers. As you continue to use them, it's important to remember what you learned during our earlier time at the crossroads. The people in our lives influence our beliefs. And one type of person holds the most sway—the Givers. But here's where it gets tricky. Some gifts help us while some hinder us; some we've simply outgrown.

In the next chapter, we'll take a closer look at who your Givers are and what gifts they're offering. Doing so will help you better understand the beliefs behind your confidence level.

WHO ARE YOUR GIVERS?

Discerning Between Gifts of Insecurity and Gifts of Confidence

As we learned at the crossroads, who we allow into our life influences our beliefs. There's one type of person who holds even more influence than most. I define these individuals as Givers. A Giver, as the word implies, gives gifts. These gifts influence and define our sense of identity. Some help, some hurt, some shift over time, and some are useful for a season, but not so much once we outgrow them. Givers may be parents, teachers, coaches, counselors, friends, guides—people who cross our paths and see us. What they offer us comes from their perceptions of us or hopes they have for our future. They contribute to how we see ourselves and relate to others.

Knowing more about who our Givers are and the gifts they offer helps us understand the beliefs that affect our confidence level. If we have low confidence, for instance, likely it is linked—at least in part—to having the wrong Givers in our life. I saw this as an educator and encouraged parents to celebrate the strengths in their children rather than overly focus on their weaknesses. Good Givers call out the strengths in people and help them identify their purpose in this world.

We all prefer good Givers over bad or manipulative ones. The challenge is recognizing which Giver is which early enough to choose well. On the surface, they're often hard to distinguish. And most of us lack the tools to consistently make the choice we need.

The Six Signs of a Good Giver

What makes a Giver good? Learning to assess how we feel as well as what is happening around us helps us identify good Givers.

From my years as a professional coach and educator, I've identified six traits that good Givers possess. Each trait is helpful on its own, but taken together, they are invaluable in separating the healthy and unhealthy Givers.

So here they are, in no particular order.

1. GOOD GIVERS HONOR YOU AS A PERSON WITH HIGH VALUE AND GREAT POSSIBILITY.

These Givers often come from unexpected places. When I was launching my coaching company, a friend discussed my services with a CEO, Jon, several states away.

He flew in to talk with me. As we discussed the issues his company was facing, I grew uncertain about my ability to meet the needs of a company so vastly outside my area of experience. My focus had primarily been in leading teams around nonprofit work, developing women for leadership roles, consulting nonprofits in human service industries, and training educational groups. This company was a long-standing, multi-million-dollar operation with over 300 employees in a mechanical and technical service industry several states away—with the majority of the employees being men.

I was suddenly faced with numerous variables outside of my comfort zone. Yet Jon believed in my capabilities and saw the connection between my experience and what the company needed. He asked me to consider working with a leader in his company that oversaw forty employees.

Honestly, I was tempted to decline and stay safe with my status-quo work. Yet, I knew this was a great opportunity to stretch by stepping outside of my comfort zone. So I agreed. Five years later, I am deeply embedded in the leadership development of this company and thoroughly enjoying my work. I've helped them build trust and open lines of communication. Through my talents, I've been a part of creating a thriving culture with consistently healthy employee growth. How did this happen? By a Giver seeing something in me that I hadn't yet seen in myself.

Jon was an unexpected Giver in my life who offered three gifts. First, he honored my current expertise in coaching human growth and development. Second, he tapped into my possibility to excel in a new, unproven opportunity. Third, he used his position of influence to open doors for me. That's a powerful triad combination to bestow upon another. And I'm still grateful to this day.

2. GOOD GIVERS OFFER NEW BELIEFS AND CONSISTENTLY NURTURE THEM IN YOU UNTIL YOU'VE GROWN INTO THE PERSON YOU ARE MEANT TO BE.

My husband Darren is a great example of this trait. We've known each other for nearly thirty years. In addition to being

CONFIDENCE

my spouse, he's one of my oldest friends and knows me better than anyone.

For more than two decades of marriage, he has been a consistent source of support and a True North compass for my beliefs. When I'm unsure about something and begin to express a false belief, like "I don't know if I can run my own company" or "write a book" or "get a PhD," he gently but stubbornly pushes back against these lies and helps me course correct through true beliefs that get me back on track.

Once, when I realized my fear of selling and marketing were slowing my growth, he used his business background to show me how to write contracts and proposals. After two years of "trying to write a book" (really, just talking about it), he put me in touch with a writing coach. When cost was the biggest deterrent for me pursuing my PhD, he encouraged me in taking out loans while expressing his confidence in my ability to finish a doctorate and eventually pay it off. And he was right! I paid off the loans in under two years with money earned in my new coaching company. His belief in me gave my confidence the boost it needed to push forward. He took my longings and dreams seriously, but not just from the sidelines. It was his active participation that helped me push past my false beliefs blocking my potential while he found ways to support me in nurturing the true beliefs regarding what I could attain.

3. GOOD GIVERS CONTRIBUTE TO YOUR LIFE AND DREAMS WITH NEW MOMENTUM THAT MOVES YOU FORWARD.

What kind of Giver helps you move forward when you are stuck? If you immediately imagine a person, you might want to expand your vision. In my life, it wasn't only an individual but a large nonprofit that had a reach of over 20,000 people. They were committed to empowering their leaders and invited me to teach leadership workshops on 3C Living. What interested me even more was that they wanted me to create an experiential environment for attendees that included creative exercises that engaged the right side of the brain with art and music, something I had been doing for a while with small groups and retreats.

When I said yes, my speaking world instantly opened up from doing workshops in small groups to presenting to thousands of people over the next several years. And it began when this Giver saw a need for their people and recognized my skillset as being a good match to bring the dream to reality.

It became a mutually rewarding connection for both parties and was a catalyst for huge momentum in shaping me as a coach.

4. GOOD GIVERS ENCOURAGE YOU TO RISK IN NEW BUT HEALTHY WAYS.

A leader came to me after I'd had early success in my career and asked, "Why do you only offer these workshops and retreats to women?" It was a big question that caught me off guard.

This Giver saw untapped potential in me that he cared enough to address. And he did it not by just asking a question, but by then telling me (rather intensely) that he felt like the men were getting "ripped off" by not being given the opportunity to receive what I was offering.

To be honest, I assumed only women wanted to hear my insights. To be more honest, I believed because I was a woman, that my words and experiences would only be relevant to women.

Trusting him, I partnered with his organization and held a full-day conference for both men and women. I remember

CONFIDENCE

feeling both surprised and encouraged. His belief in me, coupled with his ability to open doors, gave me the opportunity to risk in new ways for the first time. His gifts produced long-term results for me. I now regularly speak to men, women, or mixed audiences while remaining true to who I am in each setting.

This Giver invited me to step out and risk in new ways. And this is important to note: while I was nervous, I knew it was a healthy and needed risk for me. You know that feeling deep down in your gut that you will regret it if you don't do it? I've learned to listen to this feeling. It helps guide me in wise risk-taking. Unfortunately, there were plenty of times when I had to learn the hard way that I should have declined or recognized that I was not set up for success. Recognize when your values and/or experience do not align with the invitation and avoid those Givers.

5. GOOD GIVERS KNOW THE END GAME IS TO LAUNCH YOU—CHEERING YOU ONWARD AND UPWARD—EVEN IF IT MEANS WORKING THEMSELVES OUT OF A JOB.

I'll never forget the time when I was between jobs and having an identity crisis in my midlife. I was desperately trying to figure out next steps. While I'm a successful coach now, I had no idea then what a professional coach was or did.

About that time, I hired my own coach. He became an influential Giver in my life as he introduced me to coaching and encouraged me to consider it as a profession. Not only did he suggest the idea, he generously shared his own coaching platform and mentored me in the field until I was ready to launch my own coaching company a year later.

Throughout our work together, he demonstrated an altruistic desire to see me be successful. He gave me the confidence to believe in my abilities while mentoring me along the way and then cheered me on with each step forward as I started my coaching company. Even as it worked himself out of a job as my coach. It's one of the greatest gifts a person can give or receive.

6. GOOD GIVERS DON'T TAKE THE CREDIT FOR YOUR HARD WORK.

This one makes me think of the team working with me to publish this book. I wanted to write a book for as long as I can remember, but continued to just "think" about it for over two years. My husband helped me realize that if I didn't get some help, it would never happen.

But who to help? And what kind of help did I need? I knew my challenge was to make the manuscript clear and compelling. I didn't want future readers feeling like they were plodding through an academic paper. But how? All I'd been trained in was research writing, and I don't see a lot of dissertations hitting the bestseller list.

I needed help to write differently. The team of Givers began to appear. A writing coach came alongside me, and eventually an editor. Each read through my manuscript, line by line, chapter by chapter. They offered content editing that allowed me to learn the art of voice and arc and flow. In short, they helped me find the right way to convey my message in the most compelling, authentic manner.

After working together for several years, I remember finally reading the revised chapters with relief. This was a book I would want to read. It was powerful to see it flow and take shape. This team took my thoughts and ideas, helped me re-fashion them, and then handed them back to me, ensuring the work was still mine.

CONFIDENCE

Helpful and Unhelpful Givers

The above six traits will help steer you to good Givers. But as I said earlier, the process can be confusing because, especially at first, it's hard to discern a Giver's motive.

I'll share two contrasting stories from one area of my life, school sports, to cast light on the difference between helpful and unhelpful Givers.

I vividly remember when I was thirteen years old and the high school softball coach called me aside from my middle school PE class to teach me how to throw a softball. I'd never learned how to shift my body weight and hold a glove in my left hand as I threw with my right hand. It was exhilarating to watch my throw change from what would best be described as desperate fumbling into a high-powered fast ball.

Recruiting me to join the high school softball team the following year, he coached me in fast-pitching. Between his consistent guidance and my hard work, l went from learning how to hold a ball one year to team captain and lead-off pitcher several years later. I eventually pitched a no-hitter and led the team to the state championship. Who knew that was possible? I sure didn't. There's no way I could have predicted this. But over several years, my confidence grew and what I believed about myself changed from, "I don't know what I'm doing" to "I think I can do this" to "I can be a leader in this sport!"

Notice how a good Giver can affect our confidence. It starts with someone believing in who we are *and* who we can become. False beliefs gradually lose their grip. And new, true beliefs are formed that impact our confidence. Something magical happens when a kind-hearted person cares enough to believe in us and call out potential we didn't even know we had. A good

CONFIDENCE

Giver is someone who offers a gift of new beliefs that helps us move forward and discover untapped potential.

In contrast, I had a PE teacher from my younger years who often mocked my lack of athletic ability and even ridiculed me for "throwing like a girl." He was polluting my mind with his false beliefs about my potential or lack thereof. Later, when the high school coach that believed in me and my untapped potential entered my life, I was offered radically different true beliefs about my ability that opened up a whole new world while countering the false beliefs the PE teacher had created (Quick shout-out to all the *great* PE teachers out there working hard to help coach their students. I know you're working hard.)

I've lived long enough and worked with enough people to know that no one gets through this world unscathed. Unfortunately, we'll all encounter, sooner or later, Givers who dole out false beliefs. Be on alert and eject from those situations as soon as possible. Remembering that many of these people were also once the recipient of this painful behavior allows you to have compassion for the false beliefs that haunted them throughout their developmental years.

But when we are given the opportunity to believe something better about ourselves, do we consider new possibilities and hold higher hopes in who we are meant to become? Do we step out and take new risks? Or do we hide behind the false beliefs that keep us stuck and feeling small? This choice is what makes or breaks our confidence level. At some point, we need to take the risk to boldly embrace the true beliefs that allow us to become who we've always longed to be.

CONFIDENCE

Can a Good Giver Stop Being Good for You?

The short answer is . . . yes.

This is where the topic can become confusing. Good Givers can change to not-so-good Givers. We and our situations can change as well. When that happens, the season with that particular Giver is ready to conclude. Otherwise, what was once helpful can become unhelpful.

Here's a great sign to prove our hunch. A good Giver will always step aside when asked or when the time is right. An unhelpful Giver can be demanding, clingy, and manipulative when we attempt to move on.

This will play out differently for each situation. Maybe you knew a Giver who once embodied all of the above six traits, but then the relationship began to change. Perhaps they're going through something personal, have shifted in their thinking, or had extenuating circumstances come up from the ever-changing seasons of life. When what once seemed helpful turns unhelpful or even harmful, it can be confusing and rock our confidence. But it is important to recognize so we can respond in a healthy manner.

I experienced this with a friend who was the poster child for good Givers. She excelled at all six traits until, without warning, she began to do the opposite of each trait when around me. As my life became more successful, she became more threatened. She found subtle and not so subtle ways to put me down and sabotage my forward momentum. It was confusing, and I initially gave her the benefit of the doubt since these recent actions were so unlike her.

Once I recognized that our friendship had shifted from helpful to harmful, I had to address it. Sometimes being honest with the other person serves as an opportunity for them to course correct because it brings questionable or hurtful behavior into the light. That's the best-case outcome but can only happen if the Giver will humbly see the hurtful nature of their behavior and truly commit to change.

Unfortunately, in this case, the Giver refused to take responsibility for any harmful behavior. It's always more painful this way. The honest discussion served as a catalyst that confirmed the relationship was no longer helpful or even good for either person. And when this happens, often the best choice is to temporarily step back from the friendship or even permanently end the relationship with the Giver—for your sake and theirs.

And in extreme circumstances, where the Giver is abusive or destructive, a conversation isn't helpful or even safe. In those cases, it's best to move on without trying to make them understand or hoping against hope that they will change. Our top priority is to protect ourselves.

We spent earlier chapters mastering clarity. Clarity is needed to distinguish between helpful and unhelpful Givers. Practicing using our voice around this will increase our confidence as we embrace what is true and reject what is false.

Smart Brain Wayne

As we discuss the traits of good Givers and how to distinguish between helpful and harmful ones, I hope something else is becoming clear. Not only do we get to watch for good Givers in our lives, we get to decide the type of Giver we want to be to those around us.

The hard reality is that each of us, to some extent, has already been both helpful and harmful as a Giver. Up until now, you might not have understood how others are Givers—or seen yourself as one. Whether a teacher or student, a coach or player, beginning your career or the CEO—you get to choose the type of Giver you'll be as well as the type of Giver you'll attract. Our choices are dependent on the level of awareness we hold about who our Givers are as well as understanding how to be a good Giver.

Reflecting on the type of Giver we want to be is just as important as analyzing the type of Givers we have in our lives. Will we be one who honors the value of others and cheers them on . . . even if they pass us? Or will we be the type of Giver who is threatened when others experience more success than we do?

Good Givers learn how to foster the six attributes and recognize their power in standing for true beliefs. Being a good Giver is an active posture. It requires us to proactively pour into those we care about or who are under our care. Not speaking up isn't okay because that can signal our agreement with a false belief—and it breeds confusion and doubt rather than clarity and confidence in the receiver.

This reminds me of a student I had in my early years of teaching. Even as a third-grader, he was already showing the signs of being beaten down by life. It's heartbreaking to see young children with broken spirits, but that describes Wayne. Each day he'd shuffle into the classroom with slumped shoulders. He avoided eye contact with me and the other kids. It was clear he had a learning difference and struggled with self-acceptance.

I was determined to know his story and try to help. I called him to my desk one morning during the first week of school and asked what made him sad. He said some of the other kids called him names. My heart sank. I asked him if he'd share some of those names. He looked at the floor as he softly repeated a long list of false beliefs that had been tattooed on his heart: "Stupid. Idiot. Dumb. Lame. Retard . . ." His voice tapered off as the hurtful words hung in the air.

I placed my hands on his little shoulders and quietly said, "Today, I am giving you a new name. From here on, you will be 'Smart Brain Wayne.'" For the first time, he made eye contact. At first, to see if I was mocking him, but then because he felt truly seen. A shy smile appeared when I explained that nobody was dumb, but that each of us simply learns differently and together we were going to figure out how he learned.

From that point forward, that was the name I called him. He even began to write Smart Brain Wayne on the top of each paper he turned in. I watched his confidence grow steadily with his new name.

I got to be a good Giver who gave a struggling student the lifeline of a true belief. It was so rewarding to speak life into this young boy. I had the unexpected honor of being his teacher for three years—third, fourth, and fifth grade. He went by this name all three years.

My favorite story about Smart Brain Wayne happened one day when I was walking from my classroom to the office. Wayne was playing tether ball with another student named Jimmy. Not knowing I was near, I heard Jimmy yell, "Wayne, you are so stupid!" I froze, about to jump in with all my teacher authority to make things right, when the most incredible thing happened. Wayne grabbed the tether ball by the string and as he held it over his head, yelled at the top of his lungs, *"I'm not stupid! My name is Smart Brain Wayne!"* He then smacked the ball with all his might. And shockingly, it bounced off the top of Jimmy's head, knocking him to the ground. Clearly, I was not needed. So, I turned and continued walking to the office.

CONFIDENCE

Justice had been served and the situation had worked itself out without me.

This was in my first year of teaching, but I never forgot the important lesson. Speak out true beliefs to replace the false ones that have caused a person to feel stuck or broken.

I wonder, who can you rename and what beliefs can you offer to the hurting world around you? There's more opportunity than you think.

Becoming a Good Giver

To be a good Giver, it's essential you be aware of your own places of insecurity. When we identify where we're insecure, we ensure that we don't give out of our insecurity. Tragically, those Givers who aren't aware tend to give gifts tainted by insecurity rather than confidence.

Let me explain what I mean. I'm a parent of teens. When I'm having a hard day or feeling insecure about my place in the world, I can inadvertently start to look to my children to fill this insecurity.

When that happens, I begin to give out of an expectation for them to meet these needs. It can play out in any number of ways. Perhaps I make them breakfast but feel slighted if they don't hug me or thank me. Yes, we need to teach our children gratitude and respect, but if I'm not taking care of my own needs and staying mindful of my internal state, I can put an unfair burden on my children. That happens when I give gifts with certain expectations attached because of how I'm feeling or my need for a confidence boost.

When I'm in this state, I'm giving out of my insecurity rather than out of my confidence. But when I recognize my true need, I can address it appropriately through activities such as calling a friend, spending time in meditation/prayer, or getting a massage. (Sometimes it's a simple as going out to a "sit-down restaurant" to be served my own hot meal!) Then I can give from a place of confidence that synergistically breeds confidence in my children. By the way, this isn't limited to parenting. It applies to every type of relationship, from spouse to coach to employee to teacher to friend. Learning to give from a settled place allows our gifts to instill a healthy confidence in those we care about. It also ensures our gifts have no strings attached—which always tangles things up.

Staying Open to New Types of Givers

Opening up our circles to attract new Givers is also important. I discovered this when I was a junior high teacher in East LA. I loved working with this age group. I may have learned more from them than they did from me, at least when it came to being a good Giver.

I was on lunch duty one day when a dozen girls gathered nearby in conversation. I was enjoying the light banter going back and forth between them. It's so fun to listen to kids' perspectives! If you ever get the privilege to be allowed to listen in, consider yourself lucky.

When I wasn't teaching them, I liked to enter their worlds and ask questions about the latest music and fashion styles as it made me smile and helped me get to know my students beyond the classroom.

That day during lunch duty, they invited me into their discussion. At some point, they started talking about "white people." Being a white teacher in a 98 percent Latino school, I

CONFIDENCE

found this fascinating. For several minutes, they discussed how stuck-up white people were, and I laughed at their antics of prancing around with their noses up in the air, refusing to talk to one another. I did not know that this was their perception of white people and was getting a sneak peek into their world. Suddenly, one of the girl's eyes grew wide. She got a panicked look on her face and whispered anxiously to her peers, "Shut up, Mrs. Penny's white!"

Everyone immediately stopped their funny imitations and began to apologize. I told them it was fine. Their insights offered a gift to me—a teachable moment that helped me see my race in new ways through the eyes of others. And my kind response was a gift back. By not being offended, but laughing and wanting to learn, it allowed them to see their blanket perception wasn't a valid stereotype about an entire race. We offered each other the possibility of new beliefs. Ones that helped rather than harmed. Ones that moved us all forward and out of our comfort zone.

I love this story because it reveals our human potential for seeing possibility in others. Good Givers learn to offer kindness, patience, and acceptance outside our realms of experience, comfort, and background. We need to be receptive to giving and receiving from one another with grace and curiosity. After all, we don't know what we don't know. Staying open to helpful new Givers will radically change our perceptions as we exchange false beliefs for true beliefs. It's the path forward that leads us to the life we're made for.

CONFIDENCE

CONFIDENCE QUESTION
How have the Givers in your life influenced your confidence?

Who are your Givers? It's a great question. The names you choose will dramatically impact the trajectory of your life. Let's spend a little more time on this front.

Who has been a good Giver to you? What true beliefs emerged from that relationship?

Who has been an unhelpful Giver to you? What false beliefs resulted from that?

Which of the six traits of a good Giver was most surprising to you? Why?

Who can you be a good Giver to? What true beliefs do you want to offer?

CAUTION: It's essential to remember that not all gifts are truly gifts, nor are all Givers good. Thankfully, you have the tools to discern the difference between helpful and unhelpful Givers now that you understand the six traits of good Givers, know to be aware of the Giver's motive, and are in touch with what season you're in as you discern who can best help in that phase of your journey. Never forget that you—and you alone—have the power to choose your Givers *and* choose the kind of Giver you are to others. Doing each well will fuel your confidence, so choose wisely!

CONFIDENCE

The next chapter's topic may surprise you. Many adults forgot how to do this long ago. It's the practice of receiving well and will prove a huge boost to your confidence.

THE ART OF RECEIVING

Developing the Faith to Say "Yes"

magine we're at a park. It's a beautiful day, and it feels great to be out in the sun.

I suggest we play a simple game of catch and reach for a tennis ball from my backpack. We walk over to the field and stand about ten feet apart. I toss you the ball and you catch it. We're off to a great start.

But when you toss it back, I just stand there. I don't try to catch it or even acknowledge that we're in a game. *Plunk.* The ball bounces off my shoulder and falls to the ground. You're not quite sure what to do so you walk over, pick up the ball, and go back to where you were.

"Um, okay," you say kindly. "Let's give this another try." And you toss me the ball again, more gently this time.

I just watch the ball go past me.

Now it's getting awkward. But thankfully you're a good sport and don't want to embarrass me.

"My bad," you say as you run after the ball. But after a few more times of chasing the ball as I stand there passively, you're huffing and puffing and starting to break a sweat. This isn't much fun. And it certainly wouldn't be called a game of "catch." Tired of what feels like a pointless exercise, you look at your watch as you clear your throat. You let me know something's come up, and you really need to get home.

I wave bye, confused why no one ever seems to enjoy playing catch with me.

Now at this point, you're probably thinking, *Come on, Heather. Who would ever do that?*

The short answer is, we all do it. Not with a ball but with gifts. Even if we're a good Giver, we tend to be less skilled receivers. It may surprise you how many times you've missed gifts that others have tried to toss your way. You can even have a master sage offering you a gift and still blow it by not receiving well.

It's time to learn the lost art of receiving well.

A Leap of Faith

While we're on the topic of playing catch, let's go back to a real example from my life playing softball. You'll recall from the prior chapter how I had two coaches. One was a good Giver— the other, not so much.

The good coach offered me new beliefs, but he couldn't make me into a new player. I had a role to play, and it started with how I responded to his gift. How was I going to handle the new beliefs being offered (tossed) to me? Was I going to catch them and believe? Or was I going to reject them and let the gift fall by the wayside?

What about you? When you're offered the gift of a new true belief, what do you tend to do with it? How well do you receive it? There is an art to receiving beliefs. When we do it well, it vastly influences our confidence. If that sounds a bit vague, let's get specific. You can actually measure it by these two filters:

1. Does the new belief resonate deep down with who we are or want to be?

2. Does it move us forward into the life we want?

Don't just read those words and move on. Pause and think about these two questions.

Here's a disruptive truth. Before things can change, you must dare to believe that life can be lived better. I distinctly remember standing on the precipice of this choice—and the vulnerability I felt in wanting to believe something vastly contrary to what I'd been told. In fact, I remember the uneasy feeling that maybe I was overreaching or buying into something that wasn't true just because I wanted it to be true. If we stay in that place for long, we become paralyzed in the status quo and fail to receive the gift before us.

The art of receiving requires a leap of faith that becomes visible by the choice we make.

We must actively choose to reject false beliefs *while also* embracing true beliefs. Maturing in our confidence is about learning the importance of being both on the offensive (receiving true beliefs) as well as the defensive (rejecting false beliefs). Otherwise, we constantly ping-pong back and forth between the two beliefs, never learning to hold the tension of rejecting and receiving. This is a vulnerable process that plays with our insecurities and messes with our confidence, especially if we've

CONFIDENCE

lived with the false beliefs for some time. Whether they were handed to us, or we came up with them on our own due to life circumstances, learning to risk embracing the true beliefs requires a whole new level of faith.

I distinctly remember this moment as a young girl when the two coaches were offering me two different narratives. One that kept me small and one that invited me into more. One that dared me to move forward and one that kept me stuck.

Choosing the option that challenged me to move forward was not easy, but it was worth it. Especially when I was steeped in the insecurity of not being athletic. Deciding to believe in a new possibility didn't just help me in the moment. It prepared me for bigger challenges that awaited me as an adult.

Thankfully, I received well in that situation. Yet I've failed to do so in other situations. We all have. This happens when we cling to the false beliefs out of a fear that the new beliefs are either too good to be true, we don't deserve to get more, or that we will fail miserably if we step into the unknown.

There's no doubt that the process of trading false beliefs for true beliefs can be intimidating, risky, and stressful. There are no upfront guarantees or money-back offers.

It requires a whole new level of faith—and confidence—to step into the life we are created for.

A Context for Failure

The journey of learning to receive something I'd never dared to believe about myself required a large dose of good old-fashioned grit. By that, I mean the type of determination we only find by digging down deep, day after day, and daring to believe we can be more.

What has been helpful for me in these moments is developing a context for failure. I'm talking an epic, fall-on-your-face type of failure.

I know, that doesn't sound very encouraging. But stay with me.

It's essential that we learn how to fail well.

Why? Because failure is inevitable. So learning how to navigate and recover is invaluable.

When I was that young girl learning how to pitch, I had two things going for me: a formidable coach who believed in me—and a lot of determination. But that didn't mean I got a golden ticket to success. I still had to learn how to fail well and keep going.

In the first game I pitched as a freshman, I made a big mistake. I delayed letting go of the ball by just a bit. The softball left my hand at eye level instead of at hip level—and went over the backstop! This mistake cost me big—mostly in my pride. I could hear the snickers from the other team.

I was totally embarrassed. The umpire had to stop the game to retrieve the ball . . . further humiliation as we waited for the runner to return with the rogue softball. From the mound, I could hear the ridicule. I glanced at the faces of my teammates and saw the embarrassed looks on their faces. This is the moment where false beliefs can surge.

Thankfully, the coach kept me in the game. Walking back to the mound, I said to myself, *Okay, it can't get much worse from here. Hold your head high, stay in the game, and release at the hip like you've been taught. You can do this.*

From the sideline, my coach smiled as he yelled a reminder of when to release the ball, his humor somehow signaling his belief in me and engaging my confidence that all would be well. His choice to keep me in was the gift I needed. But I had to choose to receive the gift. Do you see how his belief in me mingled with the wavering belief I had in myself? I never forgot the life lesson this taught me.

It was the gift I needed to stay on the mound and finish the game. To this day, I still have people remind me of this mistake. Isn't it funny how people remember the epic fails more than our soaring times of success? Sigh. But here's the good news. It doesn't sting anymore when they bring this story up because I know how it ended. I remember that I stayed in the game and grew as a successful pitcher.

How many times have we not known how to receive the gift in front of us because our shame and humiliation of the failure serves as a catalyst to believe in the false beliefs? I know this has stopped me more than I care to remember. But this time, I chose to receive the gift, and it set the groundwork for a steady increase in the confidence I would need from that day forward.

Even today, I will talk myself through an epic fail with this type of inner dialogue; *Well, you threw that one over the back stop—I mean wow—it was nowhere near the strike zone! Way to go big or go home! Okay, don't worry, we've been here before, Heath, and the humiliation doesn't last forever. You will not only survive this but be wiser and stronger because of it. Remember this no matter how much it stings. Let's regroup and see what you can learn from this and don't let it take you out.*

Pitching it over the backstop was a valuable learning experience that taught me the art of receiving by having a healthy context for facing—and overcoming—failure.

Receiving Another Person's Belief

"I like teaching, but I'm tired of following someone else's curriculum."

After I blurted that out, I waited in silence for my leadership coach to respond. This moment of confession happened in the middle of one of my weekly calls during a hard season in my life. Looking back, I'd call it a midlife crisis, or to be a bit more optimistic, a midlife opportunity. I was at that crossroads of wondering what the second half of my life was going to look like—and feeling boxed in with the choices before me.

After a moment of silence on the other end of the call, I continued. "I want to teach on what I want to teach on. I'd love to design my own focus and talk about new conversations beyond 'a well-written essay.'" I sighed. "I know that I'm made for more. I just can't figure out what that 'more' could be."

Though I didn't voice this part out loud, deep down I had the sinking feeling that not only was I never going to figure it out, but I was too scared to actually try something new. It was a confusing season where my confidence was fragile and vulnerable. In the midst of that, I was grateful to have someone I could lean into who would walk out next steps with me.

My coach's response rocked my world. "Perhaps you should try being a professional coach."

Now there was silence on my end of the phone. I'd not considered that idea. But my breath caught in my chest as I excitedly considered this new option before me. Coaching would allow me to create my own "curriculum" and teach on my topic of choice. I was drawn to the possibility—but did I have the confidence to see it through? To truly be all in and venture out?

I had to start with a basic true belief that would become the grounding for me to even consider it. (If you haven't noticed, I'm

CONFIDENCE

quite the cautious creature.) Daring to start my own coaching company, stepping away from the professional career path I had been on since my twenties, and choosing to call myself a coach was overwhelming. I felt like I was going to break out in hives.

But my true belief saw me through. *I am being led and guided. I will receive this council and see where it takes me.* So I leapt out and started my own coaching practice.

As a new coach, I immediately felt the pressure to be successful and attract a steady flow of clients. Being fresh out of my doctorate and trying to start my coaching company was exhilarating on my best days and terrifying on my worst. The success rate for coaches is not high.

Fear-based mind chatter began to race through my head like a flock of birds.

What if I can't make money to pay back my schooling?

What if no one wants to hire me?

What if I don't know what to say?

What if I don't attract the clients I want?

What if I don't attract any *clients?*

My fears were crippling. The what-ifs could easily rule each waking moment if I let them. And it was easy to let them. After all, this was my "big leap of faith," the first time I'd dared to step away from a traditional career route to do something on my own full time.

I knew I needed something new. Chanting affirmations of "I am enough" or "I am successful" weren't cutting it and,

CONFIDENCE

frankly, only stressing me out more. I had to go deeper into the core of what I truly believed and identify what was harming me and what was helping me.

What you're going through likely looks different externally but is provoking similar fears. For you, it might involve the risk of a relationship, or a move, or recovering from an unexpected crisis or illness. Don't let the uniqueness of your situation isolate you from the help of this chapter. Know that wherever you're feeling restless, this can apply.

You Gotta Have Faith

If you're over forty, I'm guessing the George Michael song is now stuck in your head. You're welcome.

But it's true. We've gotta have faith. My coach helped convince me of that. Even so, I had a hard time believing—and thus receiving—it.

Big exhale. Okay, let me pause here and admit something. Don't worry, I don't sing George Michael songs at karaoke parties. The very thought of karaoke makes my palms sweat! What I have to share makes me feel far more vulnerable than even that. Faith has never come easy for me—not in the past and sometimes not in the present.

Any of you have a magical faith button that stays easily locked in when doing something big and scary in life? Not me. I felt like each day I was standing on the edge of the cliff. Inside I was screaming for some sort of safety net or parachute. The idea of me "having faith" was not in the least bit reassuring. My faith button felt broken. The moment I would press it, the button just popped right back out. Faith felt so . . . fuzzy. Give me something concrete.

CONFIDENCE

Thankfully, when my coach saw my lackluster response to his calming challenge to have faith, he switched courses. (Thanks for reading the room, Coach). He explained that a concrete way to grow my faith and keep me rooted in it daily was to anticipate what was to come.

It was as if a lightbulb switched on. When faced with a daunting situation, I hadn't understood how to engage my faith, because I wasn't anticipating my future. Rather, quite the opposite. I was spending my days fretting, avoiding, nail-biting, and dreading all the possible scenarios for failure.

If I was going to grow the confidence I needed to move into the life I was made for, I had to have faith. Why? Because faith fuels confidence. But let's get specific. Faith in what?

Faith in my abilities.

Faith in the journey.

Faith that I was being led and guided.

Faith that I could take the steps needed to get me closer to building the coaching company I dreamed of having and the coaching presence I desired.

Faith that my quality of life could remain intact.

Faith that my voice—which I was still figuring out—was wanted.

See what I mean? Faith was sorely lacking in me. I instinctively knew this was critical to grow my confidence but the word *faith* felt unattainable. Security, control, strategic success, clear logic and rationale—these were all words that made sense to me. But faith? How in the world do I put that into practice?

Thanks to my coach, I decided to do something about it. Where I wanted faith, I replaced my fear with anticipation.

I ~~fear~~ anticipate how my abilities will grow in my new profession.

I ~~fear~~ anticipate each bend in the journey.

I ~~fear~~ anticipate how I am being led and guided.

I ~~fear~~ anticipate knowing which steps I need to take daily to get me closer to building the coaching company I dream of having and the coaching presence I desire.

I ~~fear~~ anticipate how I will foster my quality of life as I build my company.

I ~~fear~~ anticipate finding a new voice to offer people.

I ~~fear~~ anticipate offering new "curriculum" that I want to teach.

See what I mean? It's got a bit more grit to it. And it gave me more to hang onto each day as I batted away the worries, what-ifs, and false beliefs. You just gotta have faith.

Gratitude—Thank You Very Much

Now, each time I feel fear rising, I use it as a trigger to move me into anticipating. This practice helps me receive the gifts of true beliefs I so desperately need to grow my confidence.

Plus, I found something to combine with anticipation that further enhanced it. Kind of like how combining peanut butter and chocolate creates something way tastier than either alone.

At least that's what millions of Reese's Peanut Butter Cup lovers believe!

What I combined with anticipation was even better than peanut butter or chocolate. And it had fewer calories. It was gratitude.

Now, as I said what I was anticipating (even though I felt the butterflies of fear in my stomach), I also expressed my gratitude. My new version sounded like this:

I anticipate how my abilities will grow in my new profession.
I am grateful for all that is opening up for me.

I anticipate each bend in the journey.
I am grateful for this exciting life!

I anticipate how I am being led and guided.
I am grateful for this unexpected adventure!

I anticipate knowing which steps I need to take to get me
closer to building the coaching company I dream of having
and the presence I desire.
I am grateful that I get to dream and anticipate how
I will be able to move forward one step at a time.

I anticipate how I will foster my quality of life
as I build my company.
I am grateful for how much I am learning and growing.

I anticipate finding a new voice to offer people.
I am grateful that I get to explore new depths within me.

Do you see the power of this one-two combination? It takes all the pressure off me to manifest some big, dramatic life and allows me to partner better with myself as I replace fears and worries with anticipation and gratitude. It takes humility to recognize we can't carry the weight of the world—or even our own dreams—on our shoulders. We need help . . . and gratitude. That's the art of receiving.

But there's another benefit at play. When I combine anticipation and gratitude, my faith grows. It helps me move forward in belief of what can go right rather than being paralyzed by fear of what may go wrong.

This is the formula that led to a tremendous breakthrough for me:

ANTICIPATION + GRATITUDE = FAITH

And guess what. As I practiced it, the clients started coming. My coaching dream became a coaching reality!

Nothing Stays the Same

There is a haunting poem from Robert Frost that was referenced in the book *The Outsiders* called "Nothing Gold Can Stay."[5] Every time I read it to my students over the years, the words seemed to hang in the air. What it captures so well is the bittersweet ache of life.

If you aren't familiar with it, read these words slowly and allow yourself to feel the gravity.

"Nothing Gold Can Stay"

Nature's first green is gold,
Her hardest hue to hold.
Her early leaf's a flower;
But only so an hour.

CONFIDENCE

---

5. S. E. Hinton, *The Outsiders* (New York: Puffin Books, 1995).

Then leaf subsides to leaf.
So Eden sank to grief,
So dawn goes down to day.
Nothing gold can stay.[6]

My students understood this simple poem. They related to *The Outsiders'* protagonist, Ponyboy, as he described the poignant sadness it evoked in him after losing his parents in a car accident and having to be raised by his older brother in the harsh poverty of Tulsa, Oklahoma.

Life doesn't stay static. It is dynamic. We all know it. But certain moments jar us awake and we see with clarity that life is constantly moving and growing. Right when we've got everything sorted out, life usually throws us a curve ball. Nothing models this more clearly than parenting. Just when I had figured out the toddler years, my kids needed something totally different in their grade-school years. Then I was doing well in those years when the preteen and teenage years hit.

The very moment when we think we have a stage figured out, everything changes. Life presses ever onward. My husband and I sometimes long for a do-over in parenting with the sobering awareness, "If only we knew then what we know now."

Life is a teacher that doesn't slow down. Staying present with our beliefs is what allows us to grab all we can in the precious moments that make up our hours, days, weeks, months, and years. And faith can be the security blanket we need not only to step into the life we want, but the life we need.

That certainly played out in my coaching business. After several years of steady growth, I soon had more than I could

CONFIDENCE

6. From *The Poetry of Robert Frost* edited by Edward Connery Lathem. Copyright © 1923, 1947, 1969 by Henry Holt and Company, copyright © 1942, 1951 by Robert Frost, copyright © 1970, 1975 by Lesley Frost Ballantine. Reprinted by permission of Henry Holt and Company, LLC.

manage. And a new challenge for my faith emerged. But rather than allow fear to creep in, I steadied myself with the combination of anticipation and gratitude. It sounded like this:

> *I anticipate how I will change my business model to keep up with the growth. I am grateful that I am being led and guided in this, and I will know what to do.*

See how faith (anticipation and gratitude) helps us grow the confidence we need? And addresses the changes required?

As the poem reveals, life doesn't stay static. As we grow in confidence at one level, then we find ourselves at new crossroads. I'm now writing the book you hold in your hands. And I am pushing away fear and embracing faith. That's what gives me the confidence to put into words what I've learned in my life and from the many sojourners who have graciously shared their stories with me. And it feels good!

Change does not have to bring fear. But often, it does. Choosing to see change as an opportunity to engage new beliefs allows us to adapt and find the life we want.

Change We Don't Choose

Change always comes at a cost. But there are most certainly different levels of cost and loss. Having a busier life versus losing a loved one is not even in the same stratosphere.

Which brings us to an important topic. How do we handle changes we would never choose?

When my father passed away several years ago, the loss cut deep. To simply grab onto a new belief in the middle of my sorrow would have dishonored my heart and his memory.

CONFIDENCE

But as time went by, I allowed it to change me for the better. I wanted to honor the vast hole his death had left in my life by observing how this would forever change me. I grew kinder, more compassionate, and slowed down to simply "take life in." I observed the gray squirrel in my front yard as he tapped down his acorn for the winter with his tiny paws. I watched the movement of the trees and how the wind created a rhythmic swaying. I compared the varying levels of green from the grass to the bushes, to the leaves on the great oak in the park across the street. It was as if I was seeing everything for the first time in living color.

My grief was costly . . . and yet it changed me for the better.

It brought new beliefs. I understand more deeply how precious life is and how it should be savored. I know the pain of unresolved goodbyes. It slowed me down and made me more mindful. In the middle of a full and busy life, I now stop and watch seven tiny yellow finches feast off the berries on the tree I see from my office window. Before, I might not have noticed them much less taken the time to count them. Or they might have only held my gaze for seconds. Now I lean back in my chair and observe them for minutes. And in doing so, I know this is how I've changed for the better from a heart smashed with the weight of deep grief. I now notice and look for little delights throughout my days that I did not savor before.

Dear reader, I can say with love that now, having been through significant losses, I eventually anticipate how moving through deep grief will change me for the better. And I'm grateful—not for the loss, of course—but for how healing from loss teaches me to live differently, better. And there is an art to receiving in the pain of life.

These new beliefs also influenced how I lived through loss. For instance, after my father passed away, I stepped back from the world where I had been building, developing, speaking, striving. I set a slower rhythm so I could enjoy my clients, my family, my days, and my friends. Life became simpler. All this from change I did not want nor would have chosen. We get to receive the gifts we are given, but sometimes we have to look a little harder as we honor the pace of what we are facing and how our hearts are responding.

Leaning into the change that swirls around us, with anticipation and gratitude, allows us to build the confidence we need to move through life. But honoring how we do this is critical. We cannot simply slap on faith the same way every time. Preparing for a job promotion and recovering from the loss of a loved one are completely different. Yet both require faith. And, like it or not, both ends of the spectrum eventually require us to practice anticipation (for what is coming) and gratitude (for how we are being transformed through the loss and for what is yet to come). This is the root of how we grow our confidence.

The Underdog in Each of Us

People are inspired by watching others respond to loss in ways that shape them into better people. Whether a true story or fiction, what is one of your favorite movies about a most unlikely person emerging as a hero? It probably wasn't hard to come up with it. These kinds of stories stir our hearts and our belief in overcoming seemingly impossible odds.

One of my favorite movies is *Rudy*, a 1993 film that ESPN named one of the Top 25 Sports Movies of the Past 25 years. It is set in the late 1960s and is the true story of a young man named Rudy who—against all odds—finally got the chance to play in a Notre Dame football game. It was a huge, impossible victory. A goal that he'd dreamed of and worked hard for his entire life.

These victories are happening all around us if we only look for them. Just last football season at my kids' high school, the stadium went wild when the game was stopped to put an autistic student in to run a play. Each game, he had been suiting up and hanging with the football players on the sidelines. But this game, it was arranged by the coaches on both sides to have him run a play and get a "touchdown" as the crowds stood on their feet cheering him on. Not just our team's fans, but the fans on both sides. As the sweet boy ran his heart out, the players dramatically blocked and refused to catch him. I was weeping, cheering, and so ridiculously proud of the school, players, and coaches! I loved witnessing this beautiful display of humanity. And to watch him receive it without inhibition or insecurity was even more inspiring.

Why does this move us so much? Because there's an underdog in each of us longing to make the play. But will we receive what we are given or reject it out of insecurity, fear of failure, or the pain of vulnerability? We have each dreamed of success and have been shot down more times than we can count. Getting up again and again and again is painful. Boldly receiving what we are meant to have is risky. Yet even though we know the odds are stacked against us, even though fear haunts us late at night, and even though we can still taste the humiliation of failure—we can receive the hope of more. We hold faith by anticipating and expressing gratitude. That process also grows our confidence along the way. And then one day, usually when we least expect it, we get the win we've longed for.

We must choose to suit up for each game with no guarantees. We must choose to anticipate and be grateful and practice confidence. We must avoid comparison, for no one gets to live our particular story except us.

Only then can we fully receive what is being offered.

The Challenge of Receiving

The art of receiving well depends on two variables: time and consistency.

First, give it time. It won't feel like much growth in the moment, but it will later when you look back and see where you came from. Many times, clients will come to our conversation the next week and express amazement in their growth. And that's in one week's time!

Certainly, you can experience immediate improvement, but oftentimes, a day or a week is too quick for an accurate evaluation. Give it about three months and then evaluate how your confidence is growing and where it is showing up in your life. I think you'll be pleasantly surprised.

And then there's the power of consistency. Stay at it because, like a tree, it does not grow overnight. We cannot see what a seed is doing underground. But it is busy growing roots to support upward movement. And it requires water, nutrients, and sunlight. Our faith is like a seed. Keep feeding it with the nourishment of anticipation and gratitude and our confidence will grow. Within weeks, we'll see a tiny sprout. Keep feeding it for years and the roots will grow deep. Stay at it for another two decades and we will have a tree big enough to hang a tire swing on.

Where do you want to grow? Focus on it. Receive the gifts you are being offered in this season. Increase your faith by anticipating and holding gratitude when the worries pull at you and the insecurities threaten to derail you. This is the art of receiving well. This is what roots your confidence to support you moving forward into the life you want.

Just don't forget to periodically look back to see how far you've come.

CONFIDENCE

CONFIDENCE QUESTION

When have you missed the gift of confidence and what caused you not to receive it well?

These five questions will help you master the art of receiving.

Do you generally consider yourself a good receiver? Why or why not?

Does faith tend to come easy or hard for you? Why is that the case?

Where do you need more faith to grow your confidence?

Name an area where you're currently anticipating.

Name an area where you're currently grateful.

CAUTION: While this chapter was written to help you learn the art of receiving, you also have the chance (and eventually the responsibility) to pour into others so they can receive. Make sure that as you learn how to receive, you also practice the art of being a good Giver to others. This accelerates the growth of our confidence.

CONFIDENCE

I'm anticipating that your sense of confidence is growing! And I am grateful to be on this journey together. Well done. Yet, over time, many experience a loss of confidence that takes them by surprise. In the next chapter, I'll reveal why this happens—as well as how to stop this drift.

STOP THE DRIFT

Charting a Course of Kindness

You step onto the deck of the boat and let out a sigh of relief and joy.

The day has finally arrived. It's going to be the trip of a lifetime!

You've been juggling so much, wondering how to get away from it all. Not for good, you love your life and your job, but you need a significant break, one long enough to fully recharge. And now you're about to do so.

Your good friend just happens to own a boat and be an experienced sea captain. Her invitation for you—and your two dogs—to join her on an eighteen-day leisurely cruise around the Tahitian Islands in the South Pacific took your breath away. It seemed too good to be true.

But now it's beginning. On the boat, you marvel at how it's packed with supplies for every possible need. The weather is perfect and the air is electric with excitement as you set sail on your first day from the Hawaiian Islands to start your much-anticipated adventure.

Except things don't quite turn out like you had hoped.

Within days of your departure, disaster strikes. A storm relentlessly batters the boat for over three days. To make matters worse, the engine floods, making it impossible to steer or generate energy. With no power, the boat begins to drift. In the middle of the South Pacific with no land in sight, what should have been an eighteen-day trip turns into six months on the open ocean. You're completely adrift.

What would someone do in that situation? We don't have to imagine an answer. This actually happened to two women (thankfully, not me!). In the true story, they eventually were found off the coast of Japan, thousands of miles off course and heading in the wrong direction. They'd lost all control to direct their boat and were at the mercy of the wind and the waves. After drifting for six months, they were spotted by a fishing vessel out of Taiwan who sent an SOS call to the Navy. They were rescued the next day.[7] (If you're wondering how they fared, don't worry, upon rescue they were in good health—and so were the dogs!)

Yeah, but that's a pretty extreme example, you might be thinking. *When am I going to take a boat out and get lost in the South Pacific?* Most of us will never experience being adrift in that specific way. But you can relate, right? Isn't that how life feels more times than you wish? You plan for a big adventure, set your course, make your plans, and then crisis strikes. You try to stay on course but find yourself drifting aimlessly. Except there is no Navy or random fishing vessel rescuing you.

7. Associated Press, "Women Lost on Drifting Boat in Pacific Ocean for Months Tell Their Incredible Story," *The West Australian*, October 28, 2017, https://thewest.com.au/news/world/women-lost-on-drifting-boat-in-pacific-ocean-for-months-tell-their-incredible-story-ng-b88643376z.

Recognizing when you are adrift is half the challenge. The other half is knowing what to do to get back on course so you can arrive at your intended destination.

What takes the biggest hit in these instances is often unnoticed—but it's costly. It is our confidence.

Starting Well and Drifting Quickly

Let me offer an example that hits closer to home.

What about that plan in January where you're going to change the way you exercise and eat? You're positive that this year is going to be different and begin with inspiring resolve. Yet somehow, once again, the motivation only lasts for a few weeks.

This is true for me. I can get so inspired reading about the massive benefits of fruits, vegetables, and whole foods. I'm invigorated by the research about all the benefits—from cell rejuvenation to more energy. I vow to eat more whole foods, *forever*. Recipes and meal-planning inspirations flood my mind and Pinterest boards. I'm going to be a changed woman! My family will be the healthiest on the planet, thanks to my new knowledge. I share all my inspiring facts over steamed Brussels sprouts and tofu, ignoring my teen's expression of "Here Mom goes again with her health fad." I dismiss the looks as I pat myself on the back. *I am ushering everyone here into a new season of health and happiness. You're welcome, family.*

It starts so well. Until weeks later I find myself enthusiastically chowing down on pizza, tacos, and burgers. Huh? What happened to the motivation that inspired me to explore more whole foods and nourish my family in all new ways? When did I start drifting?

CONFIDENCE

The same is true for so many things we know are good for us, whether it's exercising more or fearing less. The list of possibilities is endless, but our commitment isn't. The problem isn't knowledge. It's drift. We may change how we live . . . for a time. But then we find ourselves falling aimlessly back into old habits.

We won't attain the life we want until we learn how to stay on track. Many people fail at this stage because they lose confidence. What's important is to notice why confidence fades. Sometimes it's due to comparing ourselves to others who seem to have it all figured out. But more times than not, it isn't about them . . . it's about us. Because of so many past failed attempts, it's easy to lose our confidence.

Let's begin by exploring what causes us to drift off course. Then, I'll share how we can get back on course.

Why We Drift

It's that sinking feeling we all dread. The moment we find ourselves right back where we swore we'd never be again. Shame hits us like a cold wave. We're embarrassed and disappointed with ourselves. We feel trapped in a story we don't want to be in.

When we drift away from the life we want, it's a sign we need to do three things:

1. Shut down false beliefs.

2. Invite in true beliefs.

3. Evaluate what's working and what's not.

Let me share three tangible, unique examples of how this can play out. As you read these stories, do so from a posture of better understanding your own drift. In other words, what triggers you to let go of your truths and start believing other stuff that isn't true?

I'll start with my own story. It began with my commitment to get into better shape. Yes, this was probably one of those "January New Year/New Me" resolutions. I was determined to see results but the strangest thing happened. Even though I was working out, I kept gaining weight.

Why? Well, it has to do with brownies and fresh baked cookies. Yes, those innocent looking sweets were the cause of my drift. I'd tell myself I deserved a treat for working out. Then I'd indulge and put all the calories I'd burned right back on.

I had to shut down that false belief that I deserved sugary rewards after working out. Then I had to invite in a true belief to replace it. In this case, I changed my belief to "I get to enjoy my workouts and find good-tasting fuel and clean foods to nourish my body." As helpful as that was, the process didn't end there. I had to keep evaluating what was working and not working to head off future drifting. It's an ongoing process.

That's just one example from my life. But there are so many ways drift can happen.

Amber was one of my coaching clients. It was a joy to help her chart the life story she wanted to write, and we'd been working together for many years. Growing up in an abusive home, she had struggled with believing what was true. Her false belief was, *I don't deserve to have what I want. I must take care of others to earn love.* Over time, we'd made progress in exposing and shutting those lies down. We replaced those lies with her new true belief, *Loving myself means taking care of me. I get to have the life I want without guilt.*

This powerful shift helped her step into the life she was made for. Amber moved to a country she had always longed to

CONFIDENCE

live in, finished her Master's degree, and was in a loving relationship she'd hoped for. Her life was going swimmingly . . . until she took a trip home.

Now to be fair, our family of origin—as much as we love them and would die for them without hesitation—hold a power that can cause us to digress faster than anything else. It's amazing how we can feel centered and powerful, but with one look, comment, or sigh from a family member, we're suddenly twelve again. Amber and I had prepared for this phenomenon, especially since she'd grown up in a family with so much unhealthy behavior.

When I talked to her two weeks later, she was, let's just say, quite adrift. All her true beliefs had gone out the window. She felt worthless, unloved, and completely powerless. What had happened? As the two weeks unraveled, Amber had stopped shutting down false beliefs, stopped inviting in her true beliefs, and stopped evaluating what she needed. She lost confidence, which caused her to drift into old patterns as if on autopilot, doing and saying things just to survive.

Can you relate? I sure can. It goes from bad to worse when we shrug away course corrections and simply live adrift without acknowledging how bad it is. Like an ostrich with its head in the sand, we avoid the issue by convincing ourselves (and others) that all is well. Even though we know in our hearts nothing could be further from the truth.

See if you can spot the drift in Steve's story. Outwardly, he and Amber couldn't be more different, yet no one is immune to drifting.

Steve grew up in a home where he was loved, but often not validated. When he tried to share what was important, he was usually dismissed, shamed, or corrected. It's not hard to see where his false belief—*I'll never be heard*—came from.

Given that, it may surprise you to learn he grew up to be a president and owner of a successful company. Unfortunately, this damaging belief from childhood was now hurting his ability to run his company with confidence. Where once he had confidently led a small team, he now had a team over ten times the size due to the company's prosperous expansion. This created immense pressure. And the false belief had started creeping up. (Side note, this is a common occurrence. Our false beliefs can sneak back up, and even multiply, when the pressures and demands of life increase.) As the leader, his presence and voice were highly needed, but his false belief was blocking him from speaking up. He was avoiding conflict, not initiating difficult conversations, and resisting the uncomfortableness of holding individuals and teams accountable. His results began to dip and his team was suffering. And he knew it.

This is when I entered the scene.

As Steve and I worked together, we identified his false belief and the pressures that were exacerbating it. He shifted to a true belief—*I get to be heard and valued for what I offer*—and the situation gradually began to change. Practicing this new belief, he leaned into relationships instead of disengaging; initiated difficult conversations instead of avoiding them; and stayed present with direct reports, colleagues, and friends. All around him his life began to change for the better. The company success resulted in higher profits and increased employee morale. More importantly, his confidence returned. And when he started drifting back to old beliefs under times of increased pressure, Steve knew what he needed to do to get back on course. Facing those pesky false beliefs sneaking up to taunt him, he invited in true beliefs and made sure to evaluate how things were going. He even started offering these true beliefs to his leaders to grow the company culture.

I hope you found these three examples helpful in seeing the various ways we can get pulled off course and start drifting. The good news is that we can get right back on course by practicing these three steps. We can often do it in less than a minute, which is even better news. The quicker we notice the drift, the quicker we can reach for what we need to get us back on course.

The hard part is knowing how to notice.

Noticing When You Go Adrift

"Anxiety can be a gift."

Does that sound like a true or false belief to you?

Perhaps surprisingly, this is a true belief. It's one I started engaging when I realized I was spending too much energy on managing my anxiety. When I shared this personal belief with a client recently, she stopped the conversation with a shocking, "Huh?" followed by, "Please explain."

We often fear anxiety. But another way to look at it is that anxiety is a signal to you that something is wrong. In that sense, it can be a gift if we'll listen to it. Stay curious and ask what it's alerting you to notice. This is a process known as "befriending your uncomfortable emotions."

Anxiety, fear, and dread are all examples of uncomfortable emotions trying to signal you that something is off. Now, to be clear, I'm not minimizing or dismissing the arduous and painful journey many of us take in dealing with severe anxiety and panic attacks. I've been there, so I know. But one thing I have learned is that my uncomfortable emotions do not need to be feared but, rather, respected and paid attention to. Staying curious about my anxiety became an important belief to help me better understand when I was off course.

CONFIDENCE

I first discovered this when I was a young teacher in my twenties.

I struggled with growing anxiety. It was miserable and the vulnerability I lived in was terrifying. I spent years trying to manage it, control it, and dismiss it—but it wasn't until I decided to really listen to it that I discovered the gift of my anxiety. It was telling me that I was not wired to work with people, in person, day-after-day, in a role that demanded I teach and plan five days a week. Some people are wired to do this daily, but I am not. And worse, I felt guilty that I couldn't. I kept shaming myself. *I should be able to do this like everyone else. What is wrong with me that I can't?* I felt bad that I couldn't keep up and stay in the game like everyone else around me (or so I thought). Obviously, this only increased my anxiety. As my anxiety went up, my confidence went down. And the vicious cycle kept going.

It wasn't until I let go of the guilt and shame—while staying curious—that I was finally honest with myself and discovered what I needed. I craved solitude, "think time" alone, breaks from face-to-face conversations and being responsible for continuously leading people.

Pause. Read that again. That action shifted my entire life. A similar action can change yours as well.

I knew I loved teaching and truly enjoyed my students, so the solution wasn't to stop doing that and sell t-shirts on the beach (although at times that does sound pretty good!). It was the environment and frequency of teaching that needed a shift. So I moved to the university level where I could teach three days a week rather than five. Doing so provided much-needed breaks between classes, which allowed me to refuel. Eventually, I created a coaching practice that allowed me to engage in a way that fed

CONFIDENCE

my spirit. Because I knew what I needed to thrive, I set up my schedule in a way that was life-giving. I chose to conduct most my conversations over the phone, realizing how much energy face-to-face required of me. I didn't avoid face-to-face meetings, but chose selectively when and where and how many were helpful. If you're not wired this way, I confess it may sound odd. Perhaps I'm an introvert. I may have heightened sensitivities. I've studied lots of theories around this, and I'm still not sure, to be honest. But I am confident of the results when I recognize and care for my needs in this area. I live most of my days peacefully. In fact, my true belief is that I am a peaceful person highly sensitive to what ripples the peace. Now, when any uncomfortable emotions come up for me, I use it as a signal to pause and listen to what I am observing so I can course correct and get back to heading in the right direction. Peacefully and confidently.

Staying on Course

One of my all-time favorite phrases came from my husband. He has this uncanny ability to listen to my verbose monologues and then succinctly capture it in one sentence.

When I was recently bemoaning the fact that I was doing what I didn't want to do and frustrated with my lack of follow-through, he listened for some time (quite a while, actually). Then he sagely replied, "Yep, we don't drift into the life we want, do we?"

His simple insight left me momentarily speechless.

It was such a powerful statement because it revealed how the life I wanted required me to live intentionally and, at times, be willing to fight for it. Without that, I would drift into a life I didn't want. Honestly, I didn't like this new revelation at first. It shed light on how incredibly unrealistic my perspective had been. And it made me wonder—how long had I been fighting the way life worked?

There are reasons why we drift. And understanding this is what will help us get back on course.

Shockingly, I saw the reflection in the mirror with Darren's poignant statement. What I was really hoping for was that it could all be easy and just come to me—preferably with rainbows, unicorns, and a choir of singing angels exalting me. Don't laugh! You know what I'm talking about. That desire to drop those extra ten pounds with a smile on my face, attract ideal clients with ease, build my dream company with a flick of my wrist, and be the wise, loving mother for my children who would one day praise me for feeding them healthy foods and helping them to solve all their problems. Oh, and I wanted to do it all with joy and boundless energy.

Darn it. My husband's comment revealed how my expectations didn't line up with reality.

I didn't like having to be so intentional. I wanted to magically drift into my dream existence.

And when it didn't happen, I wasn't just complaining. I was losing confidence because my expectations were unrealistic.

It's not easy to grapple with the reality that when we stop living intentionally, we drift into a life we don't want. We end up getting completely off course only to find ourselves somewhere we don't want to be. I feel empathy for people in this situation. Taking responsibility for setting the course and then staying on it is hard. We all have to contend with the actuality that life is challenging. It won't be easy pursuing that big dream or important relationship. That won't just happen. Though we wish it were otherwise, we can't let go of the steering wheel and expect to arrive at our desired destination.

CONFIDENCE

Getting the life you want requires paying attention to your whole being—intellectually, physically, emotionally, and spiritually.

And giving yourself what you need along the way. Otherwise, you will drift. This is a reality you need to consistently face.

Throughout it all, your confidence will take a beating. Even so, stay hopeful and be intentional. It's the key to staying on course.

The Unkindness of Comparison

As we continue to build our confidence through creating a strong belief system, one of the strongest pulls that causes us to get off course and lose confidence is comparison.

Many don't recognize this issue in their lives because they think comparison is easy to spot. But it comes in all shapes and sizes—from jealousy (*Why don't I look like her or have what he has?*), to toxic self-affirmation (*Well, at least I'm not doing that!*), to unhealthy victim mentality (*Why does she get to do what she loves, and I don't?*).

Notice this the next time you are on social media. How we compare our lives to others in what they are doing or not doing, distracts us from moving forward. Worse, it causes us to slow down and start drifting as we focus on what others do or have compared to us.

This runs rampant in our society. We disintegrate our confidence when we compare ourselves to others. In my practice, I often encourage clients to step away from social media or even the news so they can focus on charting their own course instead of getting stuck in one place or drifting aimlessly at sea.

So, how do we not only intentionally arrest the drift, but stay on course? It starts with how we live out each day—moment by moment, hour by hour. These practices are the equivalent of course correcting by small navigational degrees. In the moment, no single decision seems dramatic, but together, they keep us on course to where we want to go.

For the sake of clarity, I'll reduce it to this simple formula:

KINDNESS + STRUCTURE = STAYING ON COURSE

It requires our head and our heart to be fully engaged. What do I need to stay on course and take that next step today? Is doing so kind or harsh to my heart?

For instance, think about how we start a new year. January is the month where we make new declarations of how we'll intentionally improve our lives. We enter the first Monday in January with zeal and a committed resolve to get the life we want. It's when we plan to start that new diet, meditate daily, be more patient with our kids, lose fifteen pounds, find a new job, and become an entirely awesome, wonderful, perfect creation. The pressure is almost paralyzing.

We need goals and the goals I named (well, except for the last one) are admirable. But when we turn them into our measuring stick, they aren't very kind or forgiving.

If you're like me, somewhere around Tuesday afternoon, my Monday resolutions have already faded and the new year looms ahead feeling like a sentence to be served. *Only 360 days left,* I gloomily think.

But what if we created resolutions and daily patterns to support them filtered through these three questions:

1. Am I being kind to myself?
2. Is this a simple, sustainable, and enjoyable way to live?
3. Am I moving forward in the right direction?

Answering yes to these three questions fuels confidence, slows drift, and generally makes life (and ourselves!) more enjoyable. Let's take a look at each of these three questions.

FIRST, are you being kind to yourself?

I always ask this question first. Why? Because whenever I try to do things in an overachiever manner, I set myself up to fail. It's that voice inside that sounds overly driven and harsh.

I'm going to lose ten pounds by Friday, so I'll grit it out and go to the gym every day, pushing my lazy self to burn at least 1000 calories off my out-of-shape body.

That's slightly exaggerated, but you're familiar with the cruel voice of self-talk. You know that feeling you get when you're just so disgusted with yourself that you set these ridiculous goals with no margin for mistakes or grace for setbacks?

I'll let you in on a secret. The voice and the words come from what I call shame-thinking.

I heard this voice the other day. *"You have been way over-enjoying holiday eats. You better pull yourself together. Look at that scale! You should be ashamed of yourself!"*

Ouch. We would never talk to anyone else the way we shame ourselves, would we?

It may get results for a brief time, but doing so makes you—and everyone around you—miserable. That's not the way I want to achieve results.

It's time to replace shame-thinking with a kinder dialogue. Challenge yourself to believe that kindness will help you move forward into the person you want to be and the life you want to live.

For instance, as you step on the scale, try this: "*Wow, you gorgeous human! You really had fun this past month, didn't you? Way to be all in! Worth every bite, huh? Okay, now it's time to deal with this. But don't worry, I'm here with you. I'll make sure to help you in a way that feels kind.*"

And to make it even kinder, you can invite kind people to join you. A kind resolve might sound more like this, "*I'm going to lose ten pounds in three months and enjoy how I do it, both in my exercising and my eating.*"

See how this simple mind-set can set the tone for how you treat yourself all year long?

This is how we want to grow. Caring for ourselves mentally, emotionally, spiritually, and physically. It's the whole self that needs attention as we step into new ways of living. This is the kinder way.

SECOND, is this a sustainable, enjoyable way to live?

As we think about what we need to support our goals and stay on course, we have to listen to what works for us. What do our hearts, minds, and bodies need in this season to sustain themselves?

Finding ways to care for ourselves in simple and sustainable ways will help us stay on course and not give up. Our confidence will rise as we make wise choices that not only work for the moment, but for life.

We know this, but short-term fixes have, at best, short-term results. We can pull an all-nighter once by overloading our system with caffeine and loud music, but try going without sleep for several nights and we'll see how unsustainable that is.

When we go for quick fixes while ignoring what's truly best for long-term success, we start to drift. Usually this begins

CONFIDENCE

when we set unachievable or unrealistic goals out of a need for immediate approval or validation. Along the way, not only do we drift, but we become miserable and ultimately lose more ground than we gained in our momentary burst.

Choose instead a path that is sustainable and enjoyable. For instance, I want to eat more plant-based foods. I've tried pursuing this before the wrong way. But this most recent time, I approached it mindful about my motivation. Doing so changed everything. I enjoyed not only how these foods made me feel but the taste as well. To keep it sustainable, I decided to commit to it for six weeks—not six months or the rest of my life. To keep it simple, I had foods prepared ahead of time that I enjoyed and could easily reach for throughout the day. To keep it enjoyable, I did it with two others on similar health journeys, so we could encourage one another and share creative recipes we enjoy. Most important, I declared perfection was not the goal. So once a week I enjoy a day off and eat whatever I want.

Isn't this a kinder, more inviting way to stop the drift?

THIRD, are you moving in the right direction?

It's good to monitor progress. That's what can help identify and stop drift. But trying to track our results every hour or day is exhausting and can actually create burnout and eventually lead us astray.

Remember, we're looking for the trajectory rather than the minutia. It's important to get a little farther out than this moment for a better read on where things truly are. If we assess too much in the moment, it can turn hypercritical. This is not kind and can backfire. Choosing to evaluate results over a longer period minimizes the momentary setbacks and allows us to see what's really happening, with a healthy dose of grace.

In my personal coaching, I don't assess a client's progress until weeks or even months out. In fact, I don't even work with someone unless they commit to several months. Why? Because patterns don't change overnight. It's unrealistic to assess in one or two conversations whether a person has changed. We have to give ourselves time.

It's the small, daily steps—like navigational degrees—that will keep us on course and get us closer to our destination. Yes, absolutely we can monitor where we're heading to stay on track. But we do so in a way that is kind rather than exhausting.

Don't just take my word for it. There's substantial research that supports how it's the small steps over a period of months that lead to long-term change. Dr. Caroline Leaf is a leading neuroscientist specializing in changing mind-sets. I've mentioned her studies a couple of times already—if you can't tell, I'm a big fan of hers. She sums up this issue in a powerful way: "Our minds need time to understand what the spirit already knows." Brilliant, isn't it? Your spirit knows what you need, but your mind needs time to make the change and create the daily support systems to help you shift. Understanding this is critical to arresting drift.

Don't Go It Alone

Remember how I began the chapter with the story of being lost at sea? What I loved most about that story was that there were two of them, along with their trusting canine companions.

Can you imagine what their days and nights must have been like as they spent months together in uncertain, dangerous conditions when they were only prepared for a two-week journey? I wish I could have been a fly on that wall to hear the conversations they must have had.

CONFIDENCE

They went through a life-and-death situation that was hard on their minds and bodies. Yet, the picture in the newspaper shows a close-up of the two of them together with huge smiles on their faces. That's due in no small part to them having each other throughout the tumultuous journey.

So, allow me to ask: Who's on this journey with you? Who is the person or group of people committed to helping you get where you want to go? Who will stick it out with you when it becomes longer and more arduous than you expected?

I'm blessed to have several people like this in my life. I'm smiling now as I think about a dinner I had recently with a friend where we laughed hard and cared tenderly for some challenging situations we're navigating. Something that I thought would be a quick and easy journey has turned out to be much longer and more difficult than I imagined. Knowing I had a fellow sojourner to listen eased the loneliness and encouraged me to stay on course. Over our favorite dessert of butter berry pound cake with an extra scoop of ice cream (I cannot stress the importance of this dessert during trying times), she asked me, "Heather, what are your true beliefs?"

I immediately chuckled because she knew my language and valued it. More importantly, she knew what I needed to stay on course, and she wanted to stand with me in it. This is the type of companion I want to be stuck with at sea. With a tired but resolute smile that immediately grew my confidence as soon as the words came out of my mouth, I responded, "I am being led and guided."

Which leads me to a prayer I wrote years ago that has great meaning for me: *Help me understand what I need. Guide me in the plans I make. Show me what is working and what is not. Thank you that I am loved, and I am supported in my success. I anticipate the partners that are waiting for me.*

We'll talk more about this in the last part of the book, but I had to mention it here. Because when we are adrift at sea, we all could use prayers.

CONFIDENCE QUESTION
How can you stay on course for the life you're made for while being aware of the ways you drift from confidence?

Where are you currently adrift?

How did this happen?

What do you need to get back on course?

Are you being kind to yourself as you reset your course?

Who are the key friends and sages with you in this journey?

CONFIDENCE

> **CAUTION:** Don't compare yourself to others when you drift off course. Recognize that you are uniquely made. Be kind to yourself as you embrace the right thoughts and appropriate actions for getting back on course.

CONFIDENCE

We've been trekking through difficult terrain here. Gaining confidence and becoming who we are meant to be is opposed on so many fronts. But now you have six powerful tools to combat comparison and doubt: Giving Self Permission, Growing Beliefs, Staying Powers, Recognizing Givers, Knowing How to Receive, and Stopping Drift. Now it's time for courage. Yes, this requires taking brave action—and you're ready for it!

PART III
Courage

The Third C: Choosing to Act

It was then that the woman realized she had a choice to make. *Shall I keep the bracelets on or take them off? If I keep them on, I have a purpose with very little risk. But if I take them off, the risk is greater. What if I don't know who I am? And what about all those I disappoint?* Then an exciting new thought began growing within her. *What if I get to know my beautiful spirit again and find a purpose outside the bracelets?*

We won't find better traveling companions than clarity and confidence. Especially in the early stages of our journeys when the road is paved and the sky is clear. Together, they help us see clearly and believe resolutely.

But a third companion is required during the more challenging parts of the journey. Times when fear is overtaking us and we're tempted to quit. Or times of overwhelming pain or grief. When all seems lost and you're sinking fast, you need another "C" at your side.

You need courage.

Because in those moments, a commitment to resting so you can have more clarity, and even choosing beliefs that impact your confidence, are good . . . and not enough. Courage is about taking action.

True courage involves facing our worst fears and pushing through them. Doing so produces a powerful ripple effect. Because regardless of whether we succeed or fail, we'll discover an inner strength. By choosing to act, we see what we're truly made of. It's only in the act of defying what's coming against us that life's full range of possibilities open up.

But make no mistake. Being courageous when it most counts is risky. Anyone can act brave when success is all but guaranteed and the stakes are low. But when the odds are stacked the other way and the pressure's on, well, that's when most fold. And that's when courage makes all the difference.

Courage, clarity, and confidence are intricately connected. The stronger your clarity and confidence, the greater your courage will be. Inversely, your courage will waver without a healthy foundation of clarity and confidence.

You might be surprised to hear that the enemy of courage isn't fear but cynicism and the haunting sense of "can't." I'll

COURAGE

explain why in the coming chapters as well as how to level up and get the traction we need, find our fuel, identify what pulls on us, transform our tension, and ultimately find our peace in being.

Now, it's time for courage.

COURAGE

LEVEL UP

Accessing Our Courage

The situation looks pretty grim.

You're alone on the empty downtown street, but you know you're being followed. You need somewhere to hide.

There's an alley between the two brick buildings to your left. It's dark, so you can't see what's lurking there. But you also can't stay in the open.

Sweat drips down your forehead as your nerves prickle on high alert.

Footsteps. You hear them echo but can't tell from which direction. Each step sounds louder than the last.

You look at the weapon in your hand. According to the green glow, the charge is almost out. You've got to move.

This is where I found myself, playing a highly stressful virtual game. Good grief, my pulse is picking up just remembering it!

My son Luke loves video games. I decided to join him in his world, playing a few rounds of some fast-paced games. Not a highly successful venture, I can assure you, but I see why it can be addictive. It's the challenge of facing that next level and the joy of victory you experience when you do. The adrenaline rush of looking back and seeing how each level was fought and won—some easier or harder than others—but each level representing your success.

This is what life is like. Courage helps us level up. And how we choose to take action is what grows our courage. Staying at the same level all the time gets boring, right? Sure, it's more predictable and safe—which can be nice for a season—but staying at one level won't get you the life you want.

What if we saw each tough experience as our chance to "level up"? That hard conversation we have been avoiding with a colleague? Level up. Learning how to love our spouses better after twelve or forty years of marriage? Level up. Facing the fears to finally start our own business we've dreamed about. Level up. Pursuing that dream we have inside us. Level up. All these acts of courage are what levels us up into better versions of ourselves.

When we avoid them, it costs us. We get restless, frustrated, depressed, and anxious.

We all long for more. But it's only those who challenge themselves to take action who grow the lives they want. Without courage, our world stays small. Worse, we stay small missing the opportunity to level up.

We're never too old to level up. When I recently turned half a century, a good friend told me with a wink that she was celebrating how I had made it to level 50! It made me smile as I appreciated this "accomplishment." You're not just getting older. You're moving up to higher and higher levels!

Courage Isn't a Scarce Resource

We see courage in the faces and actions of those we call heroes. Firefighters. Doctors. Soldiers. Police Officers. Kindergarten teachers. Their bravery may seem like it was something they were born with—a unique strand of DNA they possess that we mere mortals don't.

But that's not true. Everyone has courage reserves inside them. And we can access them . . . now.

Maybe you don't feel brave. Usually that's because you haven't exercised that particular muscle. Before we can use a muscle, we have to believe we possess that muscle.

That's what we're going to do here. Learn how to access courage. Discover why it's essential. See what it looks like. The good news is, courage isn't a complex concept. We just need to learn how to begin engaging it in small ways. From there, we can grow it with each step forward.

When I dreamed of started my coaching company, fear tried to rise up and talk me out of it. *What if I didn't have enough clients? What if I wasn't as good as other coaches? What if I didn't make enough money?* There were countless what-ifs.

I had to muster my internal courage to move away from a secure career path and toward an uncertain future. As a sole entrepreneur, I would be responsible for everything. Where before I had a resource of teams supporting me in large organizations, I now just had good ole me.

Think about all we take for granted when we're attached to a large organization—health benefits, retirement plan, marketing, tech support, business development, finance office, steady income, paid vacations, opportunities for professional development—the list goes on. I was about to walk away from all that because I believed that maybe, just maybe, I had something

COURAGE

to offer that might be unique and even needed in this world. More importantly, I knew I wouldn't be able to live with myself if I didn't try.

You know what I'm talking about. It's that deep-down desire you've felt at various times in life to run after a dream . . . but then something held you back.

So, fill in this blank: If I didn't have any fear, I would . . .

_____

_____

For me, it was working for myself and owning my own company. I had dreamed of this since I was a child. Moving forward required courage. But here's the good news. It didn't require a ton of it. Just enough to take one shaky step at a time. I see how my courage increased incrementally as I ventured out. Not with big steps. At least not at first. Usually it was just enough bravery for one more step. To grow my business in new ways such as moving from personal clients to corporate coaching, organizing conferences, leading retreats, and eventually writing a book (this book!) a decade later. See what I mean? Courage builds.

Engaging Your Courage

We get the ball rolling by engaging our courage—no matter how miniscule an amount we might have or how vulnerable we might feel. The key is to engage it. Wake it up! In doing so, we'll see it start to grow.

One day, we will look back and smile at what used to scare us. Dr. Brené Brown talks about the contagiousness of courage

COURAGE

and the vulnerability behind it in her book *Dare to Lead* as "having the courage to show up when you can't control the outcome."[8] When I remember where I started, I can now smile at my fear of wondering whether I would ever get a client when now I have more than I can keep up with. It all started with the vulnerability behind the bravery.

Here's the truth: we all have just enough courage to take that one step forward, and in doing so, it grows. But the reverse is also true. If we continue to avoid engaging the courage within us, it cannot grow. If we do not venture out one step at a time, our courage stays stagnant and we suffocate it. Each time we avoid a situation or opportunity, our courage shrinks.

I am reminded of a recent conversation I had with an executive team. We were in a meeting together when the president stopped the conversation and turned to her vice president. "I'm really struggling right now because I feel like what happened yesterday broke down trust, and I need to check it between us." I had no idea what had happened yesterday, but I sure admired her courage to address the elephant in the room. And it was contagious. The vice president responded with equal courage to share what he had experienced and how he had felt misunderstood by her. She was then able to apologize and explain her intentions. Within minutes, trust was not only rebuilt, but strengthened, and we carried on with the meeting's agenda. See what I mean? When we are brave enough to address what is happening—and not avoid it—it is a gift. This is how we level up in our relationships. And it is contagious.

Here's what I believe. It's our job to engage our courage so we can keep moving forward and growing it. More importantly,

COURAGE

---

8. Brené Brown. *Dare to Lead*. (New York: Random House Publishers, 2018) 10, 20.

it's an essential tool for helping us not get stuck, even when we fail epically.

It is when we fail that courage becomes most critical. In my earlier years of entrepreneurship, my husband and I bought a coffee shop. The "dream" soon became a "nightmare" when the business began to fold under the recession, and we were unable to earn enough to pay the bills, our employees, and the many expenses that come with owning a business. We panicked. And though we eventually sold it, I left the experience feeling weary, wounded, and financially strapped. I questioned if I would ever start my own business again. Working for "the Man" was just fine for me. It took courage to see the coffee shop enterprise as a learning opportunity for "what I did not want to do," and not as a reflection of my ability to run a business.

It was the act of engaging my courage that eventually empowered me to step out once again as a business owner several years later. The steady growth of bravery was what kept me showing up day after day—in all the ups and downs—to build the life I knew I was made for.

Where do you need courage? Engage it by taking that one step. Maybe it's having a conversation you've been avoiding, creating a vision board, whispering your hopes to a trusted friend, researching possibilities, signing up for a class, or finally asking that special person out on a date. Wherever you need courage—I am here telling you that you have it within you.

We can't wait for courage to magically appear. We must engage it for it to grow.

Everyone—and I do mean *everyone*—has courage. I hope you believe that includes you. I promise, it was never meant to be for the select few.

Stepping into Thin Air

Allow me to illustrate this with a rather visceral example.

Let's pretend your life-long dream is to parachute over the vineyards of Napa, California. You've found the perfect drop zone for landing and have studied books and videos about successful parachute jumps and landings.

Now your much-anticipated adventure is only days away. Your classes with certified skydiving instructors guiding you through all the varying scenarios has paid off. Your clarity on what to expect and how to respond is strong. You know where you'll jump, when to pull the cord, and how to land. And your confidence grows only stronger as your beliefs guide the growing excitement. This is what you have dreamed of doing, and the time is right.

The morning for the jump is here and you've systematically packed your gear. Arriving on the airfield, the plane is fueled up and waiting for you. Putting on your chute and adjusting your gear, you board the plane and eagerly wait for the engines to start up. The sound is mind-blowing as the engines break the silence, but it only serves to increase your excitement.

As the plane takes off, you watch the earth get smaller and smaller below you. Adjusting your goggles and checking your altimeter, you wait for the signal to jump. And then it happens. The pilot gives the signal! It's go time.

And you freeze.

You remember everything. Why are you clinging to the side of the plane?

The pilot frantically gestures for you to jump, but nothing is going to force you from that plane into thin air. Eventually, you pass over the drop zone and watch it get smaller. The plane begins descending. The moment has passed. You return

COURAGE

to the ground without accomplishing what you'd dreamed of doing.

Now if this has *actually* happened to you—no judgment. I'm not sure I'd be able to jump either. I applaud your cautiousness and trust your wisdom to wait.

But for the sake of diving into courage (pardon the pun), I use this illustration to highlight what is missing. All the clarity and confidence in the world cannot make up for a lack of courage. Courage is what we need to take the powerful leap of faith.

Courage is about seizing the opportunity to take action. Without it, we'll never get traction in life. Just like our parachute jumper, we won't achieve what we hope nor will we arrive at our landing spot. And the longer we fly in circles over the jump zone—knowing what we want but never jumping—the weaker we become.

Disconnected Living

Many of us work our whole lives saying what we want and even preparing for it. But when the moment to take action arrives, we chicken out.

We avoid, pull back, run away, rationalize our inaction, and our frustration grows. And again—no judgment—but we must be honest when it is happening and stay curious about why we are hesitating. Strive to understand what is behind not wanting to jump.

What do we need? It's as if we are waiting for something. But what?

In my research, there are four main reasons we don't take actions that align with our goals. I'll name and discuss them and then explain how courage is the antidote to each.

COURAGE

Most people do the opposite of what they want because they are not mindful of what they need regarding:

Affirmation

Fulfillment

Growth

Achievement

Paying attention to these four areas—what I call the Four Tires—helps us stay connected to living out the life we are made for. I'll talk about these more in the next chapter and how they help us stay on course. But for now, let's look at the stories of real people who faced—and overcame—blocks in each of these four areas. Notice how each area impacted their ability to level up. All four examples come from my research originating with women participants. As I mentioned, I initially focused on the woman's journey and what impacted her emotional well-being as well as career fulfillment, but since widening my clientele to include men, the findings have proven to be transferrable across gender. How we move forward in each of these areas applies to all of humanity.

AFFIRMATION, Callie's Story

Since she was young, Callie had always wanted to be a lawyer. But she was derailed by the lack of affirmation. Here's how she described it in her own words:

> "I had an unusual experience because since I was eight, I knew what I wanted to be. And then right before I was

to take my SATs, my dad said, 'So, what are you going to major in, and what are you going to be?' I looked at him like, *Where have you been?* 'I'm going to be a lawyer.' I don't know what happened, but he just flipped out. 'No daughter of mine is going to be a scum-sucking lawyer.' Shortly after that, he passed away, so I won't ever know why he felt that way. So I figured, well, I can do anything in the world *except* be a lawyer. But that was the only thing I ever wanted to do."

Because of this interaction, Callie changed her career focus to marketing—just like her mother. It affirmed her . . . sort of. Like a temporary fix or an inauthentic affirmation to help her feel okay, but it was not truly what she wanted. And although she was successful, she was unhappy. It wasn't until her thirties that she found the courage she needed to stop looking for others to affirm her and began to affirm herself. She went to law school. Now, she is living the life she's made for as a successful attorney.

I love how she described it:

"In my twenties, I felt like I was being pushed along by the current. But in my thirties, it was like, 'Look, I've got a paddle. I know where I want to go.'"

Don't miss the shift. Callie stopped looking for others to affirm her and instead gave it to herself. What's even more interesting is that when Callie eventually graduated from law school at the top of her class, she shocked her professors by not accepting a position at a prestigious law firm. Instead, she tapped into the courage to affirm herself in what she wanted rather than trying to please those around her.

COURAGE

Why did she accept a position at a lesser known firm? I'll let her respond in her own words:

> "I never wanted to be that ninety-hours-a-week, burned-out attorney. I work pretty much eight-hour days and then go home to spend time with my son. That's the priority for me. I can't remember a time when that balance wasn't there—when I really wanted my work to be my whole life. Even before I had kids, before I was married, there was always a balance."

Callie was able to take action that was congruent with what she truly wanted. The result was no longer being distracted or influenced by the need for outside affirmation. Rather, she learned to have the courage to affirm herself and move into the life she wanted.

FULFILLMENT, Jemma's Story

Jemma spent much of her life waiting to be happy. But once she understood the disconnect came from her lack of fulfillment at work, she turned the situation around. Here's how she describes it:

> "I started out in a field that I wasn't really interested in. I constantly felt like I was trying to be somebody I wasn't. But I was successful at it, and I was promoted a lot because I did well. In my midtwenties, I decided I'd had enough and made a scary career change right after I bought my own house. I realized I've always been a very sensitive person, but I pushed that aside to exist in corporate America. The problem was, I'd have a meltdown once I got home. As I became more comfortable with

COURAGE

who I was—a quieter person who doesn't deal with a lot of external factors or extroverted people all that well—I was able to find a job where I could work independently. Having the courage to choose a career that was self-led was what began to fulfill me."

Lack of fulfillment will distract us from having the life we want. Courage helps us do something about it. Going after what fulfills you is a brave, and necessary, act to step into the life you want. The important awareness is understanding what fulfills you. And many people struggle in this area because somewhere along the way, they stopped paying attention to this.

GROWTH, Fiona's Story

Knowing when we're going through a stage of growth helps us engage the courage we need to level up.

Before we go into Fiona's story, I'll share one about my daughter, Selah. There was a season when she was growing so fast that she experienced literal growing pains. She would wake up in the middle of the night crying from the pain. After taking her to the doctor, we understood the reason for it. Understanding what was behind the pain helped reassure us. While it didn't lessen the pain, it did take the fear away.

Fiona had a different kind of growing pain. Looking back as a young bride, she describes how she was able to recover from a life of immense hardship by embracing positive growth.

"To be quite blunt, I came out of such an unstable home situation that I was not emotionally well at all. I didn't even know what normal was. I came from a severely abusive home. I spent a lot of my twenties finding that out because my husband is so normal. He came from the dream family, so it provided an interesting balance. During my twenties, I was figuring out the basics like, what is normal, what is happy, what is the problem, and how do I fix it? Emotionally, it was not a great time but rather a season of intense self-discovery."

Eventually, Fiona created a stable home and marriage with a strong career as an educator. But to do so, she had to be brave enough to embrace new growth. As she stayed receptive, she grew into the person that enabled her to move into the life she wanted. She learned who she wanted to be as a wife, mother, and educator as she grew into the roles and relationships she valued.

Many of us fear growing in new ways because we never had it modeled for us and we avoid the discomfort and fear of the unknown. But this is a necessary growing pain that requires inner grit to level up.

ACHIEVEMENT, Ellie's Story

The fourth area involves how we experience achievement through the lens of courage.

From her midlife perspective, Ellie talked about her early years. More specifically, about her transition from college to the workforce. Notice how the themes of achievement and courage influenced the way she felt about herself, her roles in life, and even the people around her.

"It was a huge adjustment, coming from college where I had been in the top tier of my classes since high school, to having to prove myself to people in the workforce.

COURAGE

In school, I had a history with teachers and professors and didn't have to prove my capabilities over and over. But when I started in a career, it took a while for my employer to build up trust in my ability to get the job done. I didn't view that as a negative; it was a positive because I liked the challenge. I had a new goal with a new chance to prove myself."

As Ellie learned to adjust to different definitions of achievement in her new environments, she viewed it as an opportunity to succeed in learning new things and setting new goals. It requires courage to take on a new situation with a sense of excitement rather than wallow in intimidation. Initially, she was surprised at the need to prove herself but then adjusted to the task required of her. Bravely accepting the challenge of new achievement opportunities is what propelled her forward.

Aligning Our Four Tires: Affirmation, Fulfillment, Growth, and Achievement

Every person has hardships to overcome in their life story. Some big. Some small. And some people have more to deal with than we can even comprehend. Courage will see us through these difficult phases.

In the next chapter, we'll talk more about how to get traction in each of these four areas. For now, just take it all in and see what resonates with you.

As you consider paying attention to these areas, don't get stuck in a constant posture of hesitation. Remember my earlier parachute story. Clinging to the side of the door refusing to jump is not the way to courage.

COURAGE

Waiting for the right timing is good. But over-waiting keeps you stuck circling the target area without ever making the leap. When you remain in this holding pattern too long, a deep disappointment grows from not being able to step into the life you know you're made for. This creates a disconnect between who we are and how we are living.

Courage is what aligns us.

If you find yourself stuck, there's no shame. We've all lived disconnected at one time or another. The trick is to learn how to recognize it sooner so you don't keep circling the jump zone without ever taking action.

Here's an extremely hopeful, likely influential, thought: None of us is meant to live differently from the life we were made for.

Pause. I'll say it again.

None of us is meant to live differently from the life we were made for.

Do you believe that statement? Does it sound too good to be true? Perhaps this is where you first need to engage your courage. To simply hope.

But what about the tough spot you're stuck in? I get it. I've been in tough, seemingly impossible situations. I know how life comes up out of nowhere and surprises us. Eventually, though, we are given opportunities to do it differently. To get out of the holding pattern. And the way forward is always through courage. We need courage to move out and level up.

Growing Courage

Now that we know what courage is and what gets in the way, let's move to the next level.

COURAGE

How do we grow it?

Simply put, by surrounding ourselves with brave, audacious souls. Because courage is contagious.

In my research, when I asked participants what inspired them to level up, their responses were universal. Getting the right people in their corner. And specifically, they identified three things they needed from those people: the permission to fail, guidance based on personal experience, and faith in the process.

Wouldn't we all live more bravely if we had these types of people in our corner? You can see how this naturally and synergistically grows courage. And here's the good news, now that we know this, we can go find them.

Here's how I saw this mindfulness impact the life of a great leader.

Brad was an executive of a large, multi-million-dollar corporation. After working together for over a year, his clarity and confidence were strong. But in a moment of vulnerability, he said, "I know what I have to do, and I am confident it's the right decision, but I lack the courage to do it."

Can you relate? Owning it is half the battle. Being brave enough to act is the other half.

There are seemingly valid reasons why we don't want to risk doing what we know we need to do. We're scared of failing, being rejected, disappointing others, getting it wrong, or simply because it takes too much work.

For Brad, it was all of the above. Years ago, he had taken a big jump, and it had backfired on him—badly. People resigned, he was demoted by the board and rejected by colleagues despite his good intent. He endured false accusations and misunderstandings without the support of anyone in the company. It was a painful, confusing time. And worse, it was all because he

COURAGE

was trying to do the right thing for the employees. Brad took a hard hit.

Honestly, most people would have quit, but his courage kept him in the game. It was also what got damaged. It took years to recover and face the internal pain this experience caused. It fueled self-doubt about his leadership ability. Worse, it created in him a fear of jumping.

As we focused on growing his courage, we started looking at who he had in his corner.

Being honest with yourself and evaluating the people who surround you is tough. But it is the essential first step in growing your courage.

Taking inventory in both his personal and professional life, he started evaluating the people he was choosing for his team, the leaders he was hiring, and the mentors advising him.

Brad chose not only the highly qualified leaders within the company, but more importantly, those he wanted in his corner as he committed to leveling up in leadership. He began avoiding individuals who chose blaming as a way to handle failure as well as the cynics who destroyed all sense of hope. Instead, he collaborated with those who had gone out ahead of him in successful ways and provided the value of learning from failures. He connected with other leaders, mentors, friends, and coaches—both in his personal life and his professional world—who stayed solution-oriented as they built trust and united relationships.

And his courage began to grow.

Eventually Brad took the jump he needed to take. He restructured the company, had the difficult conversations, and mentored new leaders to move the organization into higher levels of success. It was not an easy fix. It took years filled with

COURAGE

highs and lows to turn the company around. But it was his work in gathering brave souls that synergistically grew his courage.

And the results were amazing. Profits significantly increased, but more importantly, the company morale grew. Teams were communicating, trust was increasing, and performance levels from each department were hitting newer and higher goals.

It's simple, really. Courage begets courage.

If you invite in brave people, you will live with more courage. And the reverse is true. If you surround yourself with cynics, naysayers, and people fearful of jumping, your valor will fade.

When we want to live bravely, we need the right people in our corner. Those who have gone out in front of us and who know how to offer needed advice. Those who help us hold the hope as we face the unknown. And those who remind us how failure is critical to learning success.

The Courage to Be Vulnerable

In the words of Dr. Brené Brown, "You can't get to courage without rumbling with vulnerability."

It's courage that takes us to that next level in life, helps us push through leadership lids, and breaks old habits we've outgrown. It's the next necessary step after developing strong clarity and confidence.

And this is a vulnerable journey. Because risking again and daring to step out when we are insecure or have messed up and failed badly is scary. It mandates being courageous enough to shut down the shame and reach for a thread of hope.

But remember, being brave isn't just needed for business success. It has the potential to transform our lives in personal ways. It did so in my life.

COURAGE

After nearly three decades of marriage, looking back I see how courage was critical in helping my marriage level up. My husband and I had each gone through hard seasons where we had to be honest with ourselves first and then with each other. Not about little day-to-day issues, like who ate the last cookie or who was picking up the kids. I'm talking big issues like what scared us, made us want to quit, and left us feeling vulnerable and alone.

Determined resolve is needed in our most intimate relationships, especially when we find ourselves wondering what those closest to us think about us or when we need to share how we feel about them. It was only through risky, honest conversation that our marriage was able to go to the next level. Courage wasn't optional. It was a mandatory part of that journey. Courage to hold onto the hope that we truly were in the process of leveling up and not falling apart. Courage to face down false beliefs we had held about one another or about the relationship. Courage to find words for emotions we struggled to understand. Courage to surround ourselves with support we needed from friends, professionals, and those we admired who were further along on the marriage journey. Courage to develop new ways of communicating and building trust.

Together, we leveled up to create a new marriage and new patterns that we both enjoy. Even more, we are better humans because of it. Win-win. Ultimately, we each became healthier people as we committed to being more honest, developing new habits, and surrounding ourselves with other brave souls determined to level up in their marriages.

Clarity and confidence are foundational, but it is courage that moves us to act in pursuit of the life we're made for.

COURAGE

COURAGE QUESTION

How are you growing your courage?

Select one area to focus on: Affirmation, Fulfillment, Achievement, or Growth

Why do you want to focus on this area? What is pulling on you?

Who are you selecting to be in your corner?

Why? What do they offer you?

CAUTION: Courage isn't carelessness, cockiness, or competitiveness. It is taking active steps needed to achieve your truest potential.

COURAGE

Now that we understand the importance of courage in leveling up and how it's synergistically connected to action, let's talk about how we do this. Rather than talking about the tires hanging on a tree, let's look at the four on your vehicle—your life. These don't gently swing back and forth . . . but get you to your destination each day. Tire swings don't need traction. The tires on your car do. You get the point. It's time to talk about how we can get traction with the Four Tires and how to check them in specific ways that are essential in helping you grow your courage.

COURAGE

TRACTION FOR A BETTER LIFE

Aligning All Four Tires for the Journey Ahead

You thought the relationship was going well. Everything was rolling along just fine. Until it went flat. And now you are in an intervention session.

The counselor clears her throat to break the awkward silence. You start to talk, but she motions for you to stop. "Let the other four go first."

"But," you object, "they are tires. This is ridiculous. Who cares what they think!"

The counselor shakes her head. "Look how deflated they are. Perhaps you've been driving them too hard."

You raise your hands, palms out. "Okay, okay. This should be interesting."

The four tires are side-by-side on the couch across from you. You roll your eyes. Why do they have to do everything together?

The one on the far left begins. "I'm the tire of fulfillment. I've felt low for quite a while."

"I feel like I'm just going around in circles," the tire of achievement says.

The one next to it chimes in. "I'm the tire of growth. But I'm actually shrinking."

"I feel invisible," the tire of affirmation grumbles. "I bet you can't even tell the four of us apart."

You sigh in exasperation. "You're right. I admit it. You all look the same to me. I expect you to be ready when I say 'Go.' And as long as that was the case, we got along fine. But it's not working anymore."

The counselor smiled. "Now we're getting somewhere."

"We are?"

"Yes. It's time for you to get to know your tires."

Spiral Up . . . or Down

I admit, my example is a bit surreal. (Okay, a lot surreal!) But there's more truth in this scene than may at first be apparent. Because, be honest, how readily can you distinguish the Four Tires in *your* life? How are you feeling fulfilled or affirmed? Where are you enjoying new growth or achievement? For most people, these four areas are considered interchangeable and rarely warrant our attention. Until a problem occurs and life starts feeling a bit off or even comes to an abrupt stop.

In my doctoral work, I spent a lot of time looking into problems. But what most interested me was finding solutions to the problems. There was plenty of research explaining why we might be stuck in life, what causes us to disengage, or even spiral down for years. I was amazed at how many articles highlighted what makes people depressed, anxious, and fearful.

COURAGE

Yet there was little conversation about what gets us unstuck and moving forward. I was more curious about what motivated folks to get back on the road and move forward again.

In other words, what causes us to spiral up rather than spiral down?

I asked my research participants to look back over their lives and share what made them spiral up when they found themselves on the side of the road, derailed by challenges, crises, or hardships.

What I discovered was fascinating. Those who spiral up from problems were—consciously or not—tapping into four resources. What they were doing was allowing their core identity to be strengthened in four interrelated areas: Fulfillment, Growth, Achievement, and Affirmation.

As I applied these research findings in my coaching practice, I began to call these the Four Tires. Just like the tires on our cars, when any of these four are not doing well, we are not doing well.

Those who understand and care for their levels of fulfillment, affirmation, achievement, and growth are more likely to get where they want to go. Others, not so much. And when we dismiss one of these four "tires"—even if we're doing fine in the other three—we're not going anywhere. Just like in life, one flat tire can stop us on the side of the road.

We often think the challenges of life are impossible to predict or even understand. We feel helpless to prevent them and hopeless once we're in them. But we can be proactive in diagnosing some situations before they turn into bigger problems.

My aim is to help you understand these Four Tires so you run at maximum potential. It's a super-helpful approach because when your tires are low, so is your courage. But once

COURAGE

you understand what needs attention, you can get going again and start spiraling up.

As we've seen, each tire is distinct. So let's get to know each of them a little better by going back to the beginning, remembering who we are and how we first showed up in this world.

Remember When?

Think back with me.

What are some of your earliest memories before the age of five? Honestly, I don't remember much, but I still hold the memory of being three and taking my first trip to the lake with my new swimsuit covered in a rainbow of brightly colored fish. I remember standing by the picnic table looking up at the ice cooler wondering how to reach the food. Another familiar memory was sitting in church looking down at my new white patent leather shoes with lace socks as my father preached—wondering how long I would have to sit quietly until my mom handed me a coloring book to pass the time. Early memories can hold a blurry, mystical, even ethereal, presence, can't they? Was that really me?

In the first 1,825 days of our life—five years—the building blocks for our identities are being formed. In fact, by the age of five, studies show that 90 percent of the brain's capacity has already developed.[9] We are living fully awake, aware, and taking in the world like a sponge, our brains being more receptive to learning than at any other time.

We naturally come into this world with our fulfillment, affirmation, growth, and achievement brimming to the top; we're

COURAGE

---

9. "Brain Development" First Things First, accessed February 13, 2021, https://www.firstthingsfirst. org/early-childhood-matters/brain-development/

unaffected by the responsibilities of life. Have you ever seen a three-year-old contemplate what gives them fulfillment or what affirms them? Perhaps how they might want to grow or achieve today? Or do they simply enjoy pillow fights, chase fireflies, build snowmen, blow bubbles, learn to read, try new foods, and create masterpieces with finger paint and pudding?

Seeing the world through the eyes of a child in their first five years is a treat! They remind us of how we once were.

We were born with an authentic ability to grow and achieve, while naturally enjoying a fulfilling and affirming life. We experienced our days with carefree curiosity as we genuinely engaged with the world around us.

As we grew, we began to better understand our place and our purpose. Taking on more responsibilities by doing homework, preparing food, completing chores, learning new jobs, and understanding what it means to positively contribute. Day by day, we naturally engaged our fulfillment, achievement, affirmation, and growth. We took pride in our first solo accomplishment of a task such as cleaning the kitchen, running an errand, or baking our first cake. We brought home A+ papers and artistic pieces to proudly have displayed on the fridge.

As we got older, we slowly forgot the rush we'd feel when we'd grow in new areas and the pride we'd have in achieving new potential. We forgot what it felt like to sit with pure authentic fulfillment as we enjoyed the wonders of the day or the affirmation of living exactly how we wanted to, doing what we loved. Our natural rhythm for authentic living got lost.

This is the reason the Four Tires idea is valuable. It is a simple metaphor to help you remember that who you naturally are gives you a way to better understand yourself. What brings you fulfillment? What do you want to achieve? How are you being

COURAGE

affirmed in who you are? In what areas are you missing the pride of growing and learning something new?

The Four Tires help you assess, as adults, what once came so naturally in childhood. It is a snapshot for what came authentically in your first five years but has somehow gotten lost. This is an assessment tool to help you better understand why you might feel sad, stuck, anxious, or depressed. Why you might be spiraling down and what you need to start spiraling up.

Understanding Our Four Tires

Why the focus on our tires? Because tires are the perfect representation for four key areas of our lives that impact courage and keep us moving forward. They provide the gateway to having even greater courage as we learn what fulfills us, affirms us, as well as where we want to grow and achieve. When these four areas are neglected, they eventually break down, as does our courage to act.

We're going to spend time on the importance of each, because only by understanding them individually and together will we gain traction. Maybe only one of our tires needs attention. Maybe all four do. But without an evaluation and alignment, we'll either remain stalled on the side of the road or be traveling out of balance.

In the sections that follow, I'll share more about how to recognize each area and why paying attention to each is so critical.

THE TIRE OF AFFIRMATION

The first tire represents an act of saying or showing that something is true. Think of it as a confirmation or ratification of truth. It is the act of affirming or being affirmed by emotional support or encouragement.

COURAGE

Here are some questions to help you determine where your affirmation comes from and what might be blocking it:

- What is truly good about you?
- What do you like best about yourself?
- What do you want to be known for?
- Where are you feeling validated?
- What is blocking you from your authentic self?
- What fear do you have about how you are perceived?
- Where are you searching for affirmation?

THE TIRE OF FULFILLMENT

This second tire represents the satisfaction or happiness that is a direct result of fully developing our abilities and character. It's the realization of something desired, promised, or predicted.

Here are some questions that will help you see where your fulfillment comes from and what might be blocking it:

- What brings you joy?
- What makes you feel refreshed?
- When do you feel peaceful?
- Where do you feel blocked?
- What do you want more of?
- What is your heart whispering to you?
- Where do you want to feel more fulfillment?

THE TIRE OF GROWTH

This third tire represents a stage in the process of maturing. It is progressive development, a producing that often comes

COURAGE

through a combination of adversity and healthy determination.

Here are some questions that will help you know where you want growth and what might be blocking it:

- Where do you want more knowledge?
- Where do you want to move forward in life?
- What are tangible next steps?
- What could you try that falls outside of your comfort zone?
- What is holding you back?
- How do you want to be challenged?
- Where do you want to grow?

THE TIRE OF ACHIEVEMENT

This fourth and final tire represents something done successfully, typically by effort, bravery, or skill. It is the process of achieving something.

Here are some questions that will help you understand where you want to achieve and what might be blocking it:

1. Where do you want more success?
2. What accomplishments would make you feel proud?
3. Where do you need to be victorious?
4. Where are you feeling stuck?
5. What skill set do you want to develop?
6. When is the last time you felt blocked from achieving something?
7. What do you want to achieve?

COURAGE

Now that you know the name and theme of each area, it's time to understand it more holistically. This helps you know how you are developing as a person and what you need more of in your life to either stop spiraling down or to start spiraling up. Whether you're suffering or soaring, understanding the "why" behind it always helps. Then you can give yourself exactly what you need when you need it. More importantly, you learn how to assess the state of your well-being so you can get the life you want. It is your overall sense of identity that will be strengthened as you discover:

- How they all work together
- Warning signs about why we might be feeling flat
- Ways to get traction

We'll begin by looking at how the areas of Affirmation, Fulfillment, Growth, and Achievement interact and impact each other.

How They All Work Together

Each tire is unique, but it isn't independent. All four are connected. Understanding how they "co-operate" gives us the best chance for a smooth, successful journey. I'll discuss some ways to check your tires and help you get the traction you need.

Let's look at some real-life stories.

We'll begin with Linda, the highly successful executive who started working with me because her life felt flat. Her children were grown, and she was advancing in the company, yet something wasn't right. Try as she might, she couldn't put her finger on what was missing.

COURAGE

That's when we decided to look at her Four Tires.

Her tires of Growth and Achievement were in great shape. She was learning new ways to lead, develop her team, and successfully lead the company. But then we got to the tire of Fulfillment, and, well, it was looking low. No wonder she felt a bit flat.

As we got more into her story, she revealed how her longing to travel had been overshadowed for decades by her need to be a provider. When she had children, her desire for adventure had to give way to being a productive parent focused on providing for their needs as a single mom.

Fulfillment requires an engaged heart.

Linda loved her role as a mother. But now that her kids were grown, she desired to be in a loving relationship, travel, and buy a home that was easy to manage—one that felt more like a retreat than a functional place to live.

With a more concentrated focus on the tire of Fulfillment, her life began to dramatically change.

We turned our attention to the fourth tire, Affirmation. It was low as well. This didn't surprise me. The tires of Fulfillment and Affirmation are often linked since they concern our "being" rather than our "doing." Linda realized that she'd been looking to her parents, her work, and her role as Mom for her primary sources of affirmation. She needed a shift in thinking.

The answer became apparent when I asked her this question, "What do you want?" (When is the last time you asked yourself this question?) This question is a powerful gateway to checking each tire.

You see, affirmation can come from areas of responsibility and caring for others. But it doesn't last. That kind of affirmation is partial. We receive long-sustaining affirmation when we participate in activities that bring us joy. It's getting in touch with our true self and what we want.

In Linda's case, she tried new hobbies and discovered her joy for volunteering, while simultaneously needing a break from the responsibility of leading in the workplace. Last we talked, she was preparing for a gardening activity with a group of mothers and their children who wanted to learn more about growing vegetables. See how she not only found a new purpose that affirmed her place in this world, but affirmed others as well? All because she got in touch with what she truly wanted.

There's a synergy between our tires. With her tire of Affirmation running well, it helped her tire of Fulfillment because, as we noted earlier, these two tires are often linked. In fact, I often visualize these as the two front tires.

Now let's take a look at the two back tires: Growth and Achievement. These can provide the traction of a 4WD, necessary for navigating the rougher terrain of life.

That was certainly David's experience. His quality of life was rich. Yet even with a loving family, ease in finances, and the ability to do whatever he dreamed, he was losing momentum. He didn't want to stop working but was bored with his job. He felt stuck.

We started by kicking his tires, looking for any that might be a bit low.

It quickly became apparent that his tires of Growth and Achievement were suffering. He had stopped growing in his career and felt like he was on autopilot. He had no more career goals or new frontiers to inspire him to move forward. David was bored and restless with his daily life.

Once we got to the bottom of what was going on, he felt the courage to initiate conversations with his colleagues about

COURAGE

new ideas, both for the direction of the company as well as his role on the executive team. As his tires of Growth and Achievement got the attention they needed, he was able to get the necessary traction to get unstuck. His outlook changed dramatically as he focused on where he could grow and what he could achieve. But don't miss this: he was only able to take the company to new heights by first caring for his own tires.

One more story. While working with a client named Tara, it became apparent that she was not finding fulfillment in her personal or professional life, nor was she was growing in any areas that inspired her as a parent or teacher. If that wasn't enough, she wasn't attaining any personal or professional goals, nor did she feel affirmed in her day-to-day decisions.

Yep, all four of her tires were flat. You may have had a time in your life when you went through this. What are we to do when this extreme situation happens? After all, no car has four spare tires in the trunk.

Ah, but every vehicle should have *one*. And we have to start somewhere.

So we pulled off the road and evaluated best next steps. My hope was that as we cared for each tire, driving would get progressively easier. For our starting point, I chose the tire of Fulfillment since this category has more to do with how we are feeling and becoming than with what we are accomplishing and doing.

As she focused on her level of fulfillment in her job, she decided to pursue her dream career of becoming a graphic designer by taking evening courses. Next, she asked her boyfriend if he would join her in working on their relationship. Six months later, they were engaged. Tara then took the big leap to start her own business and soon had more clients than she could manage. She's now expecting her second child, loving

COURAGE

work, enjoying life, and living drastically different than she had years earlier.

These are powerful examples of the exponential power of getting all four tires heading in the direction of living the life you're made for. Even when all four tires aren't working, you begin with just one, like Tara did. From there, you'll gain traction for the next. And then the next. Until all four are road-ready again.

If you didn't see your exact combination of tire problems in these three stories—or don't even know which of your tires needs attention—don't despair. The next section will help you identify *which* of your tires are low and how best to care for them. This is what I referenced at the start of the chapter as an alignment based on your specific needs.

This process will strengthen your identity and give you the courage to take the action you need.

Why Are We Feeling a Little Flat?

What are the warning signs that one of your tires has a slow leak? The goal is to address these issues as soon as possible. It's more than possible to do so . . . if you know what to look for.

Perhaps you're in a season where everything is humming along just fine. If so, consider this section a "How to Be Prepared for When Your Tire Blows" guide and keep on truckin'. But if you're wondering why life feels a little flat, here's an immediate rescue plan.

To identify the warning signs for your tires, I've created a general checklist that signals one or more areas of struggle. I offer it to help you notice when you or those around you might be feeling a little, well . . . flat.

COURAGE

- General despondency and unsure about the reason
- Apathy for life with a loss of enjoyment, zeal, or passion
- Feeling lost or confused
- Experiencing a general sense of being stuck
- Undervalued or unappreciated
- Discouraged with low motivation for setting new goals
- Loss of creativity or vision for innovative direction
- Minimal desire or anticipation for fresh experiences
- Lack of curiosity for acquiring new learning or knowledge

Heavy stuff, huh? Any of it resonate? It takes real courage to look at why you're struggling and decide to do something about it.

Let me share some examples where we can observe how the Four Tires of Fulfillment, Affirmation, Achievement, and Growth helped people not only address what they needed, but also what those they lead needed.

When I first started working with Nina, her team was frustrated and confused both about their purpose and direction. This made it hard to set and accomplish goals, which left the team consistently discouraged. The team was suffering in both their growth and achievement. And this is why Nina couldn't get traction with her team.

In one of our first conversations, I asked her the question that activates where we want to grow and how we want to achieve: "What does success look like?" She was stumped. But she quickly realized that if she couldn't define "success," how would she be able to grow her team and help them achieve the results they needed? After clearly defining success, we saw immediate traction. Within six months, she had one of the top performing departments in the company.

Austin was a new manager dealing with employee morale. He had inherited a team that seemed unmotivated and apathetic. As a new leader eager to serve, he was a bit overwhelmed with the state of his team. Usually this is connected to employees feeling unappreciated and generally uncared for—the tire of Affirmation.

I suggested that he start a strategic effort in affirming his people. He thought about what he appreciated and respected about each person and then privately pulled them aside to tell them. And sure enough, the morale and the motivation increased, bringing the results of the team with it. In fact, the results were so impressive that Austin called me. Excitedly he shared the details of his first conversation with one employee in particular. As Austin genuinely thanked Martin for his service, Martin had an emotional response. He had never been genuinely thanked in the twelve years of being at the company, and it meant a lot to be recognized by his leader. This made Austin emotional and both realized how meaningful it felt to be affirmed. Austin made the further connection that in expressing his appreciation for a team member, it increased his fulfillment as a leader. See how being aware of these areas in our relationships can synergistically influence one another?

Terri held an upper-management position in a well-recognized company. But her team was despondent, apathetic, and the turn-over was high. It took us a while to understand what was going on, so at the end of one of our sessions, I asked her to break down all her job responsibilities and bring it to our next session. When she showed up with her complex pie chart breaking down her duties, I was surprised by how much

COURAGE

she was doing. What she wanted to do and what she was actually able to do successfully were not aligned. And her team was suffering because of it. They could not find fulfillment in their work since they were trying to do too much and doing nothing well. Once we reprioritized and set realistic goals, she was able to lead her team with clear focus and measures for success. And the personal fulfillment, along with the growth and achievement of the team, increased dramatically.

See how valuing our levels of fulfillment, affirmation, growth, and achievement help us get traction? Some take pride in being strong in one or two of the four key areas, but remember, it's critical that all four areas work well—and work well together.

All it takes to disrupt a team or an individual is one flat, overinflated, or unbalanced tire. With proactive care and attention, we can greatly decrease the odds of any of these happening.

In life, what are the warning signs that one of our tires needs attention? The goal is to address these issues before our tires blow or are too flat to drive on. It's more than possible to do so when we know what to look for.

To identify the warning signs for your tires, go back to the list I've provided. Are there any you identify with personally or that you see in those you work or live with? It takes real courage to look at why you're stuck or not living at the level you want and then decide to do something about it.

Courage is what helps us identify what we are feeling so we can deal with the issues we are facing.

It also helps to view yourself in a positive light. You're not a problem to be solved but a beautifully complex, developing person.

The illusion is that every other person seems to be zipping along just fine. Don't believe that lie! I've talked with enough

COURAGE

people to know how common—and similar—our internal dialogues are around the areas of Affirmation, Fulfillment, Growth, and Achievement. The value is in understanding this so we can assess what we need and help others to do the same.

The Power of Positive Emotion

Before we close this chapter, there's one more thing we can do to help ourselves get even more traction. The Four Tires serve as the basis for how I coach people and help them engage the courage they need to take action. But getting traction is supported by an important theory developed by Dr. Barbara Fredrickson, considered by many to be the mother of "positive psychology." I found myself drawn to her discussions about how positive emotions give us the courage to act.[10]

If the words "positive psychology" caused you to glaze over, hang on. I promise to keep it as simple as possible. As I mentioned earlier in the chapter, much of the time, research focuses on the negative such as the emotions behind what causes us to spiral down. But Dr. Fredrickson's research studied the positive ways that helped people spiral up. More importantly, how positive emotions play an important role in building our resiliency and ability to spiral up in life.

Let me explain.

Many discussions and assessments are based around why we're mad, sad, anxious, or depressed (as if we need to focus more on that). But how often, if ever, are we taught how to increase our joy, peace, contentment, and happiness? Thankfully, Dr. Fredrickson took this seriously and dedicated much

COURAGE

---

10. Barbara Fredrickson, *Positivity* (New York, Three Rivers Press, 2009).

of her life's work to researching the effects of broadening and building our positive emotional reservoir. In other words, she discovered tools to help us spiral up.

She found that human strength is often demonstrated through emotional, intellectual, and physiological responses to life's circumstances. Her Broaden-and-Build Theory of Positive Emotions shows how our positive emotions can broaden the human capacity for linking what we think to how we act. This, in turn, empowers the building of personal resources in physiological, emotional, and intellectual development.

Through her research, she demonstrated how the power of positive emotions allowed people to reach new heights of potential beyond what they imagined. Talk about getting traction for our courage! Positive emotions are the secret weapon for a better life and can help us assess our Four Tires. Understanding this allows us to engage our emotions to not only cope with life circumstances, but to build resiliency and fuel for thriving.

Are you convinced about the power of positivity? If not, there's more. Fredrickson also described how positive emotions are essential for survival as well as during unforeseen life circumstances. And there's a bonus. These positive emotions are proven to have both short-term and long-term effects including an increased ability to cope and thrive with trauma and adversity.

Wow. Talk about spiraling up! You don't have to be a research geek to see how helpful those qualities can be. Embracing the power of positive emotions is worth your time.

As much as I respect Dr. Barbara Fredrickson, I wasn't just going to take her word on this. I did my own research and asked people how they managed unexpected challenges,

COURAGE

specifically as they went through career changes in life. I was curious what helped them adapt and increase their overall sense of emotional well-being and career self-efficacy.

My findings verified why certain individuals are able to adjust and adapt (align) to life challenges. Those who saw these situations through the lens of positive emotions tended to see increases in their emotional well-being—rather than their blood pressure or anxiety—during hard times.

As their fear and anxiety of the unknown shifted into one of embracing new challenges—or better, "enjoying the adventure"—participants increased their capacity to respond well to whatever challenge came at them. As this positive shift broadened, they were able to increase their overall well-being when they focused on the four universal themes of Affirmation, Fulfillment, Growth, and Achievement. As they did so, they were also able to spiral up during other difficult times, like career transitions and unexpected crises.

Now that you've learned how to observe where you are affirmed, fulfilled, growing, and achieving, you can feel more courageous about facing whatever comes at you, knowing you are equipped to spiral up as you pay attention to these four areas. You'll be amazed by all the places you can now travel.

Only a vehicle with four, well-tended, aligned tires is ready for the journey that awaits.

COURAGE

COURAGE QUESTION

What does an honest evaluation reveal about the state of your Four Tires?

Let's use the following to assess your Four Tires:

Get Centered. Clear thinking comes from quieting yourself and engaging the right side of the brain. Begin by listening to music, doodling, or meditating. There's no formula. You may want to doodle or meditate while listening to music. Spend about 10–20 minutes in this practice. This will help prepare you to hear your thoughts and feelings.

Assess. After you're more relaxed and centered, review a few questions within each of the four tire sections. Spend no more than five minutes on this. Think of this like walking around your car to kick the tires. You aren't answering the questions, just seeing what stands out.

Reflect. Now, go back and select one tire that you want to focus on. Choose one question from that tire. You may sit in this question for several minutes or hours. Or you might simply noodle on it throughout your day. Journal about it or discuss it with a close friend. Do what feels right for you.

COURAGE

Move Forward. Lastly, create one action step that will help you gain traction in this area.

CAUTION: Stay mindful about a tire you might be avoiding. This may be the very place you need to focus. But also, be kind to yourself. If one area is easier to address than another, start there. Listen to what you're feeling and thinking. Gain traction there and take on the more challenging tire later, when you're ready.

COURAGE

We're on the journey to engaging more courage. In the next chapter, we turn our attention from aligning tires to finding the right fuel. You'll be amazed at what happens when you fill yourself with the fuel it was designed to run on.

COURAGE

WHAT FUELS YOU?

Finding Your Optimal Pace and Place

You're driving down a scenic road, listening to your favorite band, and enjoying the view. You've got nowhere to be and are in no hurry to get there.

But then something odd occurs. Your car starts to go faster. Your foot isn't on the accelerator. How is that possible? You tap the brake, but the car doesn't slow down. In fact, the speedometer is moving steadily to the right, approaching 80 mph.

You push the brake all the way to the floorboard.

Multiple times.

Nothing. Soon you're at 95 mph and survival options start to race through your mind. None seem good. You can't slow down your vehicle. Reaching for the keys, you try to turn off the car, but they are stuck in the ignition. There's no off-ramp for runaway vehicles and no way to exit the car.

The images on either side of you are now a blur. Your hands

are glued to the steering wheel, trying to keep your car on the meandering road.

The good news is the speedometer is no longer moving. The bad news is it's stuck at 125 mph.

This isn't sustainable. There doesn't seem to be any good end to this story.

But what can you do? *Really. What would you do?*

For one particular driver, this was no imaginary question. Yep, this scenario really happened. Not on a country road but on an interstate. Miraculously, no one was harmed. The driver called emergency services, told them his situation, and was escorted by several police cars during the harrowing experience. The officers managed to keep traffic cleared to accommodate his "stuck speed" as well as get him safely through three toll booths.

You're probably wondering how they finally stopped a vehicle going 125 mph. The real-life nightmare only came to an end when the man's vehicle finally ran out of gas . . . 150 miles later![11]

What a ride, huh?

(As a side note, my mechanically-minded husband was distracted with this story and wanted to make sure that I referenced an important detail for all the curious readers: the car was designed for a handicapped driver with specialty controls. He then proceeded to tell me several ways to stop any standard vehicle if I ever found myself in this precarious situation. Love that man! Always looking out for me.)

11. "Disabled Driver in 150-Mile Terror Drive as Accelerator Jams at 125mph on Dual Carriageway" Mail Online, accessed June 1, 2019, https://www.dailymail.co.uk/news/article-2278106/Driver-trapped-125mph-car-chase-accelerator-jams-dual-carriageway.html

COURAGE

Life in the Fast Lane

As I tried to envision what it would feel like to be trapped in a runaway car, I was struck with two realizations.

First, while hopefully I never experience that situation, I want the courage to handle it well. And, as you'll see in this chapter, courage does come into play, just not in ways you may expect.

My second realization was, while most of us may not drive this way, we live our lives this way. With a stuck accelerator.

True, some of us have accelerators stuck at a low speed or even one notch above neutral. Don't worry, the principles of this chapter still apply to you. Because fast or slow, most people are stuck at a speed they don't want to be going. So stop driving and keep reading.

When we can't stop or control our speed, life seems out of control. Even if we don't wreck, we'll eventually find ourselves by the side of the road, running on empty.

Can anyone relate?

I'll be the first to raise my hand. I sped through several decades of my life in this manner and found myself totally exhausted and running on fumes.

In some ways, being stuck on the side of the road is more stressful than having a stuck accelerator. Because . . . now what? The world hasn't stopped moving—only I have. How long do I linger here?

Yes, I need to get my accelerator fixed. But while the car is stuck and my tank (and I) are on empty, it's the perfect time to consider what fuels me. Because I sure don't want to find myself in this place again. I'm guessing you don't either.

I hear many of you protesting. Sure, being in a runaway car doesn't sound appealing. But as long as I don't collide with

COURAGE

anything or run out of fuel, what's wrong with moving fast through work and life? Life in the fast lane. Going faster than those around me. Always in the lead. Setting the pace for others.

Isn't that how to get more done and stay ahead in this world?

Glad you asked. Because there are three big problems with this approach.

1. IT DOESN'T ULTIMATELY TAKE YOU WHERE YOU WANT TO GO.

In the real-world example, it took the owner of the runaway vehicle more than 150 miles out of the way. At some point, it's no longer about where you want to go but simply you trying to survive. This way of living can lead to years of traveling in the wrong direction only to end up in a place you never planned to be, wondering how you ever got there.

2. YOU ARE COMPLETELY STRESSED DURING THE JOURNEY.

Imagine the emotional and mental state of the driver in his runaway car. Do you think he was enjoying the scenery? Spending time reflecting on how to find the life he was made for? Humming show tunes? When you're in survival mode, your blood pressure, heart rate, and adrenaline are elevated. In that state, would the atmosphere inside the person or car (for those along for the ride) be calm or chaotic?

3. IT IS UNSUSTAINABLE BECAUSE YOU EVENTUALLY RUN OUT OF FUEL.

No matter what speed your accelerator is stuck on, eventually your vehicle will run out of gas. Hopefully when that happens you can safely coast to the side of the road. Yep, the vehicle has

COURAGE

issues. So do we. But let's not be too hard on ourselves about it. When we're dry, spent, and empty, it's the perfect time to find a better fuel to reignite us for the journey ahead.

What Fuels You?

I'm hopeful you don't need further convincing that living with a consistent fuel source is essential. Without it, you won't experience deep success or joy in what matters most to you.

Life in the fast lane usually just gets you where you don't want to be . . . faster. And life on the side of the road gets you nowhere.

The difference between us and the man in the runaway vehicle is that we have a choice whether or not to apply the brakes and find the fuel we need to sustain us for the journey.

How many of us even know the fuel we need?

Watching my pilot husband prep his plane for flight reminds me how important this is. Driving cars, we can pull over to any number of gas stations when we start to run low. Running out of gas can be fatal in a plane. Before we fly anywhere, I watch him calculate the fuel needed for the entire journey. And during his pre-flight check, he carefully measures the fuel in the tanks to ensure we have what we need to get where we want to go.

This little act of checking the fuel is life-saving for pilots—and their passengers.

Do you take just as seriously the issue of finding what fuels you? Do you know right now how much fuel is in your tank—or how much more is needed for the journey you're on? Knowing is critical. We get in trouble when we try to (pardon the pun) wing it.

COURAGE

The goal of this chapter is to help you learn how to check your fuel on a regular basis. To help you set your course at the pace that is right for you *before* you run out of gas. Or if you're out of gas on the side of the road, to find the fuel you need to get going again.

And this is where courage comes into play. It requires courage to pause and discover the unique fuel you need to reach your specific dreams at a sustainable pace.

Knowing and *Doing* Aren't the Same

There's a vast difference between knowing something and actually doing something about it.

For instance, we all *know* what we need to do to have a healthy body. Eat well and exercise consistently. The issue is actually making a plan and sticking to it, right? And not just for one day, but a plan that works for your body, tastes, goals, and lifestyle over time. The same is true when it comes to our quality of life. We have to plan accordingly. What makes us feel happier? More peaceful? Kinder to those around us?

We need a fuel plan for our souls the same way we need a health plan for our bodies. This is what allows us to thrive rather than just survive. If you need a refresher on why that's essential, pause here and spend a few minutes back in Chapter 5 (Survive or Thrive?).

Before we can get busy "doing," we must take the time to know what we need. Do you need to slow down or get going? Are you accelerating at a breakneck pace through life or stuck on the side of the road? Where do you feel stuck?

These are big questions. I'll ask them again. Linger with each.

COURAGE

Do you need to slow down or get going?

Are you accelerating at a breakneck pace through life or stuck on the side of the road?

Where do you feel stuck?

As you think through your answers, notice what you're feeling.

When our accelerators are stuck, it's easy to feel frustrated, offended, or shortchanged. The pull is to blame others for our choices because it can't be our fault . . . or can it? *Why can't those slow-moving people just get out of the way? When will people appreciate me for all the sacrifices I make and overtime I work? Why is it always up to me to solve the problem at hand?*

Living this way keeps our anxiety high while making everyone sharing the road with us miserable.

When we're by the side of the road out of fuel, it's easy to feel insignificant, directionless, or left behind. *Why is everyone else moving along just fine? Does anyone see me stuck here? Does anyone care? What if I don't know where to go or what I need to get there?* This mind-set is rooted in fear, confusion, and oftentimes despair. We fear we don't have what we need to move forward.

It's time to pull to the side of the road and look at our map. Not a digital GPS map but an old-fashioned, paper, fan-folding map. Our goal isn't to get somewhere faster than everyone else. It's to get to the right place as a changed man or woman—and ultimately a better human being.

That's why it's important to pull over regularly to assess our fuel level. To ask some critical questions like: *Am I heading in the right direction? What's the best route to get there? And most importantly, where do I eat, refuel, and take rest stops?*

COURAGE

Unfortunately, many of us are so determined to make something (anything) happen that we've driven ourselves, and everyone around us, crazy. We're driving fast and furious, unsure where we're headed yet determined to get there in record time. Or we've neglected the process of finding the right kind and amount of fuel we need to get where we most want to go. If you doubt that, just look at the people around you. We live in a world where most folks are always in a hurry but dazed and confused where they are really going or how they ended up in their current situation.

Rather than join them, you can choose to live at a sustainable pace that allows you time to check your fuel and know what you need to consistently pace yourself for the journey. Doing so will open up your life to more peace, greater joy, and deeper fulfillment.

No Quick Fix

I remember years of living at the mercy of a stuck accelerator. I constantly needed to slow down but never seemed to realize it until I was out of gas. I was in my twenties, fresh out of college, and trying to prove myself to the world. But I was running too fast and pushing myself too hard as I held down several jobs while finishing my graduate work.

What was driving me to push so hard? In hindsight, it was a deep-seated fear that I wasn't "enough" just as I am—combined with a zeal to grab life by the tail and do it all. As you know by now, that's not a sustainable way to live. So it will come as no surprise that I eventually found myself by the side of the road—worn out, frayed, and with no idea what to do next.

I stumbled into a therapist's office and shared the sad state of my life. In desperation, I asked her how long it would take her to "fix" me. Although the question was unfair, she sagely replied, "Give yourself two years to recover and find new rhythms to live in."

Two years? I thought, but almost shouted. It made me angry. Looking back, I laugh at my naïve response. I remember defiantly declaring, "I'll give you six months."

Good grief. Anyone relate to my strong-willed nature? You're pushing so hard. And when life stops working for you (and it always will) you then push back at anyone who dares to tell you the truth.

Yet deep down, I knew I needed a better way. I was at a crossroads in my life. Was I going to demand life work on my terms and my pace or learn a better rhythm for the journey ahead?

Sure enough, it took a couple years to reprogram my mindset. To this day, I'm thankful for my therapist's brave words of intervention. And I see my own courage in making the decision to slow down, reassess, and find the right fuel for me.

Fast-forward several decades. Now I spend my days coaching people like you on this very topic. I know firsthand how essential it is for each of us to find the fuel we need for the journey.

It's true. There's no quick fix. There wasn't for me. There isn't for you or anyone else on the side of the road. But when you know how to find your fuel on a consistent basis, it makes all the difference in the world. And it has been my privilege to come alongside people until they find the fuel they need for the pace that works for them.

Exhausted or Restless?

Finding our fuel requires that we be aware of our situation. Are we tired and worn out? Slow down and fill up. Are we

COURAGE

restored and eager for more? Let's chart our course and get going!

Let's look at examples of how each play out in real life.

Helene was preparing to work in another country when I met her. She was in the process of moving from Southern California to the Middle East when she called me. She was trying to figure out what she needed for this life-altering change and knew instinctively that she wanted support.

To be honest, our coaching relationship started out rocky. If you're running so fast that you don't keep the appointments you set with your coach, well, that's an issue. After two months together with three missed appointments, we had to talk. Let me pause to say that I have no judgment around this common issue, only grace. Remember my habit of pushing hard and running fast? It takes one to recognize one. We've all been on the giving and receiving end of situations like this.

The issue with Helene was that I was hired to support her life changes, and I couldn't do it if we weren't meeting—consistently. More importantly, I wanted her to discover whether she needed to slow down or stay in motion. In our next coaching conversation—unsure whether it was going to be our last one or not—I summoned the courage to ask some hard questions.

"Helene, are you ready to slow down to have the important conversations you say you want? More importantly, is it really what you want? What type of support are you looking for? And is it even the right time to slow down?"

I could feel the shift in our conversation as we explored these questions with honesty, curiosity, and most especially, courage. I knew she was at a crossroads, facing a critical decision for her life. I wanted to make sure I was helping her make the right one, even if it meant not working with me.

COURAGE

Toward the end of our conversation, it was clear to Helene that she was tired. Tired of pushing and tired of running fast. Slowing down to assess her course felt too good to be true.

Her fears whispered that any pause would cause her to be left behind. After all, hadn't she attained her current status by running fast and pushing hard? My suggestion that there was a better way to live was a complete paradigm shift for her. The equivalent of hearing she didn't have to travel any longer in a runaway car with a stuck accelerator.

If she had the courage, she could slow down and be okay. More than okay, actually. She could make decisions to reach her life goals from a place of peace. All she'd ever known was a fast-paced life with decisions made from fear, stress, and angst. At last, she was ready for a new way.

Dear reader, this takes such bravery . . . to reset your accelerator at a speed that's right for you. It's no longer about the speed of traffic around you or waiting for permission to slow down or speed up. It's about going the optimal speed toward the life you're made for. Not just knowing the right speed, but doing whatever it takes to finally commit to it.

Helene did just that. Through several years of working together, she transformed her life. I honestly wouldn't recognize her as the same person. She moved to the Middle East, learned a new language, finished her Master's degree, and met the man she wanted to spend the rest of her life with. What a shift from the chaotic life she had been living with unhealthy relationships and no clear goals. Helene learned to slow down and reassess not only what she truly wanted out of life, but the ideal fuel for getting there.

Derrick not only needed to learn how to slow down, but switch courses and get going in the right direction.

COURAGE

We'd been working together for over a year. He was frustrated with his leadership. Although they had reached some impressive goals this year, results were starting to slide and their success rate was dropping. As we talked, he knew exactly what was at the heart of it. "I am avoiding what I need to do, and I know it because I don't want to have the difficult conversations with individuals on my team. I have some fears holding me back, but honestly, I don't want to take the time or energy I know it requires. I need to just start doing what I know I need to do." If it sounds familiar to other examples, you're right. This is a common dilemma keeping many people stuck. Avoiding "the needed conversation." Whether in the home or in the workplace, many have the clarity regarding the issue, as well as the confidence in what needs to be addressed, but lack the courage to act on it. In this instance, courage was needed to take the necessary action that his company, and team, were counting on him to take. To lead in areas only he could lead. And to have the conversations that only he could have with key players.

Sigh. Why is this so hard? Because we don't see a clear course charted in front of us with a guarantee all will work according to our plans; and oftentimes, we simply do not want to slow down and take the time on something we don't enjoy. It's like refusing to get off the freeway at the correct off-ramp simply because we are enjoying the high-speed pace. Because, well, what if something goes wrong? Or slowing down costs us?

It takes courage to be honest enough to assess and move in the right direction. To risk failing or falling behind as you chart your own course. Ultimately, we have to make peace with that fact that there are no shortcuts. Engaging our courage requires time to take action and attention to do it well.

COURAGE

The longer Derrick avoided what he knew he needed to do, the more uncomfortable he grew. Worse, the more his team failed. He was getting distracted by looking too far down the road and wanting to get to his destination faster rather than recognizing what his team needed to get there together. This is common when we don't use our energy to do what we know we need to do in the present. We can start focusing solely on where we want to go or where we have come from rather than what is right in front us. But this only serves to increase our frustration and restlessness. As complex as our brains and hearts are, we need to care for what is in front of us to get to where we want to go. To try and do otherwise simply divides our creativity, our motivation, our loyalties, and our dreams.

Once Derrick started taking steps as the leader of his company, confronting the difficult issues with various team members, his work environment changed. He began to mentor his leadership teams in new and inspiring ways to reach the results the company needed. He had hard conversations he'd been avoiding for too long. He restructured teams to ensure each person was working in their strengths. He implemented new systems of accountability that resulted in high performance. And he started getting results. It was inspiring to witness his vision and energy for restructuring the company. Derrick had engaged his courage to slow down and set a new course. And his team was now ready to get going in a stronger direction.

It transferred over to his personal life as well. He initiated nurturing conversations with his three teenage sons and talked to them about issues he had also been avoiding. Mentoring them in new ways, he began to invite them into living a life that aligned with their potential. Entering their teenage worlds,

COURAGE

he met them on their level and helped them face their challenges with grace and compassion, knowing it was his job as their father to invite them into new possibilities for how to show up well for their lives.

Step by step his courage led him forward.

Though Derrick and Helene's journeys couldn't have been more different, both required immense risk with no guarantees other than the bravery to find the right fuel and speed for their best life.

Do you relate more to Helene or Derrick's story? The truth is, each of us has probably found ourselves in both of their shoes at one time or another.

So, how do we live in such a way that we know how to check our fuel and create the pace for our journey that gets us where we want to go?

It begins with a fueling plan.

Different Seasons, Different Fuel Needs

None of us can run at one speed or use one fuel type for all the stages of life. That's not the message of this chapter.

Just as your vehicle has different gears and can run on regular or premium unleaded (or perhaps battery), you must have the freedom to shift speeds and fuels as well. Not every few minutes, but over time based on what you're facing and what your heart needs in each part of the journey.

Each of us requires a different pace for the different seasons of life. Sometimes we are moving too fast and other times we are afraid to move out at all. And most often we vacillate between the two extremes. Both ends of the spectrum require courage—whether the need is to slow down or get going.

Power comes from freeing your accelerator to go at the pace that's optimal for you. The same is true for what fuels you. That's why pulling over occasionally is so essential. The process is designed to disrupt the status quo long enough for you to reset your speed, your destination, and your dreams. For a "crossroads" refresher, you may want to refer back to Chapter 4.

The point is to be aware and intentional in the process. Doing so requires asking yourself questions that reveal your specific fuel needs.

I'll share some relevant questions I regularly ask myself, based on the various roles I hold, the commitments I have, and the dreams ahead of me.

What do I need as a coach who engages in multiple, intense conversations each day—not just to be fully present, but to fully enjoy this trusted role I have with others?

What do I need as a wife to love my husband well?

What do I need to parent two teenage children? And the stage after that?

What do I need to enjoy the many relationships in my life?

What do I need to have energy to volunteer and give back to my community?

What do I need to feed my creative talents on a regular basis?

What do I need to pursue that next big dream on the horizon?

I call this focus on what fuels me my Thrive Plan. In the next section, we'll look at how I moved from the questions that helped me think about it to actually living it.

COURAGE

My Thrive Plan

It's time to discover how to actually live your Thrive Plan.

Two quick upfront notes. We're revisiting the concept of thriving here. You'll recall Chapter 5 was titled *Survive or Thrive?* While we're taking it to the next level here, you may want to review the foundational premise of thriving from that chapter first. Second, this process will take some trial and error before you find what works for you. So temper your eagerness with patience. The long-term results will be worth it.

Here's what my Thrive Plan (currently) looks like on a daily, weekly, monthly, and annual basis:

DAILY:

- Early morning start with a lit candle, cup of tea or a latte, meditation/prayer, and inspiring literature that feeds my soul. This can last from twenty minutes up to two hours, depending on my schedule.

- Some sort of exercise—maybe a twenty-minute run or some sort of cardio, yoga/stretching, weights, or a hike. If I'm really busy, I can usually fit in a little bit of everything in under an hour.

- I try not to work past 5:00 p.m. most days so I can be fully present when my children come home. That means I usually don't book clients past 3:00 p.m. I've found this is what I need to gently transition away from work projects to being fully present with my family.

- Nature is very important for me, and I need a daily dose of some sort of outside time. Whether it's a walk around the park across the street on my breaks or simply sipping my tea on the patio, spending time in nature is like a warm blanket on a cold night that contrasts a harsh and fast-paced world. Just spending time in it reminds me how we are meant to grow as human beings. Blooming flowers are never in a hurry.

WEEKLY:

- I began to notice that most weeks, between parenting and coaching, I was exhausted by Thursday. So I made a shift. I take clients four days a week, keeping Friday unscheduled to either catch up with work, write, or simply play. It is this unscheduled time that breathes life into me, helps me unplug, allows me to spend time on areas I've been neglecting, and ignites my creativity.

- I also try to turn off my phone along with all other screens one day each weekend. Doing so helps me live fully in the present without unnecessary distractions. Some weeks, it feels a bit like going through withdrawals, but this makes it all the more important to take these technology breaks. I don't want to live addicted to the intensity of this world, but not doing so requires intentionality.

MONTHLY:

- Taking a full day off once a month to just go play and do whatever I enjoy is critical for me. This is a time to engage with whatever makes my heart come alive. Nothing productive or responsible. Simply fun. It may be a hike, a travel destination, hanging out with a close

COURAGE

friend, cooking, hosting, gardening, painting, or simply doing things I love around the house as I take an afternoon break and catch up on a good book.

ANNUALLY:

- "MeRetreats" is a term I coined for times just for me. This usually involves an overnighter (or two) where I step away from everyone and everything. I have many fond memories of times in hotels, vineyards, beaches, and exploring little towns off the highway. It's a time to relax, enjoy good foods, appreciate nature, beauty, and all that feeds my soul. Simply put, it is a time to get to know myself outside of all the roles I hold and pressures of life that start building up. On my last MeRetreat, I found out how much I love exploring back country roads and stopping at little roadside cafés. Discovering forgotten towns, learning the history, sampling the foods, and enjoying their unique shops. Even now, I smile as I remember spending over two hours with a good book at a little café, eating one of the best sandwiches I have ever had on homemade bread with a side of truffle chips (which the locals called "crack chips") and a fresh-baked molasses cookie. Does it get any better than this? Quiet times to rest, slow down, explore, feel alive, and get to know yourself a little better are the purposes of MeRetreats. I come back filled up and ready to step back into my life with new energy and creativity.

That's my Thrive Plan for this season in life (working full time with two teenage kids); it looked much different when we had no children . . . or two toddlers. See what I mean? Knowing how to assess and create your Thrive Plan on a regular basis is an important way to refuel since life is always changing.

One of the biggest mistakes I see people make is trying to live the same way when their lives have drastically changed. I was recently talking to an overwhelmed and frustrated working mom with three young children trying to keep up with a life that she had lived before kids. She needed a new Thrive Plan that realistically matched the season of life she was living.

Now let's create yours!

Your Thrive Plan

There's nothing like a personal Thrive Plan for refueling on a regular basis. You're going to do just that in the exercise at the end of this chapter.

But before you begin, I want you to be aware of three challenges when creating sustainable Thrive Plans:

1. THE PLAN CAN BE A MOVING TARGET.

As life changes, so will your refueling plan. For instance, as I'm writing this, we are living in the middle of the COVID-19 pandemic. It is our second month of quarantining as a family and with kids out of school and my husband no longer traveling, my once peaceful life has become unusually, well . . . intense. The quiet hours I used to keep around the school schedule are now drastically different as we adjust to homeschooling and online classes. In addition, the intensity of my coaching conversations has grown both in number and heightened stress as people are coping with the changes they're incurring and the fear swirling around them.

COURAGE

My Thrive Plan to refuel had to be adjusted as I rose to meet the challenges before me. For instance, my daily time right now looks more like this:

- Getting up earlier to have closer to two hours of time in the morning where I read or listen to inspiring literature that energizes me and focuses me for the day.

- A daily two/three-mile walk or run listening to podcasts and music that feeds my soul and gets me out of the office and the home for a much-needed break.

- Winding down in the evening with a casual walk or relaxing on my front porch with my hubby or good friends.

Life is slower during this season, but also more intense with the fears of the unknown and schedule changes for clients and family due to the pandemic. Embracing this new pace of life while staying in control with what fuels me is critical.

2. LOOK FOR UNEXPECTED OPENINGS IN YOUR SCHEDULE.

These unplanned windows are perfect opportunities to refuel rather than always getting the next thing done. For instance, when a client cancels and my schedule opens up unexpectedly for an hour, I pause and consider what I most need for my heart as well as for my to-do list. What would most refuel me? Getting some work done and feeling accomplished? Or pulling back and enjoying a song or podcast that feeds my soul? Maybe a friend I want to call? There's no right or wrong about whether to be productive or pull back—both can be refueling. It's about knowing which you need and giving yourself permission to do it.

COURAGE

3. GO SLOW DURING SEASONS OF GRIEF.

All of us have gone through seasons of grieving. And, given the world we're in, there's likely more of those times (unfortunately) ahead of us. The idea of "thriving" during grieving feels cruel and insensitive. Refueling during a time of grieving looks very different. I learned this with my father passing. What I normally did on my Thrive Plan no longer worked. It was as if I had to take each day in first gear instead of shifting up to fifth gear throughout the day. Where I would normally get ten to twenty things done in a day, it was now more realistic to be fine with accomplishing three items. I intentionally slowed my life to a much kinder pace. I took on fewer clients, stepped away from intense projects, became selective about who I spent time with, accomplished fewer goals, and honored my need to simply slow down and keep life simple.

Becoming more mindful of what you need to refuel requires the same deep kindness. Stay curious without self-judgment or shame. Be intentional about what and how you need to refuel in the season of life that you're in. It's beautifully unique for each person—and awkwardly complex because we are complex human beings. But stay with it. Have the courage to find what you need to refuel and create your Thrive Plan around it. And don't be afraid of adjusting it as often as you need.

If you are weary, dear reader, like many of us are, I am hopeful that you will have the courage to find exactly what you need.

COURAGE

In the words of an old Irish blessing:

May the road rise to meet you
May the wind be always at your back
May the sun shine warm upon your face
The rains fall soft upon your fields
And until we meet again
May God hold you
in the palm of His hand.[12]

COURAGE

12. While this Celtic prayer originated in ancient Ireland, the author is unknown.

COURAGE QUESTION

What regular practices help you find the fuel
needed to grow your courage? How often do
you practice them?

Now it's time to design your personal Thrive Plan for refueling:[13]

DAILY (15 Minutes to 1 Hour)

What can you do daily that fuels you?

WEEKLY (2 to 4 Hours)

What can you do weekly that fuels you?

MONTHLY (Full Day)

What can you do monthly that fuels you?

ANNUALLY (2 to 3+ Days)

What can you do annually that fuels you?

COURAGE

13. These suggested times are just general guidelines. If you're unsure about the duration, always do
what feels right for you.

> **CAUTION:** Never stop being mindful about your need to refuel. How you do it will change with the various seasons of life. Just like a car (or your body), you have to consistently refuel. Your spirit, too, requires the same consistent refueling so you can live well.

As you refuel with your Thrive Plan, it's important to know what is pulling against you. I mean, if this were easy, we'd all be blissfully thriving, right? Clearly, that's not the case. Outside forces pull on us and distract us. In the next chapter, we'll discuss the invisible pulls and how recognizing them can lead to a greater sense of freedom.

COURAGE

THE INVISIBLE PULL

Combating the Illusion of "Can't"

I was in water up to my neck . . . and it was getting deeper by the second. The river was warm from the August midday sun blazing down.

Did I mention the river was in the middle of the Belizean jungle? Yep, my work in "education breaking the cycle of poverty" led me deep into the rain forest visiting villages and schools far off the beaten path. The beauty in the country of Belize is unparalleled anywhere on Earth.

While there, I had to get out and explore. Life is an adventure and all that jazz, right?

I just wasn't expecting quite this much adventure. But the desire of living without regret was influencing me.

What if I came to the rainforest of Belize and never explored it?

What if I was the only one of my friends too afraid to swim in the river?

What if I missed out on a once-in-a-lifetime
memory due to a lack of courage?

I knew I'd be disappointed in myself if I didn't enter the river with the group I had traveled with. And as my husband Darren had accompanied me, he was eager to get out and explore. This was an adventure I would never have taken had I been solo. But I was with good people excited to venture out and discover this exotic setting.

Still, having never been in a jungle before, my senses were on high alert. I'd heard rumors there were jaguars in the area. And I couldn't help but notice the handmade sign by the edge of the river with a picture of a crocodile painted on it. Good grief!

My pulse was racing as I continued swimming forward. I was torn between leaping out of the water and joining the small group swimming ahead of me.

I made it a little farther, coming to a stop near huge boulders that jutted out of the water. Whew! I congratulated myself for keeping calm and staying adventurous. I sighed in relief. Until I saw one of my friends next to a huge boulder that jutted into the river dive deep into the murky water. Several seconds went by and she didn't resurface. Uh-oh. I thought of the crocodile sign.

Seconds later, I heard her voice coming from somewhere inside the rock. "Come on!" she shouted. "I found an underwater cave!" One by one each person from our group dove under only to resurface seconds later shouting from inside the cave.

Did my courage increase as I witnessed this? Absolutely not. It had taken every ounce of willpower to get to this point. But now I was supposed to dive into the murky water and hope

COURAGE

I make it to an underwater cave? You ask too much, my dear friends.

I froze. Something in me longed to go forward, but there was also an invisible pull that warned me to leave this uncertain situation as fast as I could. Was this a time to be brave and push through my fear? Or listen to it and get out of there?

What Blocks Courage?

There's not always a simple answer to situations like I found myself in. Sometimes the most courageous thing to do is to decline, step away, disengage, and say NO. But there are also times when we're supposed to step forward, engage, and say YES. When we do, it's like something powerful propels us onward. And when we don't, it's like something blocks our courage when we need it most.

This mysterious force that pulls at us in both helpful and unhelpful ways is hard to explain. Whether it's to step into that conversation you know you need to have or to take that business risk that will grow your company, there's an invisible pull on each human to do more and be more. That's good. But here's the problem, what's pulling at us isn't always helpful. Other things pull at us and disrupt the courage we require to move forward and take the necessary risk. The longing and the desire to be fully present or try new things pulls at all of us at different times in our lives.

What is this force that either engages or disengages our courage, helping us sometimes and dashing our hopes other times? I call it the Invisible Pull.

And what influences it? If we knew that, we could be aware when it was an asset and when it was blocking us from the life we're made for.

COURAGE

That day in the Belizean jungle, I could sure feel it. I desperately wanted to take that dive and believed I could do it, but something was pulling at my courage.

And when something pulls at your courage, that's a sign it isn't good.

I heard my friends deep inside the cave calling for me to join them. I longed to be brave, but I was terrified. The pull comes from inside us *and* from outside us. Knowing *what* the invisible pull is and what's behind it is the challenge we face when we dare to risk.

Only when we understand what comes against our courage, can we understand what we are fighting.

In the past chapters, we've talked about what engages and grows our courage. But what about the things that wither and disengage it?

"Can't" Magnets

It's time to explore what blocks your courage so you can then reject that pull in your life.

Clearly, fear is the obvious answer to what blocks our courage. Fear has many variations. Fear of failing, disappointing, or not getting it right. But let's dig a little deeper. How does fear show itself in our day-to-day lives?

When fear pulls on our courage, we have an overwhelming sense that we can't do something—or we can't be who we need to be in that moment.

We can't hope.

We can't show up.

We can't believe in a positive outcome.

COURAGE

We can't dare to boldly step out in new ways.
We can't risk.

In my work with engaging and growing courage—both in my own journey and in the journey of others—I have witnessed seven forces that create a negative invisible pull. I refer to these seven forces as "Can't Magnets" because it's as if there's a gravitational pull under us that's so strong, we are immobilized. These "Can't Magnets" keep us paralyzed in the present, unable to move forward toward our dreams or our true potential.

Let's name these seven forces because knowing them is the first step to overcoming them. In no particular order, they are:

- Cynicism
- Control
- Closed-mindedness
- Cold-heartedness
- Complaining
- Condemning
- Criticizing

This may come as a surprise, but in small doses, the above traits can sometimes be helpful in setting boundaries, critical thinking, and avoiding the "follow the pack" mentality. Not always, but on occasion. But in large doses, not so. They each have the power to derail a team, break a relationship, and prevent you from taking smart risks to level up. And they tend to create a culture of fear.

I'll share a real-world example of how these forces derailed a once-successful company I was hired to coach. What makes this such a powerful case study is how all seven traits came together to fuel the toxic environment in this organization.

Where once conversations happened with ease, people were now gossiping about one another, betraying confidences, and blaming not just individuals but groups for all that had gone wrong with the company. I can still remember one of the leaders looking me in the eye, almost as a warning, and saying, "You don't understand how broken we are." Well, I soon found out.

By the time I got involved, they were having a rocky time creating a trust-based culture with strong lines of open and healthy communication. The leadership team desperately wanted breakthrough but were actually doing things that resulted in one breakdown after another. No breakthrough was possible until the multiple levels of breakdowns were addressed.

What had happened to cause a once strong, open, and healthy culture to turn into one that was resentful, blaming, and bitter? The entire culture was paralyzed by "Can't Magnets" that kept them stuck in unhealthy ways of relating and created an invisible pull away from courage. Over the next several months, I narrowed it down to these seven issues.

1. CYNICISM
"Things always go back to the way they were—good change never sticks here."

2. CONTROL
"Anybody who tries to help us is an outsider and can't be trusted."

3. CLOSED-MINDEDNESS
"None of these leadership tools is worth learning or applying."

4. COLD-HEARTEDNESS
"I don't care what he's going through. He doesn't deserve a break."

5. COMPLAINING
"This place can't get it right."

6. CONDEMNING
"Look at _____ always messing up. It's their fault we're failing." (Blaming and finger-pointing)

7. CRITICIZING
"It's leadership's fault—all they do is sit in their office and order us around. The core values of this company are a joke!"

These were actual statements and sentiments I heard repeated at every level of the company. You know what this taught me? Someone was starting this language, and it was contagious.

Why does this happen with people? The simple answer is this. As humans, we all experience disappointment, pain, and fear. But it's how we respond that makes the difference.

The invisible pull behind the "Can't Magnets" is pain and a deep ache from life not working out as we hoped. Over time, and often unknowingly, a toxic trade gets made.

Cynicism replaces hope.

Control replaces freedom.

Closed-mindedness replaces trust.

Cold-heartedness replaces compassion.

Complaining replaces belief.

Condemning replaces grace.

Criticizing replaces kindness.

Life becomes even harder because of our response to the pain and complexities of the human condition.

Be Heroic and Pull the Other Way

But here's the good news. Once we identify the source, we can start fighting these factors.

That begins with having the courage to believe a better option is possible. And then using that courage to take the first step. What that looks like is this. While in the midst of a hard situation, reach for hope, freedom, trust, compassion, belief, grace, or kindness. These are the antidotes to fighting the invisible pull.

More importantly, we can influence those around us as we start changing the language to one of optimism. People are waiting to be called out for hopeful options and inspiring culture. Nobody likes following negativity or joining teams stuck in attitudes of "can't." Humans are naturally drawn to positive leadership.

But remember, the company I was coaching was struggling with the gravitational pull of all seven "Can't Magnets." Before any lasting transformation could occur, I first had to change the language that was harming the culture. It wasn't just a matter of not saying certain phrases or words. I had to help create new language that not only confronted the attitude of "can't," but that ushered in new courage and a fresh perspective.

One by one, I began to call out individuals to fight against the invisible pull. Yes, there was some resistance (okay, a lot), but courage is what helped me stay the course. Over time, people began to respond as I systematically started confronting the seven driving forces that powered the "Can't Magnets" by strategically pulling in the opposite direction.

COURAGE

Change takes time. You can be part of what sustains it. (Hope)

*Outside voices help offer new insights
and fresh perspectives.* (Freedom)

*Leadership tools are critical to changing a culture,
and you get to figure out which ones work for you.* (Trust)

*We can work hard to meet people where they are in life
and still hold high standards for results.* (Compassion)

*Each of us has a critical role to play
that is part of the solution.* (Belief)

*Learning from mistakes is an essential process
for sustainable growth.* (Grace)

*It is important to have the constructive conversations
that add value to the relationship as we hold
accountability together.* (Kindness)

It took time and many hard conversations, but it was powerful to see these new phrases start to replace the old ones. Years later, I now hear hundreds of employees courageously using these life-giving terms. This was only possible when they were offered new ways to address and combat the invisible pull to break the power of the "Can't Magnets."

Just this past year, I was on-site with this impressive company and witnessed leader after leader calling out employees to proactively recognize personal areas of growth in their teams. At every level, employees were responding as their leaders infused the teams with hope, freedom, trust, compassion, belief, grace,

COURAGE

and kindness—all while holding standards high and getting big results.

This is why it is so important to understand this invisible pull against courage. When you know what you're fighting, you know what weapon to reach for.

When you feel cynical, don't stay stuck there. Understand the pain and disappointment behind it and find where you can reach for hope.

When you want to control or are feeling controlled, reach for freedom.

When you feel closed-minded and struck, reach for trust—trust in yourself, trust in others, and trust in the process.

When your heart feels cold after too many hits and disappointments, dig deep and find compassion.

When you hear the complaints coming steadily out of your mouth and growing at a surprising rate, reach for something to believe in.

When you feel like condemning your neighbor, friend, leader, or spouse, reach for grace.

And when the criticizing is coming fast and furious, find kindness.

COURAGE

Courage to pull the other way is what is needed when these harmful influences show themselves. Isn't this what our world is lacking? More courageous people who offer the opposite of hurtful behavior. This is one of the bravest choices I watch people make. Those who live heroically choose to courageously offer:

Hope when they encounter Cynicism.

Freedom when they encounter Control.

Trust when they encounter Closed-mindedness.

Compassion when they encounter Cold-heartedness.

Belief when they encounter Complaining.

Grace with they encounter Condemnation.

Kindness when they encounter Criticism.

See how you can strategically and bravely pull the other way when you identify what is coming against you? Courage is what's needed to *see* what is pulling at you and not give in—and to then *reach* for something that pulls the other way.

It's time for you to practice courage in the very areas where you are feeling an invisible pull.

The Empathy Antidote

Much of what is behind the attitude of "can't" is driven by fear and pain. It is a protective-posturing reaction to previous heartache and disappointment. Knowing this helps me meet people where they are. This can happen only when we recognize the invisible pull from courage is due to the wounds caused by things that have hurt us in life.

This is especially true with people you may know who are angry and easily triggered by anything you have to offer. They

COURAGE

have been pulled down for so long by "Can't Magnets" that it colors how they view everything in their world.

Eventually, this keeps them isolated as they slowly start to turn on everyone and everything. They need a lifeline—a way out to face the invisible pulls and the pain behind them. Empathy helps protect us from taking it personally, especially when it is directed at us.

I distinctly remember a client, Sandi, accusing me of trying to control her and force her to think a certain way. I was shocked! Immediately, I felt defensive and angry at the false accusation, but I stayed curious and then reached for empathy. Here's how the conversation went.

Me: I'm not sure why you're saying this to me, but I care. Would you like to tell me why you're feeling this way?

Sandi: NO! I'm not telling you anything! You think you can just come in here and start telling me what to do?

Nothing was making sense. *Then why did she call me?* I wondered. I also felt irritation and offense wanting to take hold of my emotions. Reactions like "I don't have to put up with this!" were trying to creep in. But staying curious allowed me to remain empathetic. I could sense the fear. The conversation continued.

Me: It always gets to be your choice. What would you like to do?

Sandi: (Silence.)

COURAGE

Me: Are you still there?

Sandi: Yes.

Me: Here's what I can promise you, if you'd like to talk, I will listen without judgment and shame and with only grace and compassion. And if at any point, you don't like what I'm saying, you get to say STOP, and I will stop and wait.

Sandi: Okay.

Me: Where would you like to start?

Sandi then began to share an overview of her story. And in minutes, I had a very clear picture. I learned Sandi had a history of controlling people—more specifically, women—in her life. Her story included many relationships where she was consistently met with judgment, shame, and guilt as a way to get her to behave in a certain way.

Aha. Now I understood what was going on. She was confusing me for another controlling woman in her life. Now I had an abundance of empathy for Sandi. Don't you? We've all felt controlled at some point in our lives. It is a powerless feeling. When it happens, we naturally want to fight it, right? To kick and scream and escape whatever is making us feel that way.

Freedom was what Sandi needed, and I was happy to help her find it. This began a beautiful coaching relationship that lasted for several years. Weekly, I listened intently as she communicated who she was and what she wanted. Empathy was what helped me value her unique purpose and identify who she was and who she wanted to become.

COURAGE

As complex as these seven driving forces can be (whether in you, others, or your workplace culture), the good news is that the antidote is quite simple. You can prevent them from infecting your courage through empathy. Yes, it's that simple.

That certainly was the case with Sandi. I feel lucky to have worked with her. You may find it interesting that she's no longer a client—and that's actually good news. Because she found the direction she wanted to go and got moving. But I do still hear from her. Once in a while she'll reach out and tell me about her latest adventure. Today, she's running a large company with several hundred employees. She's fluent in several languages and designs curriculum to support educational systems around the world. What a unique life she is living. It makes me smile.

Pilots and Mechanics

I hope you're convinced by now of the power of these seven infectors of courage. They are hard to recognize at times. They may feel impossible to overcome. And if left unchecked, they can break the spirit of a person or group over time.

Yet, as we saw with Sandi's story, empathy is what breaks the hold of this invisible pull.

This became even more clear to me while working with an organization where most of the people were either mechanics or pilots. Pause. I know what you're thinking. No, I'm not a pilot or mechanic. And yes, I was in a room full of them. To coach them.

I distinctly remember a supervisor of that group challenging me in front of the entire leadership team. He stood and loudly asked how I could be successful in helping them when I was neither a mechanic nor a pilot. With all eyes on me, I had a split second to decide how I was going to respond. I could feel the cynicism and the criticism and yet, I felt the pull of something else . . . curiosity. And with that came courage.

Did it feel good to be put on the spot like this in front of a group of people? No.

But honestly it was a fair question and remaining objective helped me not take it personally. This supervisor had the right to ask this important question. He needed answers. His team deserved to know I could handle hard questions, even when there was no easy answer. In that moment, I chose empathy. When I did, the atmosphere within me, and in the room, began to shift.

I saw the fear and knew they needed reassurance. They could put their faith in me because I knew my area of expertise and respected theirs. Without a doubt, nobody wanted me fixing or flying a plane! But I did know how to build results-driven, high-functioning teams. I empathized with the leaders in this room who were nervous about the state of their company. I made eye contact with each of them as I shared my optimism and calmly assured them we were in it together. I would have to trust them to be the experts in their industry, and they would have to trust me to be the expert in mine. Together, we had the potential to be the team this company needed to open lines of communication again and increase the trust.

Within my roughly two-minute response driven by empathy, I witnessed the driving forces behind the sense of "can't" in the room wither. And the fear previously driving the conversation was replaced with hope. The supervisor relaxed. The team leaned in. Heads nodded. And I was hired, not just for a project, but in many coaching relationships within the company that continued for years afterward. Empathy became the driving force to engage

COURAGE

new attitudes of optimism, develop strong leadership, restructure teams, and empower behavior that led to higher results.

The man's initial attitude of "can't" was based on the belief: *You can't do this because you're not like us, and you don't have our experience.* Was the invisible pull behind this mind-set discouraging? Absolutely. But rather than react to it, we can choose to courageously reach for empathy and offer an opportunity to address the fears, confront the beliefs, and ultimately build trust. Empathy allows us to see how life can break us down and stop us from hoping. In this instance, they were facing significant challenges as a group and needed to know what and who to trust to help them come up with new solutions.

See what a powerful antidote empathy is to overcome the paralyzing "Can't Magnets"? Even when I've had to have hard discussions, acknowledge the elephants in the room that people had been hiding for far too long, nothing shifts the atmosphere quicker than empathy. But make no mistake, it takes courage to do this when you might be the only one combating the invisible pull.

Back to Belize

Yes, we left me dogpaddling in the water for most of this chapter. But now it's time to continue my story.

First, let me name the invisible pull coming against me. The specific "Can't Magnets" that kept me paralyzed were control and close-mindedness. I had less control than I wanted in the situation. And my mind could not open itself to a new possibility. I longed for freedom and trust but didn't know how to summon them in a situation that was totally unfamiliar and had no guaranteed outcome.

COURAGE

Now remember, the invisible pull in and of itself is neither bad nor good. Stay curious with yourself. Sometimes this is wisdom telling you, *Definitely* do not *try this on your own; it will not go well for you.* And it is important to listen to this. But other times, you know you will be so disappointed in yourself if you did not try it.

There I was in the water. Being the only one now left outside the underwater cave, I knew I would be forever bummed if I didn't join the group in this adventure. For my own heart, I needed to try this and desperately wanted to believe I could do it. Plus, I took courage in their success. It's so much easier to be brave when someone has gone before you, huh?

I could hear my friends' voices cheering me on, encouraging me to join them, and shouting advice on how to do it. But it still wasn't enough. Trusting whose voice to listen to was critical.

It wasn't until my husband took the dive and resurfaced safely in the underwater cave that I decided I was going for it. I can still remember him guiding me through the steps in how to dive and how far to swim forward. Knowing what I needed to summon my courage, he gave me step-by-step instructions as he told me to swim a couple seconds forward before I resurfaced. If I tried to come up too soon, I would hit the bottom of the rock and not be able to come up for air. (I still remember resisting the urge to panic when he said these words, visualizing myself trapped without air.)

With Darren's encouragement, I broke the invisible pull and took the plunge.

It was such an exhilarating moment when I successfully resurfaced next to my party of friends gathered inside that underwater cave. I felt victorious! It stands as a poignant memory because I realized the courage I carried within me.

COURAGE

Remember in the bracelet allegory, the girl learns that she gets to be cherished for who she truly is without her bracelets. But she must be courageous enough to take action and do something about it.

Yes, that's it! We only learn who we are and who we are meant to be by daring to act.

This is your courage. Start doing what your true self is begging you to try. Whether it's a dive in an underwater cave, going on a MeRetreat, starting that business venture, or having a needed heart conversation with a friend.

Do it.

That's the only way to learn who you are so you can step into the life you were made for.

In the words of Coach Taylor from the television series *Friday Night Lights*: "Clear Eyes. Full Heart. Can't Lose."

Hold on to that picture of courage. And remember, I am rooting with all my heart for your raging success.

COURAGE

COURAGE QUESTION
What is pulling at your courage?

Which of the seven "Can't Magnets" pulls at you the most?

What gives that negative trait such pull in your life?

How might you use empathy more frequently with yourself and others?

CAUTION: Don't forget that the invisible pull isn't inherently bad or good. The trick is knowing how to interpret what is giving you pause—and then proceeding accordingly.

COURAGE

The invisible pull behind courage is vital to staying alert and aware, but there's one more important practical tool we must use to help us deal with the complexities of life. There are no easy answers or quick fixes for the life you're made for. But there is a proven path—and you're on it. Keep reading to understand how the necessity of holding tensions helps us balance the complexities of becoming who we are meant to be.

HOLDING TENSIONS

The Value of Balance in an Either/Or World

We spend most of our lives trying to avoid tension. You don't need me to tell you that's a waste of time.

Since we can't avoid it, we do everything in our power to minimize it. To "untense" the situation. Our average may be slightly better than avoidance. But it's probably fifty-fifty at best.

What's going on here? On the surface, avoiding tension sounds good. The less stress in our lives the better. But tension and stress aren't the same thing.

The better question is this: Is a lack of tension really a good thing?

It's not if you want to jump on a trampoline. You want the springs to pull the stretchy fabric as taut as possible. The more tension, the higher you can jump. Sometimes you even feel as if you can touch the clouds above. But when the springs wear out, the surface of the trampoline starts to sag—as does your joy.

Let's look at another example.

There's a scientific concept known as surface tension. Surface tension acts as though an elastic membrane has been stretched over the surface of a liquid, allowing items to actually remain on top of the water instead of sinking.[14] Because of surface tension, insects like "water striders" can actually run across the surface of water.

We may refer to people doing the seemingly impossible, such as "walking on water." But, at least in the insect world, it is a common occurrence.

Okay, I hear you saying, *So tension has some positive aspects. But I'm not a trampoline or an insect; how can it help me?*

I'll offer one more example. This one hits a little closer to home.

We all love a good story. Whether you prefer novels, movies, or binge-watching the latest Netflix series, a well-told story has immense power to pull us in and impact us in deep ways.

Have you ever noticed that every good story has a key ingredient—regardless of the kind of story? Give up?

It's tension. A plot without tension is a story where nothing happens.

Think of your favorite movie. And now imagine how different it would be without tension.

> Once upon a time there was a man and a woman. They loved each other, had plenty of money, and faced no problems. No loss to overcome. No dreams unfilled. No journey to take. The end.

Boring, right?

---

14. "Surface Tension," Encyclopedia Britannica, accessed January 2, 2021, https://www.britannica.com/science/surface-tension.

In the same way, your life—with no tension—would be stagnant and boring.

The positive aspects of tension is a new concept for most of the folks I coach. It's counterintuitive—and wildly helpful. Because if tension plays an essential role in our lives, the goal isn't to avoid it, but to understand it. By doing so, we can hold it in the right way.

That's what this chapter is all about.

Strength and Sensitivity

Walking into the first day of my new job was intimidating. I was a young teacher who had worked with little kids between the ages of eight and ten. You know, the cute years. They liked to hug, write you notes, and thought all your jokes were funny.

But this new assignment was totally foreign to me. I had walked into a classroom of over thirty junior-high schoolers in East Los Angeles in the middle of January. I was there because my predecessor had left abruptly. This is highly irregular in the field of education and rather uncomfortable to step into.

There were a lot of questions without many answers. Why had she left? Where were her notes? What did the students know? What did they still need to know?

And there was a lot of newness for me. New grade level. New district. New curriculum. New "at-risk" population. New language barrier. And more than 130 students waiting for me to teach them Language Arts and Drama.

Yes, this situation was filled with tension. Yet it was one of my favorite assignments. Why? Shouldn't we run from tense situations? Nope. We should run from boring, stale situations.

COURAGE

And I was getting bored in my current environment. I wasn't being stretched and, deep down, I was in need of a new challenge.

With this new urban district, I had certainly found one. After assessing the aptitude levels, I quickly realized that most of them were reading and writing at a much lower grade level, dealing with significant language barriers (over 90 percent Latino), and many were struggling with all the challenges that come into play with low socioeconomic populations.

But I enjoyed being able to step into this situation and offer help. Even more, I absolutely loved the students. Without question, they taught me as much (or more) than I taught them. We learned together.

It was in my years of teaching in East LA that I learned the necessity of holding tensions—and the courage required to hold them well. Because we all crave the resolve of an answer and quick solution. But staying in the uncomfortableness of unresolve and recognizing that life doesn't always have easy answers is hard. Courage is needed to live in these tensions—especially working with kids. Facing the challenges surrounding at-risk and low socioeconomic populations is complex and multi-faceted. Compound it with the fact that they are in middle school and you soon realize there are no quick fixes or easy solutions, but rather a myriad of tensions to hold.

The best example of holding tensions is to picture a see-saw. Remember those? I don't see them on playgrounds much anymore, and I think I know why. My siblings and I were always trying to throw each other off as we shifted our weight or unexpectedly jumped off. Now visualize Strength and Sensitivity sitting on each end. If keeping it balanced is the goal, tipping too far either way can be costly. Too much sensitivity and you'll get run over as a teacher, but too much strength and you'll overpower the students. Balanced together, Strength and Sensitivity become a winning combination that mentors and guides students to learn and realize potential. And to hold this tension well requires courage. Courage to hold authority when necessary and courage to offer comfort in moments of vulnerability.

The necessity of holding this tension and adopting this mind-set came as I found myself immersed in a cross-cultural education, low socioeconomic population who struggled with academic blocks. Plus, all the challenges of teaching at the junior-high age level. (Remember those years? Some of my most painful and awkward, for sure.) Moreover, I was dealing with external influences such as gangs, suicides, school shootings, and teenage pregnancies. Devastatingly, one faculty member committed suicide during the same era in which we experienced the terror of Columbine. It was a hard time to teach this age and this population.

Entering into this school situation, I intuitively sensed the energy and opportunity that healthy tension brought. But I was about to discover there's more than just tapping into tension. It's a matter of holding and wielding it courageously.

And that comes from better understanding the two attributes of Strength and Sensitivity.

Before going further, let's pause and separate them so we can understand their unique attributes and individual benefits. I'll use my school situation to illuminate each since that is the real-world training ground where I learned how to hold the tension of strength and sensitivity.

We'll begin with Strength. In my East LA classroom, strength meant having the courage to:

COURAGE

- confront disruptive behavior
- maintain high standards
- expect students to work hard

I wanted these students to succeed, but the answer wasn't in lowering the bar on expectations. It was raising the bar on what was possible and then helping them meet it.

It requires strength to ask for more than what seems possible at first glance. It takes courage to not simply shrug and take the path of least resistance. To not just throw up your hands and let life happen. After all, what can just one person do?

But it is strength that shuts down passive ways of thinking. The students needed someone who believed in them and invited them into the seemingly impossible. That required a strong, courageous leader.

But strength isn't enough, and in fact, by itself can have the opposite effect. Without sensitivity, strength can become a cold, unrelenting force that demands results without understanding a person's story.

That's why we need the simultaneous power of Sensitivity. In my classroom, sensitivity meant having the courage to:

- build a relational bridge between myself and the students
- identify their challenging blocks
- understand their need for comfort, kindness, safety, and empathy
- foster a culture of respect

Sensitivity recognizes the importance of telling the students how much I believe in them and how their stories matter. Once they trusted that I really cared, they would write in their

COURAGE

journals and earmark a page they wanted me to read. I also kept a locked box on my desk for them to write notes that I could respond to later.

My goal was to help them feel valued and safe every time they entered my classroom. I wanted it to be their sanctuary. After researching how to engage the right side of the brain to nurture peace, I started each class with ten minutes of classical music and let them draw and write and create. Basically, a time of respite from a stressful world. It stilled their minds and hearts and helped them relax before transitioning into a time of learning.

These positive aspects of sensitivity played a huge role in transforming my class into a place of peace, personal value, and respect. And yet, I was after more than just a peaceful gathering place.

So many organizations and people today seek peace but don't realize it comes with strength. Imagine if a country said: We stand for peace. But we have no army or security forces or means to protect ourselves. We just want other nations to respect our desire to be peaceful and safe. It would sure be nice if that was enough, but it isn't. Peace comes through strength.

And in my classroom, sensitivity by itself wasn't enough either. Students didn't just need my sympathy or empathy. Yes, I wanted a place where they felt understood and safe while also challenging them to rise to new heights and reach untapped potential.

Two Are Stronger than One

Now it's time to bring Strength and Sensitivity together.

While working with this urban population, I got a firsthand look at how education breaks the cycle of poverty. My focus was to help them take pride in being productive and contributing members of society—the ultimate goal for all educators.

COURAGE

In our class, we had an average-level, statewide literature book for the students to read. But they were not able to get through it since much of the vocabulary was over their heads. That, combined with language challenges, made comprehension impossible.

The answer wasn't brute strength, demanding they just slog through it. Nor was it being so sensitive that I lowered the standards and my expectations. The solution came from a fusion of strength and sensitivity. I brought in a book more relatable to their lives and started teaching spelling and vocabulary to increase their language aptitude. And it worked.

In a short amount of time, the student passing rate in writing went from a dismal 30 percent to an impressive 70 percent. This was critical because their ability to write an essay well was key to getting them enrolled for high school. A high school diploma is what helps break the cycle of poverty—opening the door to college, keeping them off the streets, and increasing their marketability for decent jobs.

One of the hardest memories in holding the tension of strength and sensitivity occurred when a student confided in me that a teacher's assistant was abusing groups of children within the school. As soon as I was told, strength made me immediately report it to the administration. But there were children and parents' hearts at stake, too. Sensitivity was required in abundance in the aftermath.

In this same time period, the school experienced a beloved teacher dying two weeks before the semester began, the Columbine shootings occurred, and we encountered a campus-wide lockdown with a threat that had us all huddling under our desks in the dark, waiting for the all-clear from the principal.

COURAGE

These kids had experienced more trauma in a year than I had experienced in a lifetime.

I felt ill-equipped to handle many of these challenges. But during these times, I hung onto this powerful tension of holding the combined power of strength and sensitivity. I was determined to be someone strong enough to advocate and sensitive enough to create safe environments.

During the time we were huddled under our desks in the dark, waiting for the campus to be cleared, I detected some sniffles and whimpers across the classroom. From under my desk, I called out to them. They needed to hear that all would be well and that we were protected. One voice spoke up, asking if I would say a prayer. Others quickly affirmed the request. They requested the Lord's Prayer as it was what they often repeated in their homes, churches, and communities. So, under our desks huddled in the dark, I led them in the Lord's Prayer.

It's a tender memory I will never forget as they taught me that true courage is about being able to offer both protection and comfort—an important tension to hold when we feel scared and powerless. Courage helps us do this well in the moment.

I've carried that lesson with me in my coaching work with people of all ages and companies of all sizes. We all need reassurance that can only come from the combination of Strength and Sensitivity. Showing up well requires courage. Courage to say the truth, offer a hug, be fully present to the joys, pains, aches, and struggle human growth brings. Because there are some days when we want to avoid or react too strongly simply for the sake of a quick resolve rather than face the discomfort of holding a tension.

COURAGE

A Multitude of Tensions

As we focus on holding tensions well and keeping the balance between them, it's not just in the areas of strength and sensitivity. There are many tensions we need the courage to hold well.

Below is a list of common tensions I've come across in my own experience and in my work with clients. There are countless others, but these are plenty for now. Read through them slowly, considering the tension between each pair of words:

Being & Doing

Talking & Listening

Solitude & Community

Work & Play

Asserting & Accommodating

Heart & Head or Feeling & Thinking (Empathetic Response & Critical Thinking)

Objectivity & Subjectivity

Humor & Seriousness

Shallowness & Depth

Authoritative Leadership & Collaborative Leadership

Contending & Releasing

Justice & Mercy

Attaching & Detaching

Engaging & Withdrawing

Joy & Sorrow

Stillness & Activity

Giving & Receiving

Facts & Faith

Action & Rest

Individual & Group

Receptivity & Protectiveness

Individualized & Universal

Teaching & Learning

Affirming & Challenging

Leading & Following

Trusting & Doubting

Read through the list again and circle the five that you have the biggest struggle with. We'll come back to these at the end of the chapter.

We are not either/or—we are both. The more we learn to hold the balancing forces of these tensions, the more integrated and whole we live as humans. Doing so empowers us to respond well to life and offer our best. Courage comes from being willing to recognize the balance needed rather than choosing one extreme and making that your approach to life.

Do you find yourself heavier on one side of the scale, feeling unbalanced? If so, consider moving toward the opposite side to balance the scale. Yes, it will take practice. But don't get frustrated with yourself. Ample grace is needed when stretching in new ways like this. Rather than just a safe space to explore this, level up and offer yourself a Grace Space and stay curious. Give yourself the permission to not only notice it, but grow without shame.

If you are in action much of the time, integrate rest.

If you are thinking most of the time,
then try checking in with your feelings.

If you find yourself listening too much,
step out of your comfort zone and speak up more.

If most of your time is spent in groups,
give yourself solo time and try a MeRetreat.

See what I mean? There's no need to over correct in either direction. You're not trying to eliminate one side or shame yourself for the unbalance, but simply tipping the scales the other way. Recognize where you might want to move in the

COURAGE

other direction, and find your balance. This is what it means to hold tensions.

Why is this so essential? Because if we don't learn how to hold tensions, it causes us to live unbalanced. Even more, it limits who we are and who we can become.

If I'd been overly strong as an educator, I would have missed the relational needs of those around me. And if I'd been overly sensitive, I would not have held them accountable to the high standards that helped them rise to new levels of potential. Haven't we known both types of teachers? Those who were too much of a pushover and those who were overly strict? Unfortunately, these teachers became one-dimensional stereotypes rather than multi-dimensional world changers. It's the ones who learned to hold tensions that we remember with fondness. They knew how to be firm and soft so that students felt safe in the present and capable for whatever the future would bring.

Holding tensions stops us from becoming robotic and from treating those around us like robots. It helps us become more whole humans who refuse to back ourselves or others into no-win corners. It frees us from limiting our choices or marginalizing people groups. Speaking of, if you need an example of the opposite of this, just look at our political system. The political parties seem unable to hold tensions of any kind. Their way is the *only* way. And anyone who wonders about other options is the enemy to defeat. Imagine the potential for at least some common ground if human beings started acting humanely by holding tensions better.

COURAGE

Three Momentum Blockers

The inability to hold tensions actually blocks us in three ways:

1. PREVENTS US FROM ADVANCING

This is the number one block I see with people advancing in their work and growing in the direction they hope to go. The tension of Asserting and Accommodating comes to mind when I think of Bryce. As a young leader newly promoted in his job, we began to work together. His passion to lead was inspiring, but his eagerness to demonstrate his authority was backfiring in painful ways. The once quiet employee had become an overpowering leader. Although it was his strength to assert, it would turn him into a dictatorial tyrant if left unchecked. It's a common trait for many young leaders.

As we worked together, he learned to balance asserting with accommodating. As he did, his leadership grew. Instead of reacting to an employee or customer as he had, he now paused to consider whether to assert or to accommodate. This simple mind-set helped him not swing to either extreme but deal with each situation uniquely. Rather than using a rigid formula, he now had the keys to grow as a balanced leader based on what the situation required.

2. LIMITS OUR RELATIONSHIPS

This next block boxes us in—and boxes others in—while preventing our relationships from growing richer and stronger.

The tension of Talking and Listening is a common one I see in relationships, particularly in families, marriages, and long-term partnerships. In our home, we call it "sharing the talking space." Doing so instills a critical life skill that can make or break relationships.

COURAGE

We noticed this tension early on with our two children. Our daughter is an internal processor and our son is an external processor, which complicated holding the Talking and Listening tension in our family. She needed "think time" and he needed "verbal time" to process.

Helping them respect each other's style was important for our family conversations to flow smoother. She was able to ask for the time she needed to think about something, and he knew that he needed to talk out loud when he was working though something. This meant that I often engaged with my son a lot verbally, but with my daughter I learned to communicate with a journal that we would write to one another. I started it when she was five and we still continue the tradition of passing it back and forth to one another over a decade later. (In fact, she just informed me that she will still write to me in college. Lucky me.) For my son, writing seems like a form of torture, so we approach our conversations differently. I get lots of FaceTime calls from him, and I added a comfy chair to my office just for him so we could chat when he dropped by for a visit. Just knowing how to hold the tension between Listening and Talking helps us love one another better and support the styles we each need.

The same dynamic plays out in marriages. Recently one of my clients shared her awareness of how her verbal processing was causing her to overpower conversations with her husband. He loved her deeply but was simply overwhelmed by all her words. Just by being mindful regarding her length of talking and listening became a real gift in their marriage. And giving her husband the permission to "be out of words" or understanding when he was experiencing "listening fatigue" became an important way they cared for one another. It also helped

COURAGE

free her up to find other outlets and relationships to enjoy her verbal processing and inspiring connections.

3. KEEPS US TRAPPED

A "one-size fits all" mind-set is the third block that prevents us from living in freedom. It's hard to adapt or give others permission to do so when we are stuck in one gear. I think of how Inspector Javert, the antagonist in *Les Misérables*, could not integrate the idea of living by anything other than the law. He was trapped in a prison of his own making with no room for tilting the scales toward grace due to his inability to hold the tension between Justice and Mercy.

This makes me think of an amazing leader I'll refer to as Janice. She was struggling with holding the tension of Engaging and Withdrawing. As we worked together, I soon realized she had over a hundred people showing up to her office at any given time. Janice was overwhelmed at being "on call" with whoever decided to knock on her door. Who wouldn't be? And to top it off, she was an introvert who needed quiet time to think. When we met, Janice was exhausted, frustrated, and burned out. As a leader, she felt like it was her responsibility to engage constantly, which caused her to lose the tension of Engaging and Withdrawing.

To regain balance, we set up a leadership tier where the employees were grouped under managers. This reduced her communications to eight direct reports and buffered her from the department as a whole. What a difference it made! Janice was able to regain the balance of Engaging and Withdrawing by shutting her door and getting work done as she set up check-ins with her managers to keep a pulse on her department.

COURAGE

See how holding the tension of Withdrawing and Engaging helped her live more freely—not just as a leader but as a human being?

I see this tension being missed in family systems as well. There are usually unwritten rules in families about how to engage or withdraw. For instance, if you grew up in a family with many extroverts, as an introvert you might feel shame for needing to withdraw. This was the case for me. I felt guilty for disengaging from extroverted family members when I wanted to hide out in my room to recharge.

Understanding how you hold the tension of Withdrawing and Engaging is important to be aware of as you move through the various seasons of life. One of my favorite stories that illustrates this is of my introverted daughter. When Selah was three years old, we were hosting a party and, late in the evening, my dear girl climbed to the top of our stairs and cleared her throat. Once she had our attention, she pointed her tiny finger at all the guests and announced sternly in her little three-year-old voice, "You, you, and you—all go home!" I was a bit mortified with this unexpected outburst and how my guests might be feeling, but rather impressed with her authentic strength as I watched from below. Her little arm waving around the room pointing at people for emphasis until I carried her off to snuggle together in her quiet room. She had had enough and actually said what many introverts only *think*. For all my introverts out there—how many times have you longed to say this? *"You, you, and you—all go home."* (Guilty chuckle.)

Knowing how to hold tensions allows you to respond freely and authentically as you rest in the freedom that you get to do both.

COURAGE

Core Values

So why is this idea of holding tensions such a challenge?

Because everyone wants to feel resolve as soon as possible.

It takes courage to face the tensions and not turn life into an easy formula. We like the easy button. The quick fix. It's hard to have to sit in the gray zone—or as my friend Dan refers to it—the "squishy."

This is where we need courage. To wait. To resist the temptation to put everything in boxes. Unresolved issues or emotions can make us anxious and fearful of not being in control. It is the ability to stay and wait that helps us hold the tension. And that, my friends, requires courage.

But how do we grow the courage we need to hold the many tensions in life?

There are two key ways that will help you grow the courage you need to hold tensions well. The first one is what I call core values.

Naming and knowing these values help me hold the tensions I regularly face:

- Every human being has significance.

- Every human being has potential that is longing to be recognized.

- Every human being is looking for love and acceptance.

Remembering this fuels my courage and propels me through uncomfortable, challenging, and even scary human and relational interactions.

These core values are most important when we fail big and fall hard. Knowing what we value helps grow our courage in the face of conflict, relational misunderstandings, cross-cultural

COURAGE

leadership, disappointing people, and harsh rejection. It helps us get back up again. To see the situation realistically and not take it personally when things don't work out as we hoped. And to stay committed to who we are, how we want to grow, and what we want to offer.

It is during our most epic fails that we learn the importance of core values. I distinctly remember starting a company with several other partners and the intense disappointment, pain, and misunderstandings when it did not meet our expectations. Facing a pile of debt and the loss of friendships was deeply painful. It did not make me want to venture out again. But my core values gave me the strength to heal, forgive, grow, and risk again. It's what grew my courage and helped me step out when the next big opportunity came.

The second way to grow our courage and keep it engaged has to do with pausing.

Yellow Light Questions

Staying stuck in questions that require a binary switch—should I stay or go?—keeps us looking for red or green lights. Perhaps surprisingly, this can actually deplete our courage. It demands an immediate yes or no to find resolve. But life is not this simple.

Lingering at the yellow light is what grows our courage and helps us in our ability to hold tensions well. It's essential we discover how to explore questions in terms of a yellow light.

For instance, perhaps you want to leave your current job but aren't completely sure now is the time. In the first part of this book, we discussed crossroads and the group called Pausers. That is an example of the yellow light.

COURAGE

I see this all the time with my clients. Lindy found herself in this exact situation. She was stuck in the red/green-light question of "should I stay or go?" The problem was, this way of thinking was too limiting. As we worked together, we explored broader questions that did not limit her to just staying or going.

Here's a top-line synopsis of several of our conversations had over the course of many months:

FIRST WEEK

Me: What are you dissatisfied with in your current job?

Lindy: I don't like the intensity of my work day-to-day.

Me: Is it the work itself or the schedule it demands?

Lindy: I don't know.

Me: What would help you find out?

Lindy: I think I'd like to start exploring other job options.

Action Steps: Call three contacts and investigate some options on Internet job sites.

SECOND WEEK

Me: How'd it go?

Lindy: I narrowed it down to three companies I'd like to interview with.

Me: Great. How are you feeling about it?

Lindy: {Long silence} Honestly . . . tired. Really tired. It feels overwhelming to change.

COURAGE

Me: What would you like to do?

Lindy: Think on it some more and talk to a couple
             contacts who are in the field before I com-
             mit to an interview.

Action Steps: Talk to several people she trusts and listen to their
perspectives.

THIRD WEEK

Me: How'd your conversations go?

Lindy: Okay, but I wasn't really excited about it.

Me: Would you like to keep searching or stay in
             your current job and explore what might be
             making you unhappy?

Lindy: I'd like to explore my current position to see
             what is bothering me about it.

Action Steps: Journal about what was bothering her regarding
her job as well as what might be behind her unhappiness. Also,
talk with a close friend about it.

FOURTH WEEK

Me: How'd it go?

Lindy: I realized that I really love what I do, but
             I don't like being on call 24/7. The emer-
             gencies in the tech world are stressful, and I
             don't feel like I can have a life.

Me: How have you expressed it to your boss?

Lindy: I haven't.

You may find yourself sighing at her last comment. After four weeks, she still hadn't expressed her thoughts to her boss? But be careful. It's easy to expect from others what we so often don't do easily or in timely manners ourselves.

Yellow Light Questions provide space to explore what is behind the hesitation and do so without pressure, guilt, or shame. It's a space of grace we provide ourselves. One without judgment and only curiosity. And this requires courage. It puts long-term processing over immediate resolution. Sure, it may seem easier to simply move forward or pull over with a sense of satisfaction that an issue is resolved. But was it resolved fast or right? That's why Yellow Light Questions are harder and more courageous.

Let's return to Lindy. After a month of weekly conversations lingering at the yellow light, things took a definitive turn. Lindy understood she actually liked her job but struggled to speak up and express her needs. She realized this had been a common theme growing up in an addict's home. And although she had worked through much of this with counseling, she still struggled to transfer it to her professional life. She needed some new tools to help her speak up and feel equipped to address it at a professional level.

Growing up in a home where she had not been validated or heard was blocking her at work. Guilt and shame had prevented her from stating her needs. Deep down she knew this. But it was only in lingering at the yellow light that she was able to see it clearly. Had she left her job, she simply would have run into the same issue at a new job, over and over again. The issue was not the job, but her ability to communicate what she needed.

Lindy was now able to explore what she really wanted. But only because she had the courage to linger at the yellow light

COURAGE

to see what was behind her lack of fulfillment before deciding whether to stay (red light) or go (green light).

And it turned out great. Her boss was understanding and sympathetic in supporting her quality of life. Her schedule was quickly adjusted with a pay increase and a clear message to bring all concerns to him in the future. She was fully heard and truly valued.

Yellow Light Questions are so worth it. They are what help us hold tensions.

Rainer Maria Rilke, the poet, mentored his protégé with this encouragement: "Be patient toward all that is unsolved in your heart and try to *love the questions themselves*, like locked rooms and like books that are now written in a very foreign tongue."[15]

Courage, dear readers. Holding tensions can be challenging, but so worth it. Remember, navigating tension well is ultimately the way for you (like our insect friends) to walk on water!

Cheering you on.

COURAGE

---

15. "Live the Questions: Rilke on Embracing Uncertainty and Doubt as a Stabilizing Force," Brain Pickings, accessed February 17, 2021, https://www.brainpickings.org/2012/06/01/rilke-on-questions/.

COURAGE QUESTION
How did you view tension prior to this chapter? How have those perceptions changed?

Remember the five tensions you circled earlier in this chapter? It's now time to dive deeper into the "why" behind the ones you selected.

List the five tensions here.

Now take a look at the words above and circle the one to the left or right for each of the five tensions that you most identify with.

Why do you struggle with these five the most? You may have one or five answers here. Think back to your childhood or other moments that may have caused you to grow rigid in these areas.

What would it look like to grow your courage and be more balanced in each of these five areas?

COURAGE

CAUTION: Sometimes intense seasons of life cause us to lose our balance when navigating deep grief, loss, or crisis. That is okay. Be kind to yourself and recognize what tension you want to hold as you adjust, adapt, and recover. And give yourself time and space to kindly figure this out.

If you don't hold tensions well, you'll eventually become more tense. This not only gets in the way of the life you're made for, but it stops you from experiencing the peace of being, which we will discuss in the next chapter.

THE PEACE OF BEING

The Courage to Cultivate Calm

C *ourage.* The word itself is strong. Like a cup of steaming, bold coffee.

Peace. This word is soothing. Like a glass of ice-cold water. It's hard to imagine these two words coming together in a coherent way. Maybe that's why we rarely hear them spoken in the same breath. And in a world of growing tension, offense, and fracture, it seems darn near impossible to be both at the same time.

What if Peace and Courage had to live together as roommates? The ultimate odd couple, right? If push came to shove, my money (and probably yours) would be on Courage staying and Peace being tossed out the window.

Yet here in this last chapter on courage, our guest of honor is none other than . . . peace.

The disconnect and tension we feel isn't between the words themselves, but rather in us because of how we've come to "mis-know" the terms.

Let's begin with a reminder of the definition of courage. For the purpose of our journey, I've defined it simply as "choosing to take action." It requires "doing."

And peace, well, even the title of this chapter plays to the "being" nature of the word.

But Being and Doing aren't opposites. Neither are Peace and Courage.

The two terms actually go together quite well, as you're about to discover.

Selah Speed

Before we see how peace and courage are related, I'd like to tell a story about a relationship that's near and dear to me. It provides a snapshot of our deep need for peace—and how, at least for some, it is something we crave from the moment we come into this world.

It was that way for our daughter Selah. We'd waited nine years to have children. When she finally arrived, we were ecstatic. And a bit overwhelmed with the newness and work of it all!

From the start, it was apparent that Selah would be my new teacher in the importance of experiencing peace on a daily basis.

Have you noticed how some people seem to have souls that are much older and wiser than their years? Selah came into the world like a young sage, extremely intelligent with heightened sensitivities. She thrived on consistent quiet space and peaceful rhythms. I remember holding her for hours, watching leaves blowing in the trees or ants crawling across the sidewalk. Her pace of life was the slowest I'd ever encountered. I eventually dubbed it "Selah Speed." This required me to shift down to first, sometimes even park, as we enjoyed the world around us. We both learned the importance of not just calming a little soul prone to anxiety, but cultivating a peaceful being.

As new parents, there were many signs that she was unique. Being a research geek, I read everything I could get my hands on about the highly sensitive child.

For instance, from infancy Selah required total darkness and peaceful music as she settled in for sleep. She enjoyed long periods of observing and of being held. And while she exuded peace, she also quickly reacted whenever there was too much stimulant— whether it was noise, light, or too many people. All of our loving friends knew the phase "speak gently and look past the eyes" since the very act of eye contact would set her off crying. (Remember, her words to the party of friends in our last chapter?)

Selah's anxiety increased at night. The transition of the setting sun seemed to trouble her sensitive soul. I researched this phenomenon to help me both understand her and to develop ways to soothe her.

Over time, I named these our Peace Practices.

Peace Practices

In this section, I'm going to share some of the Peace Practices we used with Selah created from both personal life experience and my research. As you read them, you might also consider ways for you to nurture your own heart.

One of our Peace Practices quickly became a favorite nightly tradition. As we tucked her in bed, we would intentionally help settle her mind, body, heart, and spirit. First, we'd invite her to go to her happy place in her mind. For Selah, this was in the wild lands behind our house with her dog Beemer and Jesus. (No, I didn't even make the cut.) Then we would thank each

COURAGE

part of her body for working hard and tell them it was time to rest. Like this: "Eyes, thank you for seeing so much, it's time to rest. Ears, thank you for hearing so much, it's time to rest," etc. Then we would recite the ancient poetry of Psalms 23, telling her the Lord is her Shepherd.

When she was fully at peace, we'd gently sneak out as soothing classical music played softly in her darkened room. This process usually took 15–30 minutes. I admit there were times I was exhausted and would have rather skipped it. But it was critical for her, like water to a thirsty soul. It calmed her anxious heart. And she reset the rhythm of my heart as well.

There's nothing like a child to teach us how to live from a place of calm. They enter this world untouched and unscarred by the troubles of life. Fresh and clear, they can model what it means to listen and care for cultivating practices of peace in our lives.

But then we forget.

How many of your adult friends or coworkers actively pursue peace, or are aware of the specific factors that interrupt their peace? Far too many of us live with a constant churning in our gut, hoping nothing bad will happen but fearful it will. Perhaps that's you. Or maybe you're realizing for the first time there's an absence of true peace in your life.

Breathe.

What are some Peace Practices you could begin doing? If you're not sure where to start, ask yourself this question: When does my mind, body, heart, and soul seem most at rest? What activity causes stress and pressure to, at least for a moment, fade away? Perhaps it's listening to music. Maybe it's a workout. A walk around the neighborhood or getting lost in a good book on the back patio. Once you've identified one or two activities that bring you peace, then it's important to build those moments into your schedule. Specific is better than vague when it comes to Peace Practices. Create a specific time for them and then honor those appointments as seriously as any other meeting or commitment.

If you're having trouble finding time or motivation to believe it matters, try this experiment. Imagine how it would feel to live in a regular state of peace. See yourself doing something you love with no stress or worries. What would it be worth to have that not just be an image but a reality? It's not only possible, it's doable. But let's say you already have minimal peace. It's not a lot, but hey, it gets you (barely) through the day. If that's you, don't settle for that being as good as it gets. You have the ability to increase your current level of peace.

Unfortunately, it doesn't just happen automatically. Wishing it were so is a good start, but you have a part to play in the process. Experiencing greater peace requires us to first slow down externally—and internally—to Selah Speed. In a world that's constantly spinning faster and expecting you to do the same, purposely downshifting your speed isn't easy.

But that's okay. Easy is overrated. Hardly anything that matters is easy. That's especially true when the goal is transformation through greater peace.

So while this process isn't easy, the good news is that it does work. Countless people regularly experience the benefits of these practices. You can too.

As I write this, Selah is a securely grounded eighteen-year-old. She's recently graduated from high school with honors, a varsity dancer on the school team, and highly social with a beautiful group of friends starting her first semester in college. Just writing this makes me smile.

COURAGE

I'd be remiss not to mention the meaning of Selah's name. When we named her, we had no idea of her personality or her needs. It turns out the name Selah refers to a specific occurrence in music when there is . . . a pause. And the ancient Hebrew meaning is to "stop and think." How beautifully poetic is that?

Speaking of poetry—although I'm no poet—this was something I came across in my journal that I wrote years ago experiencing motherhood for the first time.

SELAH SPEED

I learn from my child . . .

To shift down from fifth gear to first gear . . .
    and sometimes even getting out of the car altogether.

To laugh at silly things over and over and over . . .

To meander places instead of getting to the destination
    as fast as possible.

To release time.
To release money.
To release control.

I realize my high value on efficiency . . .
    and how ridiculous it is in a child's world.

I stand . . . I sit . . . I rest . . . I relax . . . I play . . .
    I embrace unproductiveness.

I watch her eyes . . .
    I watch her movements . . .

COURAGE

I watch her pace . . .
And I emulate her.

She likes me better . . .
others like me better . . .
and I like myself better at Selah Speed.

Aren't we just more peaceful humans when we slow things down? Going slow when the world is speeding up requires living with internal courage.

Real Peace Requires True Courage

Now it's time to connect peace and courage more directly.

We now understand the importance of peace. But why is courage needed in our pursuit of peace?

Two reasons:

- to know your true self, and

- to strengthen the identity of your true self

We'll unpack them one at a time.

FIRST, we must find ways to know our true self.

Getting to know who you are and doing what my friend Kelly calls our "growth work" is a life-long journey. As seasons change, we change.

It's important to know who we are at the core of ourselves. Most people go through life never knowing this. And without it, we are chameleons changing into whatever others want us to be when we are around them. This is a miserable way to live.

COURAGE

But let's say you already know who you are at a core level. That's fantastic. You're already ahead of most folks in this area. But there's more. We aren't static beings or statues. We are dynamic and fluid—ever-changing and growing. So it's equally important to recognize that you can choose and influence who you are becoming.

Will you be a person who offers grace or shame? Will you forgive or choose revenge? Will you act from a foundation of love or hate? How we respond to life and all it throws at us is a powerful way we can get to know our true self.

But don't just take my word for it. Take in this tale of three sisters and see what you think.

This isn't a fairy tale or fable. It's a true story involving three sisters I knew personally. When their father became ill, it was obvious that he had very little time left. Each sister responded differently in her father's last days.

The first sister took the opportunity to tell her dying father of the injustices she suffered at his hand.

The second sister expressed how frustrated she had been with his passive response to her pain over the years.

But the third sister was different. She did not come with a sense of justice toward an imperfect father.

She did not exert her right to being heard. Rather, she visited him with grace. And the effect of that courageous moment of peace was stunning. In a moment of deep shame and pain, he sobbed an apology to his daughter. Her peace opened the door for him to express sorrow over the pain in his fathering. In response, she offered only love. This sister offered grace as she reassured her father that he had done the best he could.

Her choice provides a poignant reminder that we have options in who we are—and who we become. The story calls

COURAGE

attention to what was already in the third sister's true self, which was a desire to be a person of grace, love, and forgiveness. And, it needs to be said, the other sisters weren't "wrong" or "bad." Harsh, perhaps. But maybe that was exactly what they needed to be their true selves. Though the first two sisters' words didn't bless their father, it may have been the only way they knew to resolve their pain of him, while he was still alive.

The higher goal is to ultimately learn that true courage is about the ability to both bless *and* release those who have caused us pain. Is that hard? You bet. Does it seem impossible at times? Absolutely. But when we have the courage to do this, we will find our peace.

That's why this invitation is coming within the courage section of the book. It's why peace and courage go together. Courage to look bravely in the mirror and see what you like, where you want to grow, what you want to call out, and what you want to nurture. We often don't like the reflection we see staring back at us. Yet it is this befriending of ourselves that allows us to develop peace in who we are and who we are choosing to become.

Once we actually get to know our true self, and what made us the person we are today, we are ready for the next step.

SECOND, we must find ways to strengthen the identity of our true self.

We've all been in relationships where the other person just wants us to agree with them. Any feedback or challenge is received as a threat only to be rejected, shamed, or even punished.

I encountered this with a woman who talked incessantly about whatever was on her mind. She was unaware of her unrealistic expectation for people to listen. What made it really

COURAGE

uncomfortable was her misplaced belief that her perception was always accurate. After one of her more outrageous comments, I at last spoke up to question the validity of where she was getting her information. And it ushered in immediate peace.

If only.

What actually happened was she directed her rage at me. In her world, she had to be right. If others wanted to be in relationship with her, it required them to listen and affirm her every comment without dispute. I realized the only way to be friends with her was to give up my opinions, values, and beliefs. No thank you. That is not a relationship.

It's never worth giving up your true self simply to stay in an unhealthy or toxic relationship with someone who doesn't value what you have to offer or who you truly are. Healthy relationships do the exact opposite. They help you strengthen your connection with others and with your authentic sense of self.

Here's an example of what I mean.

At age fifteen, my son Luke found himself in a major dilemma. He'd waited until the night before it was due to begin a huge school project. All the parents reading this know where this is going. The project was impossible to do in one evening. When I found out it had been assigned weeks earlier, I could feel my exasperation rising.

Immediately I jumped into taking responsibility and asked, "What are you learning from this predicament?"

He sighed. "To start the project earlier," he replied robotically in a singsong deflated tone.

Something felt off. "Hang on, Luke. I don't want the expected answer."

"Well, I thought that's what you wanted to hear," he responded.

Warning bells started going off because he was giving up his sense of self to make me happy. I don't want anyone to ever just give me the "correct answer" at the expense of their authentic thoughts and feelings, especially someone close to me. As an educator, I often hold a high standard for supporting our teachers. Luke knew this, which is why he offered the "right answer" of taking responsibility and keeping the real story bottled within. But I also know that teachers are not perfect and need the support of parents to offer insight when a student is suffering. I tried again with a different tone.

"Luke, what's really going on?"

He then expressed the source of his frustration. It involved a teacher he'd been having struggles with all year. He felt her teaching style was unfair. Although he was at the top of her class, he still perceived himself as a failure in her eyes. The more I heard, the more I realized that her system was inadvertently setting up students to fail rather than succeed.

As parents, we stepped in and had a much-needed conversation with the educator. Our goal wasn't to accuse or stir up controversy, but to offer helpful feedback and make her aware of how her teaching style was causing many students to be discouraged. More importantly, we initiated a supportive triad between the student, teacher, and parents going forward. We respected her high standards, and she appreciated the parent feedback as she adjusted her assignments and grading based on our input.

The result? Luke re-engaged, producing his best work. And peace was restored. That was only possible by expressing and being connected with one's true self—for me as a mother, Luke as a student and son, and the teacher as an educator.

This is what it looks like to know and strengthen the identity of who you truly are. And to respect the true self of others.

COURAGE

Never Again

What gets in the way of knowing our true self and staying connected? We lack the courage to be true to who we are and match our actions with our convictions.

There are several reasons why. Some are more complex than others, but see if you can relate to any of the following:

We doubt ourselves.

We fear disappointing others.

We're distracted from what we really value.

We are focused on fulfilling someone else's expectations for our lives.

We don't want to risk messing up.

We're scared about how it will turn out.

We just don't like the loneliness of standing alone.

Hear the fear in all these? I know. I have felt all these myself and know with certainty that courage is not only helpful to cultivate a life of peace and calm—it is required.

My clients teach me this over and over. The wife who risks speaking up to her husband about how she has been hurting after trying to dismiss it for years; the leader who is terrified of public speaking but addresses his team by calling out potential and vision; the mother confronting her teenage sons after years of avoiding them for fear of confrontation; the president holding her leadership team accountable in new ways that cause uncomfortable disruptions; and the couple who chooses to live abroad in spite of homesickness and severe anxiety. In each of these examples and many more, people courageously chose to face what has haunted them (even hunted them) and kept them disconnected from their true selves.

And I've witnessed the peace that comes with having the courage to face it. This requires a deep commitment to risk. To face down the fears.

As I witness humans turn to face what has chased them and kept them running in fear, it makes me courageous, too. And I am inspired to never again avoid or miss the chance to bravely face what I need to address. Because ultimately, this is what brings peace.

We won't achieve perfection every time, but hanging around courageous people helps. And the higher the cost, the more important it is to be honest. It's only when we have the courage to see accurately what we did and where we went wrong that we can learn from it and course correct. Sadly, some let these painful realizations paralyze them from seeking a cure. Rather than risk more, they play it safe and stop trying. Lacking the courage to learn from their mistakes and do something about it, they simply give up. And with it goes their peace.

When we listen to the advice of those living in fear, we stop listening to our true self. It's the brave ones who dared to stand on their own regardless of the cost. This is where we need our courage. To listen to our true self and voice what we know to be right, as well as learning to listen to those who share our values. In an ideal world, we should be able to trust those close to us. But we know that is not always the case, and sometimes the core values of those closest to us can be in conflict—and when this happens, we may listen to, and trust, the wrong person.

Confronting our own actions with powerful phrases such as, "I will never again stay silent when I know I should speak up," or "I will never again compromise my values for fear of disappointing others" keeps us grounded and helps us stay committed to our courage.

COURAGE

Speaking courageous truth solidifies and strengthens the connection with our true self and fosters inner peace.

Choosing to stay true to who we are is the essence of what brings peace of being.

Peace, in the very core of our being, comes from knowing the right thing to do and then courageously doing it.

This is how we step into the life we know we are made for.

Whole, Brave, and True

As I write this, our nation and world are spinning more and more out of control. There is little peace. Wisdom seems lacking. Courage is desperately needed. Courage for people to stand against injustices. Courage to own their wrongs and make things right. Courage to offer hope and healing. Courage to build communities of equality, kindness, and respect. Courage to build bridges.

How do we do this? What helps us have peace in our very being? And how can we offer it to others?

Here are three proven ways forward.

1. DO THE WORK.

Honor your true self by doing your inner growth work. We have never "arrived." We are never done. I am writing this from an airport waiting for my flight after a week with a mentor helping me sort through the landscape of my inner life. What a gift to have a sage listen, guide, and honor my story. I liken it to a massage for the soul. It's so important that you find guides in life that help you see who you are and what is blocking your true self from being even more free. They may be mentors, coaches, teachers, counselors, or pastors. But make sure they are people who honor

COURAGE

your strengths, provide ideas to expand your thinking, and offer practical life tools to grow stronger. This world desperately needs you to show up whole, brave, and true.

2. DON'T GO IT ALONE.

Build bridges to one another where it isn't only the differences that are respected but the commonalities of what makes us human are strengthened. Each of us needs love, respect, freedom, and connection. This is what makes us each human. And we need one another in kind and valuing relationships.

Cultivate your relationships. Find people who love and support you as you are (not who they want you to be). A dear friend was recently grieving the loss of her father. I asked her, "What was it about your dad that made you feel safe?" Here is what she said:

- He let me explore questions and didn't shut down my curiosity.

- He affirmed who I was at my very core.

- He helped provide context for hard topics with no easy answers.

- He joined me in whatever stage I was in and didn't talk over my head.

- He was an anchor to me.

- He was curious about me and wanted insights into whatever I was thinking.

- He was approachable.

My heart grew full just listening to her describe him. Oh, to have more fathers like this. Yet the sad truth is that many

COURAGE

of us don't. Friends, it is essential for you to find people who honor who you are and help you know and connect to what you value. Keep your standards high and be selective. Be clear on who shares your values, for we take on the qualities of those we surround ourselves with.

3. MATCH WHO YOU ARE ON THE INSIDE WITH WHAT YOU DO ON THE OUTSIDE.

This requires learning how to be comfortable with who you are on the inside and owning it. Oftentimes, our courage is halfhearted. Yes, we are taking action, but we are not living authentically. You're taking a job because it's what your father always expected of you. Or you're dating the person all your friends like, but you're not so sure. What brings peace is being comfortable with owning who you are on the inside and letting your actions match who you are, what you believe, your core values, the opinions you hold, and where you choose to be responsible. This is true living and it takes courage to face the disappointment of others or to stand alone as you go against the expectations of what people may have for you. But it's ultimately where we find our peace. And it is so worth it.

There is only one you. And the world is waiting for you to figure out your best because it desperately needs you to show up in all your brave-hearted wholeness.

Courage isn't about being defiant. The pursuit of peace helps us defy that way of thinking. As it turns out, the very best form of courage is one that is infused with peace.

One of my favorite poems by Rumi talks about a courage that dares to connect from the deepest and truest places within us and describes it like this: "Out beyond ideas of wrongdoing and rightdoing there is a field. I'll meet you there."

COURAGE

Dear readers, we can create these peaceful spaces to meet one another. Spaces of grace that encourage personal value and respect for the sharing of individual perspectives. "Fields" that honor one another and strengthen the *peace of being* who you are made to be. I'd like more of these places. But it will require our courage.

Shall we meet in the field together?

COURAGE QUESTION

How can you grow stronger by courageously pursuing peace?

At what speed would you say you're currently doing life? What would shifting to Selah Speed look like for you?

Name two or three Peace Practices you can begin doing in the next week.

As you pursue your true self, what is something you need courage to never again find yourself doing?

COURAGE

CAUTION: Engaging our courage can feel terrifying. Doing so from a posture of peace can make it feel even more impossible. This is normal. If it wasn't daunting, we wouldn't need courage. As always, be kind to yourself and take baby steps as you venture out.

We're coming to the end of our journey together. Well done finishing this last "C" on courage. Remember that each of us has courage, but it's those who choose to reach for it that get the lives they are made for.

SOME FINAL WORDS
FOR YOUR JOURNEY

There are some parting words I want to offer on a more personal note. Remember when I mentioned in the introduction that my faith is important to me? In the spirit of full transparency, I want to mention it here to share what I have found in aligning my clarity, confidence, and courage with a loving force that I call God. Honestly, I want to give you every advantage possible and not hold back what has worked for me and what I have witnessed working for others. But please take it or leave it as you see fit. Faith is sacred territory, I know.

For me, it started with learning to trust that there is a Someone (bigger, smarter, and more powerful than me) who is for me and wants to see me grow my 3Cs to live in new and fuller ways. Feels too good to be true, to be honest.

But I have found it to be true over the years and witnessed it countless times in my work with people. And what a relief I have discovered this to be—just knowing that I am not meant to manifest the 3Cs all on my own! In fact, holding the 3Cs all by your lonesome can not only be hard work, but terrifying. So, may my experience in faith offer you deep hope as you start your journey with 3C Living.

When I think of how my relationship with God has influenced my 3Cs, the word "exponential" comes to mind. The dictionary defines it as "rising or expanding at a steady and usually rapid rate."

That's helpful but not particularly motivating. I believe a story will do a much better job of illustrating it. Perhaps you've heard this tale before. Numerous versions of the legend exist. Details change between them but they all involve a king, a chessboard, and the jaw-dropping power of exponential growth.

As the story goes, a man arrived at a king's palace with a new creation. It was a board game he called "chess." The king was so fascinated by it that he told the man to name his reward for this invention.

Okay, wait. Pause.

Before I continue the story, imagine being asked by a king of immense wealth, power, and land to name whatever reward you want. What would you ask for—and why?

As the fable goes, the man shrugged. "I'd like one grain of rice placed on the first chessboard square."

The king leaned in, incredulous at his request. "One grain of rice? That is all you ask?"

"Well, that and then double the number of rice for each square. Two grains on the second square, then four grains on the next. Do that until you get to the last square on the board. That is all I desire."

The king smiled. "Consider it done!" He ordered his treasurer to initiate this process and told the man to come back in a few days.

When the man returned days later, the king welcomed him. Being a man of his word, the king told his staff to pay the inventor.

The treasurer, with sweat on his brow, entered the room. "My king," said the treasurer, "your request is impossible to fulfill."

"How can that be?" the king demanded. "My kingdom is one of great abundance. And all this man has asked for are grains of rice. Get a bag and bring his reward to him."

"But your majesty, there are 64 squares total on the chessboard. When you double the quantity of rice on each square, by the end that comes to," he swallowed hard, "18 quintillion grains of rice. That is 210 billion tons! No kingdom in the world has that much rice."

At that moment, the king realized he'd lost a much bigger game than chess—all because he failed to understand the power of exponential growth.

Don't you love that story? Does it enlarge your understanding of exponential impact?

That's what my faith in God has done. It has increased the results of my 3C Living in meaningful and purposeful ways as I learned to trust Someone bigger than myself. Exhale. Just writing this made me relax a bit more knowing that it doesn't all come down to me—I'm not the only one to depend on. Someone bigger than me is able to care for me, protect me, and guide me. In the allegory of the girl with the bracelets, she heard the Voice in the Wind.

It is the Voice that knows me and believes in who I am made to be. It blocks out all the lesser voices of fear, shame, and guilt. And it's this Voice we need to hear in order to live *big* lives because it inspires us to see beyond the current reality and empowers us to bravely lead. It offers unconditional love and calls us out to be more.

You may not consider yourself a person with any particular faith. That's okay. I'm simply sharing how I've found breakthrough and who I am because of that. It is my way to be true to myself and everyone (including you) reading this book.

It is through a relationship—or a friendship—that I've come to know God. Not some far-removed judge in the sky sorting out who is good and bad as many of us have been taught. But a friend who knows me, created me for a purpose, and loves me exactly as I am.

In earlier years, it was easy to lose faith and think life was all up to me. It was this strange combination of expecting God to come through and yet assuming there probably wasn't anyone caring enough to pay attention to what I really wanted and needed.

But it took years for me to finally realize the power of being still. It was time under the stars where I got to know God.

When we are still, we talk less.

When we talk less, we hear more.

When we hear more, we learn more.

And we get challenged with fresh perspective.

This simple act of stillness helped me manage my expectations and emotions. I learned the importance of not expecting an answer on my timetable but of waiting.

Over time, I saw that if I would still my heart, I would feel led and guided. But it was up to me to make the space to listen and trust. And I found that God's voice is pure love and wisdom, encouraging me to take off my bracelets and reminding me of my true value. Over the years, a trust and friendship has developed with my Voice in the Wind. And I believe this same presence wants a relationship with all of us. We just have to make the space to listen and dare to believe that God has good plans for our future. That our Creator holds the manual for our lives. I like this thought a lot. God, who is love, holds the manual for my life. In fact, the Creator is someone who knows better than me my potential and believes in who I can become.

Let that sink in. Someone powerful and all-knowing believes in who you can become.

So, as you're pausing and camping at the crossroads of life, you can take this one step further and slip away to lie under the stars and listen for the Voice in the Wind. This will give you the opportunity to anchor your spirit to a Voice of Love while simultaneously unhooking from the growing fear that can build from the days and years of wearing so many bracelets.

This is often where I hear my True Beliefs and confront the False Beliefs that have kept me less than who I am meant to be.

There are poignant moments in each of our lives when we catch that whisper on the wind—the pull that there is more for us. Be brave enough to trust it. Be present enough to not miss it. And be hopeful enough to not simply ignore it, thinking it's "too good to be true."

Doesn't knowing that make you breathe easier as you step farther into the life you're made for?

It's been an honor traveling with you. As we conclude this journey, remember, you get to live the life you were made for. It's a life of freedom, not stress. So let go of the pressure of trying to remember everything. You never "graduate" from 3C Living. These topics aren't "one and done."

That's why we have our tire swings and the stars—to help us slow down and take the time to remember what we know deep down to be true. There's no expectation to do everything perfectly. And there's never a need to keep bracelets that no longer (and perhaps never did) fit. That's how you'll discover the freedom to be fully you. It doesn't come from some huge, once-in-a-lifetime moment, but through the small daily choices toward clarity, confidence, and courage made consistently over time.

Along the way, you hold tight to you. Listen for your Voice in the Wind. It's a relief to believe that you are never alone.

Finally, breathe easy.

The life you're made for is your adventure. And yours alone. Own it boldly and unapologetically.

My heart is *with* you and *for* you.

Close

SHE WAS NOW IN HER FAVORITE SPOT—gently swaying in a hammock under the stars. It reminded her of the tire swing, but was a bit more comfy for spending time under the stars. And she smiled at who she had become. What a different person she was now.

Overhead, the sparkling, shimmering lights were dazzling in brilliance. Too many to count. The stars reminded her of her dreams. So many beautiful ones had come true. Others were in process. And she believed more were still ahead.

Her gifts of clarity, confidence, and courage had brought such freedom into her life. She raised her arms to stretch. Only a few bracelets now. They were her favorites. The process of removing them had become easier as she was able to identify the impact of each bracelet.

With her clarity, she now saw who she truly was.

With confidence, she believed in who she was meant to be.

And with courage, she had learned to take the action she needed.

She found this an amazing combination. The more she used these, the more there were. The only way the 3Cs started to disappear was when she forgot to use them.

As a girl, she used to think the more bracelets she wore, the less alone she would feel. But instead, she had felt even more lonely as she tried to prove her worth through the many bracelets. At least that's what she used to believe.

She now felt freer and lighter, free to enjoy her life and who she had become. And she was painting more—something she used to love doing as a girl. Mixing colors and creating art on a blank canvas brought her life.

She had learned a lot about her bracelets. Choosing only the ones to keep that reflected her strengths— and her true self. And she was wiser now as she understood how to evaluate each one and what she needed.

Over the years, the young woman grew into a leader of great character and stature. She continued to nurture her 3C Living and invited others to join her.

And it took her far. Living out her dreams was her new reality.

She glanced down at her arms. The few bracelets that graced her wrists were intentionally chosen for the value they added. None wore her down or were worn from a sense of obligation or striving.

It had been years since her first encounter with the Voice in the Wind, but now she heard it often under the stars. Tonight, it asked, *Do you ever miss all the bracelets?*

The question caught her off guard. It had been so long since her arms were weighed down with bracelets that she had to search her memory. "I don't miss them at all. I used to think they added significance to my life. Or told me who I was. Now I am clear on my purpose and value."

That's good. I never wanted you to be burdened with so many bracelets. Clarity, confidence, and courage help you break free from the chains that hold so many back.

She looked at the few remaining bracelets on her arm, wondering about them as well. She never wanted to be defined again by the trinkets she wore.

But she felt reassured in knowing that she would have the clarity to know, the confidence to believe, and the courage to act when she needed it.

The woman smiled in anticipation of all that was to come. She felt the peace grow as she thought about her future. Yawning, she gently drifted off to sleep under the stars.

In her dream, she saw herself as a Good Giver, helping people everywhere access the clarity, confidence, and courage they held inside. She never stayed long. She didn't need to once people understood what lived within them. Plus, she knew there was a far better guide than her.

You can often find her under the stars . . . and yes, on the old tire swing hanging from the great oak tree on the top of the hill.

~~The End~~
The Beginning

NOTES

Introduction

1. Listed here are three influential studies regarding the emotional health of high-functioning women as they transitioned from college to the working world:

Fiebig, J. (2008). Gifted American and German adolescent women: a longitudinal examination of attachment, separation, gender roles, and career aspirations. *High Ability Studies, 19*(1), 67–81.

Hook, M. K. (2000). *Let me show you: Mentors, role models and multiple role planning of gifted young women.* (Doctoral dissertation). Retrieved from ProQuest Dissertations and Theses. (Publication No. AAT 9976780).

McDonnell, V. M. (2005). "I used to be gifted": Case studies of lost potential among adolescent females. (Doctoral dissertation). Retrieved from Dissertations & Theses: Full Text. (Publication No. AAT 3218380)

Chapter 2

2. Leaf, C. M., *Switch on your Brain.* BakerBooks, 2015.

Chapter 9

4. Gardner's Theory of Multiple Intelligences. Accessed August 2019, https://www.multipleintelligencesoasis.org

Chapter 11

5. Hinton, S. E. *The Outsiders.* Puffin Books, 1995

6. Lathem, Edward Connery (editor). *The Poetry of Robert Frost.* Copyright © 1923, 1947, 1969 by Henry Holt and Company, copyright © 1942, 1951 by Robert Frost, copyright © 1970, 1975 by Lesley Frost Ballantine. Reprinted by permission of Henry Holt and Company, LLC.

Chapter 12
7. Associated Press, "Women Lost on Drifting Boat in Pacific Ocean for Months Tell Their Incredible Story," *The West Australian,* October 28, 2017, https://thewest.com.au/news/world/women-los t-on-drifting-boat-in-pacific-ocean-for-months-tell-their-incredible-story-ng-b88643376z.

Chapter 13
8. Brown, Brene. *Dare to Lead*: Random House Publishers, 2018.

Chapter 14
9. First Things First. "Brain Development." Accessed February 13, 2021, https://www.firstthingsfirst.org/early-childhood-matters/brain-development/.

10. Fredrickson, Barbara. *Positivity*: Three Rivers Press 2009.

Chapter 15
11. Mail Online. "Disabled Driver in 150-Mile Terror Drive as Accelerator Jams at 125mph on Dual Carriageway." Accessed June 1, 2019. https://www.dailymail.co.uk/news/article-2278106/Driver-trappe d-125mph-car-chase-accelerator-jams-dual-carriageway.html.

Chapter 17
14. Encyclopædia Britannica. "Surface Tension." Accessed January 2, 2021. https://www.britannica.com/science/surface-tension.

Chapter 18
15. Brain Pickings. "Live the Questions: Rilke on Embracing Uncertainty and Doubt as a Stabilizing Force." Accessed February 17, 2021, https://www.brainpickings.org/2012/06/01/rilke-on-questions/.

ACKNOWLEDGMENTS

I am deeply grateful to my writing coach for taking on this project and committing to it wholeheartedly. Your partnership cheered me on when I needed it and provided clarity where it was fuzzy. Thank you for your tenacious fortitude.

Many thanks to Natalie Hanemann. You were more than an editor for my grammar and syntax. You caught what I was communicating and helped me say it better. And you did it with such grace!

To James Warrick, my coach, who first asked me, "Have you ever thought of coaching?" and who generously invited me into the field of coaching with clarity, confidence, and courage.

Thank you to all those who supported the final steps in the publication and launch—Kristen Ingebretson for your book cover and Lorie DeWorken for your typesetting. UNCMN Creative Works for your videos, marketing, and overall friendship cheering me on. The Amazing Book Launch Team lending their energy to share so freely with us. And to my team, Nicole, Natalie, Jenny, Christina, and Amber—words are not enough. How many zoom calls, texts, and emails flew between us to get this off the ground? Thank you. Let's celebrate!

And to Bob Goff who kept encouraging me to dream big and replace all fear with pure joy. What exuberance and energy you lent me when I needed it to propel me forward!

A special thanks to my 3C Living companions who were "doing life with me" during the writing of this book. You challenged me, encouraged me, and told me the truth when I needed it. Thank you for your character and modeling 3C Living. The Thirsty Thursday families, the Hoop Sisters, 50th Birthday Crew, Neptune Leadership, Arise & Be friends, Misty-lena, Sami, Joe, Havah, Shelley, and Shelly—just to name a few—you participated in developing this 3C Living language by inviting me into your lives.

Finally, as a former teacher, I always have to give a nod of acknowledgment to all the students I taught over the years because I also learned from you. Both children and adults. "Mrs. Penny" is a name I still hear fondly and think of you.

Grace Space

The spaces within us impact the spaces we step into.

Grace Space will provide concrete examples for how
we can foster spaces of grace using seven principles:

#1 Responding vs Reacting

#2 Questioning vs Accusing

#3 Receptivity vs Defensiveness

#4 Constructive Language vs
     Destructive Language

#5 Connection vs Protection

#6 Freedom vs Control

#7 Trust vs Fear

Part of the 3C Leading Series

Images courtesy of Freepik.com